THE
MEMORY
PALACE

THE MEMORY PALACE

TRUE SHORT STORIES OF THE PAST

Nate DiMeo

RANDOM HOUSE

NEW YORK

Published in the United States by Random House, an imprint and division of Penguin Random House LLC, New York.

RANDOM HOUSE and the HOUSE colophon are registered trademarks of Penguin Random House LLC.

Library of Congress Cataloging-in-Publication Data
Names: DiMeo, Nate, author.
Title: The memory palace / Nate DiMeo.
Description: First edition. | New York, NY: Random House, [2024] | Includes bibliographical references.
Identifiers: LCCN 2024015299 (print) | LCCN 2024015300 (ebook) | ISBN 9780593446157 (hardcover) | ISBN 9780593446171 (ebook)
Subjects: LCSH: United States—History. | United States—Biography. | United States—Anecdotes.
Classification: LCC E179 .D525 2024 (print) | LCC E179 (ebook) | DDC 973—dc23/eng/20240509
LC record available at lccn.loc.gov/2024015299
LC ebook record available at lccn.loc.gov/2024015300

Printed in the United States of America on acid-free paper

randomhousebooks.com

2 4 6 8 9 7 5 3 1

FIRST EDITION

For Leila and Quinby and Mom and Dad

A Welcome

Something moved me once. That's how all these stories begin for me. Some historical something, some fact or anecdote, came into my day—usually unannounced, over the radio, at a museum, in a text from a friend, on one of the seven hundred tabs open on my browser, or embedded in some larger work—and changed it. Somehow managed to cut through the whirr and sputter of life and moved me. Often I don't know why. That fascinates me. Why this story? Why this video? Why has some other person's experience and memory, from some other time, made their way into mine? Why, in the rushing, roiling stream of information that inundates pretty much all of us, pretty much every day, pretty much all day long, was this bit of the past the thing that glinted and caught my eye and connected, snapped me into presence, filled me with wonder? And why was this the thing that stayed with me, sometimes for years, these things that moved me once?

So often, I think, the answer to that question comes down to this: In that moment, I knew that that thing about the past was real. I got it. I felt that flash of connection. I understood that that person in that story, or who made that object in that museum, or who was on my screen in some archival footage Lindy Hopping or walking down the street with their child on their shoulders, had once been alive. They felt pain. They experienced joy. They had a body and senses. They had dreams, and some of them were fulfilled and some weren't, and some were so dear and deeply felt that maybe they couldn't admit they even had them. Maybe that person was Teddy Roosevelt; maybe that person spent much of their adult life traveling between midwestern Coca Cola bottling plants, servicing conveyor belts. They were as real and as human as any of us. And that is, of course, a preposterously basic idea. But it is also one of the hardest to hold.

Each episode of *The Memory Palace* and each story in this book was written as an attempt to take one of those things that moved me once and make other people feel that way too. I want to conjure the peculiar magic that comes in those rare moments when we understand that the past was real.

I have been doing this for a long time. I started right after my daughter was born; as I write this, she has just turned fifteen. And through all those years, I have found the act of writing these stories personally valuable. Because it requires this odd act of empathetic imagination through which I try to catch a glimpse of an answer to that most fundamental of questions: What is it like to be someone else? Doing so, or at least doing so well, requires that I reconnect to that initial feeling of wonder, and of understanding, however briefly, the reality of the past, and that reminds me that our present moment is itself historical. And that determines what work we can do, which diseases will and won't kill us, whether we are safe from conflict, whether we can afford a home, what clothes we wear, what art we enjoy, how we clean ourselves, what we smell like, whether we are free, whether we can marry the person we love, what is in the air we breathe. All the things that make up our fleeting moment. And I have found that for these stories to work right, I need to find my way back, again and again, to that feeling of connection. And to remember—to know—that our time is short. That this (he says, waving his hands to indicate, like, everything) is what we have to work with and make of what we can.

And so I try to figure out what it meant to me—this anecdote, this artifact, this set of facts—and figure out how to turn it into a story that might mean something to you too. A short one. Something that can sneak into your life unannounced. A concentrated shot of feeling. Maybe it will change your day. Maybe it will stay with you.

There is nothing comprehensive about this book. *The Memory Palace* is more a cabinet of curiosities than a scholarly museum. There is no table of contents. It isn't organized by era or subject matter or any of the time-tested, thoroughly useful ways that other nonfiction books are. Because the utility of the stories is different; I think people come to *The Memory Palace* to feel things rather than learn things. So the order of the stories is, as we say as I write this, in the early days of 2024, just vibes. It has been chosen according to considerations of rhythm and pacing and mood and other things that, I hope, will help make the reading experience as enjoyable as possible as you move through the book from beginning to end. But it also means you can just drop in anywhere. Flip the book open and start at any story. Read them in any order. Wander through as you will. See where they take you.

This is *The Memory Palace.* I'm Nate DiMeo.

THE
MEMORY
PALACE

Distance

Samuel Finley Breese Morse spent the first thirty-five years of his life learning to paint. At Andover, at Yale, in London at the Royal Academy of Arts. He studied the work of the masters. To learn how Michelangelo built bodies that seemed to pulse and shudder out of mere oil and shadow and crosshatch. To learn how Raphael summoned the spark of inner life with a single stroke of pure white in the dusky ocher of a noblewoman's eye. To learn how to create illusions of space and distance. To learn how to conjure the ineffable through the mere aggregation of lines and dots on stretched canvas.

In 1825, Morse was living in New Haven, Connecticut, with his wife, Lucretia, and two sons, with a third child due any day now, when a courier delivered a message. The city of New York wanted to pay him a thousand dollars to paint a portrait of the Marquis de Lafayette. The hero of the revolution was coming to Washington to celebrate the fiftieth anniversary of the start of the war and he would sit for Morse, if the painter could leave right away. Morse packed his easel and his brushes and his paints, and clothes good enough to wear when meeting a great man of the age, and kissed his pregnant wife, and left that night.

A week later, Morse was in his rented studio in Washington, preparing it for the arrival of his distinguished subject the next morning, when he heard a knock on his door. Another courier, this one breathless and dirty from a hard ride on a hard road, handed him a note, five words long: "Your dear wife is convalescent." Morse left for home that night.

He rode for six days on horseback and in the backs of juddering wagons, wrapped in blankets against the cold wind of the October night, and when he made it to New Haven and ran through fallen leaves up to the house on Whitney Avenue, he learned that his wife was dead. In fact, she had died before the courier knocked on his door. In fact, she had already been buried, one morning while he was on the road. While he was racing home to be by her side. Thinking she was getting better.

Samuel Finley Breese Morse spent the next forty-five years of his life trying to make sure no one would have to feel what he felt that night ever again. He spent the next forty-five years inventing the telegraph, to turn real space and real distance into an illusion, and inventing a code: dots and lines that could transmit the stuff of life and of dying wives.

Gigantic

S he first set foot on *America* in November of 1795. We know this. It says so in the logbook of a trading ship called *America* which set sail from Calcutta a month later. We know that the ship's captain paid $450 for her, a big investment. Add to that figure the cost of food and of revenue lost by taking up space that could have been stocked with barrels of spices and bolts of fabric and other nonperishable things, instead of using it to transport a live elephant.

The captain had big plans for her. We know this, too, from letters he wrote to his four brothers. He thought people would flip out about an elephant back home. There had never been an elephant anywhere on the continent of North America. He figured that had to be worth more than a crate of cardamom or Darjeeling tea. He bet he could turn his four hundred and fifty bucks into five thousand, easy.

We don't know if he did. The historical record loses track of the elephant after a while. Newspapers tell us she drew crowds in New York right after *America* returned to America. She stood tied to a stake at the corner of Broadway and Beaver, downtown. People paid to see her stand there. We also know that the captain brought her down south when winter came, to get her out of the northern cold; the Carolinas were as close to India as he could offer. After that we don't really know what happened to her, for a while. But we do know about Hachaliah Bailey.

Hachaliah Bailey's family owned a farm in Somers, New York, now a bedroom community an hour and change from Manhattan on the Metro-North commuter line. In his early thirties, Hachaliah worked as a drover, bringing cattle into the city, such as it was at the start of the nineteenth century (it was a longer trip then). At some point during one of his cattle drives, Hachaliah became enthralled with one of the animals that lived at the stockyard in Manhattan. He'd talk about her all the time when he was home, and he'd go to see her every time he came to town. We don't know how she came to live with the cattle and pigs and sheep and goats, or how long she lived there, but we know that, around 1807, Hachaliah Bailey bought an Indian elephant for one thousand dollars and brought her home to live on his farm in Somers. He called her Betty.

Hachaliah had never liked farming. It took forever for things to grow. It took forever to plow a field with a team of mules. But with an elephant? He ought to be able to cut that time in half.

We don't know how well that went. What we do know is that an Indian elephant in rural America draws a crowd, especially in 1807, and Hachaliah Bailey soon figured out that there was more money to be made by drawing a crowd than by increasing agricultural output through elephant-based efficiencies. So Hachaliah Bailey and the elephant he now affectionately called Old Bet hit the road.

For the better part of a decade, the pair toured the Northeast, commandeering town squares and barns and charging admission. Eventually, Bailey expanded the operation, turning it into a full-on traveling circus. He added a horse and a dog and a goat, which everybody had, but an elephant? No one had an elephant.

Here were farmers and coopers and their wives and their neighbors. Here were people who hadn't left their fields or their towns since they'd first immigrated or since they'd gotten back from the war. Here were children who'd never been anywhere, never seen anything, beyond the world of their farm and their neighbors and their woods past the wall of stones their grandfather had laid. And into that world walks this creature. Into that world walks the world.

We don't know how much money Hachaliah Bailey made off Old Bet. We know there were times when the two of them would roll into a town and people couldn't scrounge up even a little money, so they'd trade him farm tools and booze for a peek at the pachyderm. And we read, though we're not sure we entirely believe, that the Indian elephant developed a taste for Jamaican rum. We know Hachaliah Bailey started walking her from town to town in the middle of the night so people wouldn't get a free look along the way. We know he was successful enough to sell two shares of Old Bet for twelve hundred dollars apiece. We know those things.

And we know, and are sad to report, that Old Bet died in Alfred, Maine, in 1816. She was shot by a farmer who felt it was a sin to charge people to see an animal. We don't, of course, know how Old Bet felt about anything.

But there are some things we do know:

An Indian elephant in the wild can live up to seventy years. Evolution has made them fundamentally social animals. They eat, they breed, they find water, and they protect themselves and their young and one another from predators by working as a group. We know they communicate through body language, by secreting bodily fluids with decipherable odors, and by growling and stamping and trumpeting and shrieking and emitting sounds at frequencies so low they can't be heard by humans, but which vibrate through the ground to be picked up by other elephants as far away as six miles.

We know, too, that their social order, and group and individual survival, hinge on their famous memories. Researchers have seen elephants, reunited after twenty-six years, signal that they recognize one another as family, and all elephants can remember and recognize as many as two hundred individual elephants.

So which did she remember?

Which did she look for among the cattle and hogs of the Manhattan stockyards?

And to which elephants did she send subsonic messages to radiate out through New England soil, only to fall seven thousand miles short?

What did she remember?

Of the ship's hold?

And the salt air of the Indian Ocean?

And the Cape of Good Hope?

And the mouth of the Hudson?

Of the countless days spent tied to a stake?

Of the green hills of North Carolina?

Of the faces in crowds?

Of the nights spent walking under stars, and quarter moons, and North American elms?

On her way to yet another strange place with no elephants.

The Nickel Candy Bar

I'm just going to take a few things here, tie each one up in a bow, then attach a small parachute and throw them out and let the wind carry them where it may.

The first thing:

There were the peanuts. They are really what did the trick. Otto Schnering was a baker in Chicago who invented this treat called a Kandy Kake. It was a chocolate bar with a tiny pastry in the center. It was delicious. So he put a label on it. Changed the two *c*'s in "candy cake" to *k*'s because why not and founded the Curtiss Candy Company. Curtiss was his mother's maiden name, and it sounded way better to American ears than the German name Schnering, at the start of World War I. And the Kandy Kake did pretty well for the Curtiss Candy Company. Better than its Polar Bar or Honey Comb Chip or its Earth-O-Nutt Dip. Well enough for Otto Schnering to expand his factory in the 1920s and automate much of its production, and bring himself closer to his greatest dream: the five-cent candy bar.

The competition's candy bar cost a dime. But the Curtiss Candy

Company couldn't make the Kandy Kake on the assembly line. The pastry inside was too delicate to be made by machines. So what if instead Curtiss just threw some peanuts in there? No one would care if a peanut broke while bouncing along on a conveyor belt. Plus, peanuts were cheap. Then he whipped up some nougat, eventually swapped out expensive sugar for syrup made from corn grown right there on his farm, and he had nailed it: the nickel candy bar. It needed a name.

You can believe he was so taken with Grover Cleveland's daughter—who had been born some thirty years earlier and had died, at age thirteen, a full seventeen years prior to Schnering figuring out the whole peanut-and-nougat thing—that he decided to call his candy bar Baby Ruth, because Ruth Cleveland's name just happened to be on everybody's lips then. You can believe that.

Or you can believe he named his candy bar after Babe Ruth, the affable Yankees slugger who was on the front page of every newspaper nearly every day, every summer, back then, a hero to children in every corner of the country, and the single most famous person in America. You can believe instead (as certainly seems most likely) that Schnering tweaked the name of his candy bar in a cutesy way because he couldn't afford to license the Babe's likeness and didn't want to be sued. Either way, he knew he had a winner. He just needed people to try it.

The second thing:

There was Doug Davis. All he wanted to do when he was a teenager was to learn how to fly, and then get himself to Europe in time to shoot down the Red Baron. So he enlisted and learned to fly biplanes. He did barrel rolls and split S's, the high yo-yo and the low yo-yo. But when he graduated from flight school at the top of his class, they told him he was more valuable as an instructor than as a pilot, and he stayed stateside. Then World War I ended and that was that for his dogfighting dreams. But he could still fly. He bought a surplus plane from the army for a few hundred bucks. Then he started to make that money back, five dollars at a time. He took passengers for ten-minute trips soaring over the hills of Griffin, Georgia. He took his plane on tour. He bought a few more planes and started a flying circus. He hired retired army pilots who didn't want to give up the thrill of the open-air cockpit quite yet. He hired Mabel Cody, a daredevil, a great one, to do tricks while walking on the wing of his plane. It was an extraordinary thing to be out pitching hay or shucking corn or hanging laundry on the line on your farm, in your town that was barely a town, and have a circus land in a field by your house. These brave men and women literally came out of the blue to do a show for you in machines you might have only read about. They went skimming just above your head and buzzing through the open doors of your neighbors' barn, scattering chickens, then pulling up and climbing up and up and spiraling down and down and up and up again, over a landscape you'd seen all your life, that you wouldn't ever see quite the same way again. Damn.

The third thing:

Otto Schnering hired Doug Davis to make Baby Ruth a household name. Here was the idea: a series of publicity stunts all over the country. A product giveaway on a scale the nation had never seen. Doug Davis would fly over American cities. Fairgrounds. Festivals. Places with lots of people, lots of potential customers. From a flyer promoting one of the giveaways: "Yes sir! It's going to rain candy from the sky."

And so it did.

Baby Ruths, in red-white-and-blue wrappers tied with string and strung up with tiny parachutes, floated down through the sky over

Pittsburgh. Drifted past office windows. Draftsmen looked up from their tables as something caught their eye. Then ran over to the window. White parachutes by the dozens. Kids in the streets below, looking up, eyes wide, hands outstretched, the best thing they'd ever seen. Traffic stopped on Liberty Avenue. Women laughing, having caught a surprise dessert on their lunch break. And then a plane, right by the window, a man in a plane right by the fifth-floor window. It looked like he was laughing.

That is the thing about those old planes. There was no cabin. No protective dome. And they were just about as long as three grown men laid end to end, and you could see the pilot from the ground as he banked to take another pass. Could have seen Doug Davis tossing out Baby Ruths, maybe caught a smile as he circled, did a gratuitous roll to give 'em a thrill. And he could see them on the ground, see kids looking up in wonder, or looking down, scampering for a nickel candy bar. In city after city.

One time he took a kid with him, a lucky son of a gun, and dropped the candy over the Hialeah Park Racetrack down in Florida, gave the kid the thrill of his life at twelve years old—his first time in a plane, and now he was tossing candy bars into the blue skies over Miami Beach. Watching them drop and then their parachutes pop open and then tumble for a moment, then sway, and then glide away.

The fourth thing:

When candy rains from the sky, you don't merely get free nickel candy. You don't merely get wide-eyed wonder. You don't merely get a day upended by joy and surprise. You get parachutes that don't open right. Where one string snaps and the thing spirals down to the sound of rippling fabric. Or candy bars that slip their bonds and plummet, that crack people in the head, that crack windshields. You get drivers with cracked windshields who jam on their brakes and get rear-ended. In Pittsburgh, you get people reaching too far out of office windows to grab a free candy bar that they could have bought for half the already insignificant price of any other bar on the market and tumbling out, to be saved only by a hard fall onto a fire escape. You get emergency meetings of the city council to change aviation laws within city limits. In New York on a perfect beach day on the Fourth of July, you get a stampede, a crush of boys and girls and moms and dads, grown men and women clamoring for candy. You get Yetta Kerman, of 164 South Fourth Street in Brooklyn, a fifty-four-year-old woman, laid up in the hospital with a broken leg.

Another thing:

Doug Davis's Baby Ruth drops helped make him famous (he wasn't held liable for Mrs. Kerman's leg), and he parlayed that fame into multiple business ventures. He became a pioneer in commercial aviation. Delivering packages and then passengers as the lead captain of what would become Eastern Airlines. An eighty-year-old woman who wanted to take her first flight, from Atlanta to Miami, refused to board until she was assured that the great Doug Davis would be her pilot. She waited two days until he was on the schedule and then enjoyed a smooth, steady ride to the Sunshine State. But smooth and steady wasn't what Davis wanted. He had been in the business of barrel rolls and adrenaline and wide-eyed wonder. And so, to the increasing consternation of the board members of the airline, their lead captain kept entering races and stunt-flying competitions, and kept winning. Kept thrilling crowds and himself— when he wasn't keeping a commercial airliner steady, looking for smoother air for his passengers, up high where folks below couldn't see him smiling. Until one day he banked too hard in the fifth lap of an air race in Cleveland and stalled and spiraled and was killed instantly, set aflame in a field in front of sixty thousand people.

One last thing

    to tie up with string

        and toss into the wind

and see where it lands:

The boy in the plane with Davis in Miami, who dropped candy on the crowd and just loved it. He loved it so much he became a pilot. He named his plane after his mother, Enola Gay, and dropped an atomic bomb over Hiroshima.

Hercules

ercules was a real, live man.

There are a number of reasons we know for sure. His name (just the one name, just Hercules) shows up in tax records. He's there among a list of taxable property in a census conducted in 1787: He is listed as a cook. He is mentioned in a handful of diaries and letters. There is a portrait that people thought was almost certainly of him, a Black man in a white chef's coat, his hair barely contained by his tight white chef's hat—but they're now pretty sure is of someone else entirely. But Hercules was a real man.

We have the evidence. We have that evidence, the records, the diaries, the probable portrait, because George Washington owned him. And when you are George Washington, people save your stuff. They keep your writings. They keep the diaries and letters that your friends and your family wrote, just in case you, the first president, a Founding Father, a hero of the revolution, show up in those diaries. Just in case you answered their letters. So historians and biographers and the Mount Vernon Ladies' Association can tell your story. So they can give a full accounting of your life, can catalog its moments and chronicle its days. Hercules was enslaved by George Washington, so we know he existed. Though we don't know much beyond that.

Hercules was born sometime around 1754. He was married, though we don't know when, to an enslaved woman named Alice. They had three kids, Richmond and Eve and Delia. George Washington bought Hercules from the guy who lived next door to Mount Vernon. He put him to work running a ferry across one of the rivers that ran through the estate, and then at some point Hercules was transferred to the kitchen.

He took to the work and became the head chef. Hercules made the food that George and Martha Washington and their family and their guests ate. Washington loved Hercules's cooking. So much so that when Washington became president, he took Hercules with him to be chief cook at the presidential mansion. This was back before they built the White House, back when the capital was Philadelphia.

Here's the thing about Pennsylvania back then: It had a law that said any slave who lived within its borders for more than six months would be freed. The president wasn't above the law. But let's be clear: The president also didn't want to free his slaves. So every six months, George Washington would send these people back home to Virginia for an interregnum, a period that would allow them to comply with the letter of the law, and then rotate them back in for another six months so he could continue to own them. After six months, he sent Hercules back to Mount Vernon.

It was a bummer for Washington. He was going to miss Hercules's cooking, but the law was the law. He wasn't the governor of Pennsylvania.

So Hercules went home, but, with the lord and lady of the manor out of town, they didn't need a chief cook in Mount Vernon, and he was put to work in the fields. He was a big guy. He was called Hercules for a reason. So they had him build a brick wall. He was back in Virginia—having been sent away from the job he'd thrived in and possibly enjoyed, within the limits of bondage; the job that gave him status (he had even been allowed to sell leftovers, and he'd used the money to buy things for his family, and some fancy clothes for himself), from a city where several thousand Black men lived free, where they were their own masters—because George Washington wanted to make certain he could remain a slave, rather than let him live as a free man, even as an employee in the same position.

Hercules ran.

George Washington was a real, live man. We know this because every ten years Americans have to fill out a census form; he started that. And because there's a presidential cabinet that has real meetings and real staff who collect real paychecks funded by taxpayers, and who create policies that have real impacts on people and upon the natural and built environment. We know this because Native Americans no longer own what we call downtown Chicago, or most of Ohio. We know this because there is a United States at all.

Then there are all those paintings, evidence of days in which Washington sat in a room with another real man. We know this, too, because we have his teeth, his dentures anyway, which are actually teeth of other men and pieces of teeth from horses and cattle and elephant ivory. He didn't put them in very often, because they couldn't really open and close and they hurt, besides, but there were times when those fake teeth were in his real mouth. And we have his hair. So much of it. Kept by his barber. Cut off by his personal assistant before he was buried in the ground, because people had been writing for years to both the assistant and his boss asking for a lock of Washington's hair as a souvenir, as a real relic of this real man. They wanted some tangible connection, because otherwise he was just an idea, a memory, an image that can be conjured just by invoking his name.

George Washington.

See?

There he was for a second. A presence that can be summoned at will, to pair with some inspirational quote on liberty. To make some point about America, or Americanness, or leadership, or honesty, or bravery, or dentures, or the Delaware River. But he was a real man once.

He was once mad that another real man he supposedly owned ran away. Mad because his family missed the man's cooking, and mad because it made him look bad. He had been telling people that he would never purchase another slave, and he felt pretty good about telling people that. But this thing was really putting him in a tough spot. Here's a quote: "The running off of my Cook, has been a most inconvenient thing to this family; and what renders it more disagreeable, is, that I had resolved never to become the master of another Slave by *purchase;* but this resolution I fear I must break."

In several letters, written over the course of more than a year, Washington kept pushing people to try to find Hercules. In them, he kept suggesting places he could have gone. Methods of capture. Names of people who might have leads or could otherwise assist in the search. Meanwhile, people at Mount Vernon were suggesting he just hire a new cook. They had a nice white woman in mind. But the president wanted Hercules back. He liked his food. And Hercules worked for free.

At one point, possibly as part of Washington's efforts to track Hercules down, an aide to a prince of France who was staying at Mount Vernon tried to get information from Hercules's six-year-old daughter. He asked: Wasn't she upset that her father left her? Wasn't she sad that she'd never see him again?

She shook her head. "Oh sir!" she said. "I am very glad because he is free now."

Hercules didn't come back. For the longest time we knew nothing of where he went or how it felt to get there. We just knew he was never caught.

For more than two hundred years, his story ended the day he ran off, but in 2019 historians at the Historical Society of Westport, Connecticut, picked up his trail in a letter and various municipal records and followed it to New York City. He had been spotted there in 1801, it seems, by the mayor of New York himself, who had once eaten Hercules's food at Mount Vernon. The mayor wrote to Martha Washington with the news, but there was nothing she could do at that point to bring him back; Washington's will stipulated that the people he'd enslaved should be freed after his death. The historians search for Hercules found him in census records, in New York City, and in the records of the city's Second African Burying Ground on Chrystie Street. But a life isn't lived in a census, as it is not lived in a grave. Hercules lived his as a free man for fifteen years. He doesn't owe history an accounting of his days. Hercules was free of George Washington; George Washington should never be free of Hercules.

A Brief Eulogy Written After Noticing That *The New York Times*'s Obituary for Carla Wallenda, the Last Surviving Child of the Founders of the Flying Wallendas Acrobatic Troupe, Said That the Cause of Death Was Unknown

A crowd of Danes watched her uncle Willy fall from the high wire in 1936, hitting the safety net the wrong way and sustaining injuries that would kill him two days later.

In 1959, another crowd, this one in Mexico City, watched her cousin Gunther's wife, Margarita, lose her balance several stories above the bare ground and die when she landed.

Two years later, in Detroit, seven members of the extended Wallenda family were about to complete an astounding feat of strength, skill, and daring, in which they would attempt to cross a high wire as a unit, as they had done many times before. Four men walked the tightrope in a line, a horizontal pole connecting each pair, while a male Wallenda balanced on each of those poles and a seventh Wallenda, in the role known in the business as "the Pretty Girl," sat in and eventually stood upon a chair balancing on another horizontal pole extended between the two men beneath her, thus forming a mobile human pyramid that looks as preposterous as it does terrifying. Anyway: circusgoers in Detroit in 1962—people on dates, moms, dads, grandparents taking their grandkids out for the night, big smiles, fingers sticky, tipped pink by cotton candy—watched as Carla Wallenda's cousin Dieter, approaching the safety of the opposite platform, wavered, sending a shiver through the high wire, and the pyramid collapsed, and four of the acrobats fell to the floor forty feet below, leaving Carla's father and uncle clinging to the cable by a leg, by the crook of an arm, as they held on to her cousin Jana, whom they'd caught in midair as she fell from the top. They held her by her wrists as she hung, sobbing, awaiting rescue above the floor where her brother and cousin lay dead, and another cousin lay in agony, having sustained injuries that would leave him paralyzed from the waist down for the rest of his life.

The next year, six thousand people at the Omaha Civic Auditorium watched Carla's aunt fall to her death from atop a fiberglass pole upon which she had been balancing.

In 1972, Carla's husband, Chico Guzman, was balancing on a swaying pole, which was Carla's specialty, too, at a fair in Wheeling, West Virginia, when the pole swayed too far and struck an electrical wire and stunned him. He fell sixty feet and died.

In 1978, her father, Karl Wallenda, the

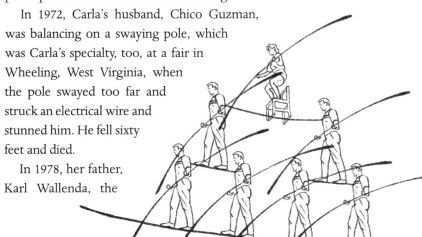

patriarch of the Flying Wallendas, was doing a quick wire-walk between two hotels in San Juan, Puerto Rico, to promote a more spectacular performance he was scheduled to give the following night under the big top. A gust of wind came off the bay and took him by surprise, and he struggled to maintain his balance as the wire swayed beneath him. Two hundred people saw him hit the sidewalk.

Carla Wallenda died on March 6, 2021, at the age of eighty-five, in Sarasota, Florida. There is no information about her death, though you can infer from the obituaries that the cause was natural, and that any witnesses to it were the types of loved ones or medical professionals we find at our side, if we're lucky, when the time comes. There is, however, a much more extensive record of the life she lived than will exist for most of us.

She appeared in two newsreels as a child, in the late 1930s and early 1940s. In the first, she is barely older than a baby, and her famous father is on the tightrope behind her, holding her hands as she toddles across. In the second, Carla appears to be five, maybe six, but not older. No one holds her as she walks the tightrope. She beams the whole time.

Her father got his start young too—when he was ten or so, in Germany after World War I. He spent his days working in a coal mine, and at night his parents would send him out to the bars in town. He'd hop up onto tables and walk on his hands and earn a few coins. There was an ad in the paper when he was twelve: A circus in another town was looking for someone who could walk on his hands. He took what little money he had and bought a train ticket. He met the owner, showed him his tricks, and the guy pointed to a wire some thirty feet off the ground and said, "Great, now do it up there." Young Karl Wallenda didn't want to, but he didn't have the money for the return trip home, and so he did it. The crowd went crazy; he fell in love with that sound.

Years later he was a star, and he had recruited two of his brothers and a pretty girl willing to stand on his shoulders as he walked the wire. He married her. They toured all over, and then one night in Havana, John Ringling of the brothers Ringling hired the family Wallenda and brought them to the States. But the net the Wallendas had ordered didn't arrive in time for their first show, at Madison Square Garden in 1928. They performed anyway. And when they had completed their high-wire traversal as a four-person pyramid, four stories above bare concrete, the audience went wild. It was like nothing they'd ever seen. And the applause was like nothing the Wallendas had ever heard. They never used a net again.

Their fame grew, and the troupe did too. The Flying Wallendas included not just Carla and her siblings, who had learned the literal ropes from their daredevil parents, but her parents' siblings. Their spouses. Cousins came out of the woodwork and joined the act. Even as some of them died, the show went on, as it must.

It didn't go on for every Wallenda, though. Carla's uncle Arthur retired young, saying he would rather be a living farmer than a dead acrobat. Her mother retired too. She'd always been afraid up there in the air, she said. At some point she stopped being able to push through it. When she quit, her fear grew, and she couldn't even watch the family act. She'd just wait in the wings until they played the music, the little triumphant fanfare that would trill as they basked in the applause and waved to the crowd.

Carla never quit.

You can go to YouTube and find a clip of her in a pink sequined leotard, doing a headstand atop an eighty-five-foot pole, with no net, as is the Wallenda way, from a TV special hosted by Steve Harvey. She is eighty-one years old.

One doesn't arrive at eighty-one able to climb a pole eighty-five feet off the ground, let alone to do a headstand at the top as it sways beneath one's weight, unless one has spent one's life in the air, preparing and maintaining one's body to do so. The stretching, the training, the rehearsals, the fittings, the falling, the getting back up. The relative madness.

It wasn't all applause, Carla's life. She had four husbands, and too many tragedies. There were many times when defying death professionally didn't pay the bills, so there were waitress gigs and odd jobs that made her feel dead inside, that weren't walking on a wire. *That.* That was when she felt alive. She said this a lot in interviews over the years, and when you read it, you believe her.

Her father had said the same thing again and again before the gust of wind came off San Juan Bay.

Carla Wallenda died at eighty-five. The cause of death is unknown to the wider public, which, in her family, is an achievement. The arc of her life was determined, as so many of ours are, by the circumstances of her birth and by the choices of her parents. Some families choose the suburbs for the schools and a decent yard, or choose the city for a shorter commute, or move to be closer to the ocean or farther from their in-laws. They choose this life to join a burgeoning field, or that one for stability. Carla Wallenda's family chose flight.

A History of Martian Civilization, 1877–1906

Giovanni Schiaparelli had spent two years waiting to aim the telescope, in the palazzo on a hill above Milan, at Mars. It was an incredible instrument, perhaps the finest in the world, and, having used it to produce his groundbreaking maps of the poles and the principal bodies of water on the fourth planet from the sun, the esteemed astronomer was eager to see even more in the winter of 1877, when its orbit brought it closer to the Earth than it had been in many years. He wasn't disappointed. The weather was good. He himself was in fine form, having abstained from alcohol and stuck to a rigorous physical regimen to make sure his faculties were in tip-top shape. His work had paid off, for at that distance, in those conditions, he could see for the first time narrow bands of shadow crisscrossing the belly of the planet. He drew the most detailed map of the Martian landscape ever produced, including a network of *canali* running between the planet's *mare*.

It was, to the people gathered around newsstands in New York and Sydney, to the scientists at symposia at Cambridge and Jaipur, the best evidence humanity had ever had that they were not alone. There were canals on Mars.

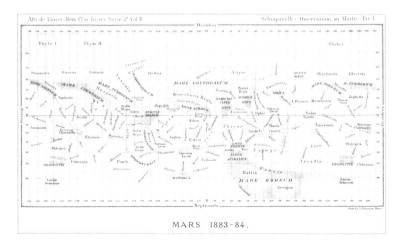

MARS 1883-84.

Astronomers the world over turned their own telescopes toward the red planet, but no one could see what Schiaparelli saw. This wasn't entirely surprising. Nineteenth-century astronomy still had a fair bit of art in its science; it was contingent on atmospheric conditions, on handmade instruments and lenses, on the variability of human perception. Schiaparelli and his telescope couldn't be beat.

Percival Lowell was the son of one of the wealthiest families in New England, and had been looking for a way to shake off the label of "dilettante" that had stuck to him as he bounced about between diplomatic postings and academic gigs. He found his calling when Schiaparelli found his *canali*. Soon Lowell's portion of the family fortune was being spent constructing the world's most powerful telescope, on a hilltop in Flagstaff, Arizona, far from city lights or industrial pollution. He threw himself into his new passion and became, before long, a real astronomer, respected for his diligence and meticulousness. Plus, he had the biggest telescope. In 1894, it helped him confirm Schiaparelli's findings: There were canals on Mars, and moreover—based on his careful observation of the planet's surface, noting the way Schiaparelli's *canali* connected the planet's large bodies of water—he reasoned they were part of a massive irrigation system that could be the work only of a civilization on par with our own.

People followed the developments in the papers, read about all of it on the train, talked about it with the pharmacist, or the bootblack, or the guy at the mill, thrilling with every new observation and extrapolation, wondering about the composition of those canals—so much bigger than any on Earth. Were they waterways? Were they used for travel? Were the circular nodes in Lowell's drawings Martian cities?

Philosophers pondered the Martian soul. Archaeologists wondered if the canals were in fact evidence of a lost culture. Maybe they were an object lesson on hubris for our rapidly industrializing planet. But Lowell put that speculation to rest when he observed new branches in the network of canals and alterations in color in the fields between them. These changes suggested that life was being lived right there, right then. He discovered a new set of canals running parallel to some of Schiaparelli's *canali,* with maybe a hundred miles between them.

These would appear and then disappear—some sort of seasonal construction, he hypothesized. He could only guess at the purpose of these new canals, but they were marvelous: Imagine what it would take to make something so massive and then tear it down—it ran thousands of miles—and do it all so quickly. It spoke of a civilization far more sophisticated than ours, with some sort of public-works apparatus that put our municipal bureaucracies to shame.

One day people read in the papers that Lowell had seen a light, "a brilliant projection," he called it, flaring at the edge of the planet.

It couldn't be natural. It couldn't be a volcano or some sort of comet. They were signaling us, Lowell declared. Mars was trying to contact its neighbor across the way. Maybe the Martians had been doing it for millennia. Maybe they'd just been waiting for us to get our evolutionary act together, to advance far enough as a species to see them. Finally, in Flagstaff, someone had.

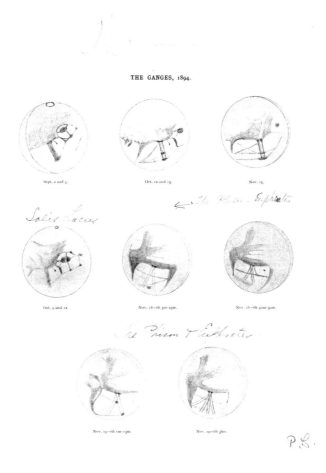

THE GANGES, 1894.

But scientists here on Earth couldn't signal back. They tried to think of a way. Global semaphore, someone proposed, would require flags the size of the state of Indiana and a flagpole that defied the laws of physics, not to mention handling procedures that would outstrip the capacity of even the most industrious Boy Scout troop. Contacting the Martians would take something else, another scientist suggested, something like draining Lake Superior, then filling it with gasoline and setting it on fire. The light could be seen from the surface of Mars, assuming folks there had a telescope at least as strong as Lowell's. But would they know it was a signal? Or would they just think we liked to set lakes on fire now and then?

But the realization set in: We were stuck, we earthlings. We couldn't communicate with Mars. We couldn't travel there. We were left to speculate from afar, left to wonder about those remarkable beings who made those canals, who might be signaling us but would never get an answer.

There were canals on Mars.

Until there weren't.

They started crumbling sometime around 1907, when a chorus of astronomers began poking holes in Lowell's findings. They didn't question his sincerity. He was a responsible scientist doing good, responsible work. Taking diligent notes, putting his findings up for review by his peers. His observations of the red planet left behind a wealth of data, and avenues of further exploration for generations of astronomers to come. He was just wrong about what was happening there. He had been from the jump. In part, this was because he, and most of the rest of the English-speaking scientific community, had misunderstood Schiaparelli: He was using the word *canali* to mean not "canals" but "furrows." Or "channels." And there *are* furrows on Mars. They are caused by an ancient flow of some as-yet-unidentified fluid. We send probes and roving robots to sort it out still. But they are *canali,* not *navigli.*

But Lowell went looking for canals, so that's what he saw when he looked at the furrows. And when he saw the parallel canals, the ones that would disappear and then reappear, he might just have been seeing things. Some trick of the eye. Could've even been seeing a shadow cast by his own eyelashes.

That was in the papers too. Insult to injury for Lowell, surely.

And people went back to the rhythm of days on Earth, set by seasons and harvests and elections and train schedules and work-weeks and baby feedings and holidays and closing times and quotas and other earthbound concerns.

But there were canals on Mars, for a while there.

Zulu Charley, Romeo, a Love Story

How can we know if it's love? How can we know if it's real? How can we know what the other person is feeling? How can they know our heart, even if it is right there on our sleeve? How can we know what they have, that couple there? Are they in love or are they performing it? How can we possibly know from all the way over here, or from right beside them?

For a dollar a week, a man named Mkano performed a life. It cost a quarter to watch him do it, in the summer of 1881, at G. B. Bunnell's Brooklyn Museum, where, amid the other human oddities—the fat woman, the skinny man, the rubber man with the stretchable skin—you'd find Mkano, one of six men known collectively as Farini's Friendly Zulus. This was a well-chosen name, certain to appeal to a white audience who liked their exotic creatures declawed and neutered. The man who chose that name was good at that sort of thing. He had renamed himself, after all, going from William Hunt, a second-tier Canadian acrobat, semi-famous for tightroping over Niagara Falls, to Signor Farini, a European man of mystery, one of the nineteenth century's most successful showmen. And so it was that the Great Farini christened Mkano as "Charley," an all-American name for an African man far away from his home in Zululand.

We don't know precisely how or when the man who came to be known as Zulu Charley came to be employed by the man who came to be known as Farini. But it happened sometime around 1879, shortly after the British were routed in the first battle of the Anglo-Zulu War in South Africa. Newspaper readers around the world were fascinated by stories of the fierce spear-wielding warriors who'd defeated the gun-toting agents of empire. Farini knew readers would pay to see those warriors up close, so he sent someone to South Africa to find some.

The lines went around the block in every city they stopped in. In London, Brits crowded in to look their enemies in the eye and size up these men who'd beaten their sons and husbands and fathers and friends at the other end of the world. In New York at Bunnell's Brooklyn Museum, Charley and five other sons of Zululand were paid twenty cents a day to live a Zulu life, or at least those parts of a life that would entertain Americans. Chants and war dances, mostly. Spear-throwing demonstrations. Day after day, all through the summer, they suffered stares and catcalls and curses. They were right around the corner from the living human skeleton. The infant elephant. The two-headed girl. Day after day. Eight thousand miles away from home.

Anita Corsini spent her days teaching piano. She was eighteen, a Florentine new to America, as so many were back then. And as so many did, she worked to help support her family, but her father let her keep some pocket change. And one July day she had a quarter in the little pocket stitched into her homemade dress, and she decided to spend it at Bunnell's Brooklyn Museum and get out of the sun for a bit. She made her way through the exhibits, past the largest living couple. Past the smallest living couple. She might have caught the cat show or the bird show or the baby show; we don't know. But we do know she found herself among the crowd gathered to gawk at Farini's Friendly Zulus. Maybe she pushed her way to the front, or maybe men made way for this pretty girl with the dark curls and the dark eyes. Maybe some watched her as she watched the show. Watched Zulu Charley and the other men with new names as they chanted and danced and feigned fighting. Maybe those men saw her dark eyes grow wide.

How can we tell if it's love? How can we parse desire? How can we separate the physical—the flush, the rush of blood, the butterfly flutter—from the romantic, the story we tell about the flush and the rush and the flutter, woven from well-worn phrases and default descriptions of fleeting feelings?

Anita Corsini called it love at first sight. She knew enough English for that. There's a phrase in Italian, *un colpo di fulmine,* a lightning bolt of love. Maybe she used that phrase when she told her father, Tomasso, a man who made display cases for a living, about how she had fallen in love with a man on display. Told her father how every free quarter he let her keep was spent at Bunnell's Brooklyn Museum, to gaze upon this man from Zululand. About how, over the course of some unknown number of visits, she had worked up the courage to talk to him, this thrower of spears and of lightning bolts, and how she'd told him she loved him, and he'd said he loved her too, and asked her to marry him. And about how she'd said yes.

Her father had her arrested. She spent a night in Jefferson Market Prison in the West Village. He wanted to send her to the insane asylum on Blackwell's Island but the police wouldn't go that far. There was nothing they could do, really. New York was one of the few states where interracial marriage was legal, so they let her go. And Anita and Mkano found a reverend in Brooklyn and got hitched on August 25, 1881. One of Mkano's countrymen served as a witness. Anita's father didn't attend.

Later that night they went back to the museum. The show must go on and all. And Anita Corsini sat in the audience in a purple dress and a light straw hat with a white plume. We know because a reporter from *The New York Herald* was there to watch the new bride watching her new groom. Anita was described as "positively handsome, with a clear and rosy complexion, large and dark languishing eyes, full rounded cheeks, and a pure aquiline nose." Mkano was described as "swarthy." When the reporter caught up with Anita after the show, he asked her about their love. "He is my Othello and I am his Desdemona," she said. When the reporter pointed out that Othello kills Desdemona in the play, Anita said, "We love each other too much for that"—"naively," as the reporter decided to put it.

Let's pause here as we read, and let you hold that moment up to the light and examine it for yourself and draw whatever conclusions you will about this couple in that moment in history, about the unnamed reporter's choices and intentions. Continue when you will.

What can we know of their love? Some historians have done their best to know as best they could. Tried to sift through the clues the couple left on the rare occasions when their lives caught the light: A "Where are they now?" article. A report from here and there when Farini's Friendly Zulus hit the road. We can find Anita in those few clips, squirreled away in some paragraph, sitting in the audience watching her husband. But we can't know what they talked about or how they spent their time.

We can immerse ourselves in context, read about the fluidity of racial identity during that period, especially in New York, and note that the Italian Anita might not have been considered white, and speculate how that might or might not have affected how she and her husband were treated when they went out into the world, or how news of their wedding was received when it was read the world over. We can interrogate, as some historians have done, the practices of sideshows and showmen and point to a number of supposed pairings perpetrated by publicists. Count the number of tickets sold to the weddings of world's smallest men to world's smallest women and the like. But we can't know what the couple thought of each other. What they liked most. What they wanted to change.

We can read about the time a museumgoer taunted Mkano—or at least the Zulu Charley who appears in transcripts of and reports on the legal proceedings in New York and London. A man called him names and slapped him on the legs and shoulder, and Mkano hit him with a club. And we can applaud the police for not pressing charges against Mkano. We can read about how he agitated for a better contract, and complained about being bought and sold like a cow by Farini. We can read in the records about how the magistrate ruled against Mkano and the other renamed men and threw out their claim. We can extrapolate from his testimony Mkano's agency, a particular drive, and piece together some fragments of the character of this man who once met a woman. We have far fewer fragments from the woman, as is so often the case. Those two lines in the paper, for what they are worth, are all the voice that history has afforded Anita Corsini. Another fragment of what little we have left of their love story. These two people who found each other when both were so far from home.

We can't know their love. We can just hold it up to the light, then let it fade. And note for a moment just how brave a thing it is to love anyone in this world.

At the White House Easter Egg Roll of 1889

B y the time the gates were thrown open on the morning of April 22, 1889, the press knew the drill. This was the eleventh White House Easter Egg Roll. The tradition had really begun decades before, when local families would gather on the wide lawn in front of the Capitol to picnic on the Monday after Easter. They would bring eggs, hard-boiled and hand-dyed, and sticks for the kids to use to push them about in the grass. But in 1878, the families had arrived, their children's fingers rainbowed with dye, giddy in anticipation of the thrill of pushing hard-boiled eggs around with sticks, and been turned away. A law had been passed that protected the Capitol grounds, which could no longer be subjected to the destructive powers of picnics and children's delight. Hearing about the disappointed families, President Rutherford B. Hayes opened the White House grounds, and thus began a tradition.

In the eleven years since that day, the White House press corps had developed its own traditions, churning out the same sorts of articles year after year in what was surely a simple and pleasant assignment. Reporters would stroll about the grounds, taking note of the weather, the children, the first family, and any innovation that distinguished that year's rendition from any other. In the articles about 1889's Egg Roll, we read of a sunny April morning with air that was seasonably cool and filled with "the merry prattle of little-folks," children who had taken "possession of the grounds surrounding the President's house early on Easter Monday and [spent] the day rolling their eggs, romping, and playing and enjoying themselves generally in their own way." One article praises the diversity of the children within the crowd of several thousand, "large and small, rich and poor, black and white," a rare thing then, particularly in a city that was predominantly segregated.

Having ticked off the boxes of the weather and the children, the articles turn their attention toward President Benjamin Harrison, grandson of former president William Henry Harrison, and particularly toward the recently inaugurated president's own grandson. Benjamin Harrison McKee was just shy of his second birthday on that Egg Roll morning, when the press found him on the balcony of the portico, being held by the president as "the little fellow . . . kicked and howled with delight and almost jumped out of Grandpa Harrison's arms."

This was the first public appearance of "Baby McKee," a child who would soon become known as "the most famous baby in the world." It seems that during the remarkably unremarkable administration of Benjamin Harrison, having a rambunctious, towheaded kid toddling about the White House was enough to break through during slow news days. Perhaps the high point of the family's public life occurred in 1890, when the goat-drawn cart in which the boy rode about the White House grounds took off down the road and the president himself was seen sprinting after it to rescue Baby McKee.

But of course, on that April Monday, the press could not have known about the glories to come for Baby McKee (or of his less glorious adult life, spent chasing obscurity in Europe as an escape from years spent hearing, "Hey! You're that baby!" in the United States). The press instead identified the addition of live music as the most noteworthy innovation of that year's event. The U.S. Marine Band, in red coats and blue pants and white domed helmets, played

John Philip Sousa marches conducted by Sousa himself, enchanting "little people as well as old . . . adding materially to the enjoyment of the occasion" throughout the day, before finishing with a medley of "patriotic favorites," signaling "that another frolic had passed into history."

Historians of the White House Easter Egg Roll, such as they are, seem to follow the journalists' lead and identify the introduction of the Marine Band to the annual festivities as 1889's most significant occurrence, and include it in timelines of the event, along with the two Egg Rolls canceled during Word Wars I and II, and the day Lady Bird Johnson made an intern dress up as the Easter Bunny. But I propose there was something of far more historical importance happening on that April morning in 1889 than the fact that America's foremost march conductor was brought in to conduct marches. Further, I would submit that the most important figure at that event on that day wasn't John Philip Sousa or Baby McKee or, for that matter, President Benjamin Harrison, but the man on the left in this photograph.

White House Grounds 4.22.'89

We do not know his name. But his importance is owed to another man whose name you may know: George Eastman, who that very spring was becoming one of the most famous people in America.

Eastman spent his childhood in comfort, but his father died suddenly, and he and his mother moved into an apartment in Rochester, New York. She took in boarders to make ends meet and spent her days in their tiny kitchen cooking for them. At night, after helping her clean up from dinner, George Eastman took over the kitchen, where he would tinker with formulas he hoped would pull them out of poverty. He spent years mixing chemicals that would stain her sink, and whose strange and stinging smells would permeate the apartment, until he figured out how to replace a glass photographic plate with a movable strip of paper and celluloid negatives. That experimentation would, in the coming decades, lead to the invention of the motion picture, meaning that photographs could be taken in sequence, that one could make a filmstrip that was long and sturdy enough to be wrapped around a spindle and fed through a camera that could produce twenty-four images per second, and then sent through a projector that put those images onto a screen. That

meant we could find new ways to tell stories, that we would have *Casablanca,* and Rocky Balboa, and Kurosawa, and *The Red Shoes,* and Rita Moreno, and Richard Roundtree, and the bike riding scene from *Butch Cassidy,* and *Night of the Living Dead,* and *Singing in the Rain,* and Tony Leung and Maggie Cheung, and *Do the Right Thing,* and *Beau Travail,* and Elle Woods, and John Travolta's white suit, and the Zapruder film, and *Mad Max: Fury Road,* and it would create fortunes for Eastman and countless others and would change the course of history in ways that will make your head spin a little, if you think about it for a while. And those might not even have been George Eastman's most profound contributions to human history.

In the spring of 1889, while children pushed blue and orange eggs across the green White House grass, we as a species were beginning to become ourselves. Eastman's first product, the Kodak camera, had been released the winter before. At that time, as had been true in the six decades since the invention of the medium, taking pictures was the domain solely of people with the means to purchase and maintain expensive equipment and stores of chemicals, and the expertise and skill with which to use them to create images. In one punchy bit of ad copy, George Eastman offered two incredible propositions: "You press the button, we do the rest." For twenty-five dol-

lars, his company would mail you a wooden box with a fixed lens, a single button to push, and a handle to wind the next exposure into place on strips. You would take a hundred pictures and ship the camera back to the Kodak factory. It would send you back your camera, and your photos in small, circular prints, and, for an additional ten bucks, a fresh roll of film. This wasn't cheap, but it was accessible for many (twenty-five dollars was the equivalent of several hundred today). And by the spring of 1889, after a winter spent indoors oohing and aahing over cameras received by friends as Christmas presents or bought by tech-savvy acquaintances who were raving about the product, the Kodak No. 1 was the must-have new toy of the monied class. A sunny day in April was the perfect time to get out and take some pictures.

There is an aside in the otherwise rote write-up of the 1889 Egg Roll that appeared in *The Evening Star* the next day: The "amateur photographers were almost as numerous" as the kids. The reporter must have thought he was seeing a fad, not a moment that heralded what would surely be a permanent change in the way we lived. There are earlier examples of Kodak photographs. But this photo of this unknown man, bewhiskered and seemingly bemused, is likely the earliest documentary evidence of someone doing what so many of us do multiple times a day: take a picture of our life as it happens. On an April morning in 1889, two people ran into each other and were delighted. We see it on his face, don't we? Our friend with the camera lighting up at having come upon someone else engaged in the same thrilling new hobby. Two men, both unknown, at the birth of a revolution.

The Kodak camera freed our forebears from having to go to a photo studio to sit stock-still while someone mixed chemicals and charged them a small fortune for one image. It freed them from the held pose in a stranger's room. From having a moment that was so unlike the rest of their life represent their life forever. The Kodak camera put the means of production of those most vital of things— our own images, our own histories—into our own hands. The circular photos from those first years, of people at play and at work, of the streets where they walked, of the trees and buildings that shaded and sheltered them, of children who were young once, are taken by people figuring out, for the first time, what you could do with a camera. What it did to your life to have pieces of it on a wall, or in your wallet, or to be found one day and wondered over when you're gone.

The Glowing Orbs

When she found out they were going to shoot her husband into space, Annie Glenn wanted to talk to her minister. They were faithful people, the Glenns, devout Ohio Presbyterians, believers, deep down. When John was chosen to be one of the Mercury astronauts, Annie Glenn wanted to be sure that was okay. That man could leave Earth and stay in God's good graces, that the heavens weren't actually heaven. Her minister consulted the scriptures and found no good reason to keep her husband earthbound. And so, on a February day in 1962, while John Glenn waited in a small metal capsule atop a ninety-four-foot rocket for the clouds to drift away and clear the Florida sky above the launchpad, Annie Glenn prayed for fair weather, for her husband's safe return, and for America. And then she sat on the rug in their living room in front of the TV, hugging her knees to her chest, as mission control counted down to liftoff, and watched the smoke billow and the flames flash as her husband was propelled into the blue, and into the troposphere, and stratosphere, and mesosphere, and into the black. He was to orbit Earth three times in a little less than five hours. There was much work to do.

John was a marine, a war hero, a test pilot, duty bound—"Yes, sir"; "No, sir"—and the man for the job, if the job was checking off an array of procedures and processes and monitoring the health of the spacecraft and the spaceman, all while keeping his eyes on his work while Earth whipped by his window, while dawn turned to day turned to night turned to dawn, and on and on, while white ribbons of cloud roiled and rolled and broke over Bali or Boca Raton or Dar es Salaam. Somewhere around the South Pacific, as he rounded into his second swing around the globe, something caught his eye: He was flying through a field of tiny glowing orbs. Brightly lit and luminescent. They looked like little stars or fireflies. A whole shower of them. They seemed to follow him. Thousands of them.

When John Glenn came back to Earth and debriefed the folks at NASA and met the press and the president, neither he nor any of them had any good explanation for what he'd seen up there in space. And the mystery stayed with him. It floated around his head like one of his glowing orbs. Like the ticker tape that flitted about him and Annie at the parades that the grateful nation threw in his honor. But he was a man who was comfortable with mysteries. He was a believer deep down. And he'd write that his experience in space and the glowing orbs affirmed that faith. No one could see what he saw, he was sure, and not believe in God, not believe in miracles. He said the same thing thirty-five years later, when he went into space again at the age of seventy-seven. But at that point, people had solved the mystery: The glowing orbs weren't extraterrestrial fireflies. Weren't seraphim escorting a faithful man through the heavens. Weren't some godly being or a shimmering intelligence beyond our own.

They were pee.

John Glenn's urine. Expelled from the capsule and frozen into thousands of tiny orbs that caught the sun and seemed to glow from within.

So it was no miracle. Just a forty-year-old man from Cambridge, Ohio. Taking a leak. While flying eighteen thousand miles an hour, one hundred and sixty-two miles above Earth, in a metal capsule made up of thousands upon thousands of individual parts, designed and manufactured by thousands upon thousands of individual

Americans, and flying because the winding, polyvariant histories of two nations had pitted them against each other in an odd and temporary competition at an odd and temporary historic moment, while the man's wife watched TV, knees clutched to her chest on the living room carpet. Which is close enough to a miracle for me.

The Prairie Chicken in Wisconsin: Highlights of a Study of Counts, Behavior, Turnover, Movement, and Habitat

There was the time in 1914 when Frances Hamerstrom was seven and told her mother she wanted to plant a garden behind their big brick mansion in the woods outside Boston, and her mother said, "Of course, gardening is a fine pastime for a girl, but, Frahn," she said, pronouncing the girl's name with the moneyed mid-Atlantic accent of a Katharine Hepburn or George Plimpton or Mrs. Howell from *Gilligan's Island,* "the staff will dig the holes. Your job, as someone who will someday run a household, is to instruct the help as to where you'd like to plant the flowers and how. And then later, if you would like to cut some of those flowers for an arrange-ment to brighten up the parlor, bring some cheer to the landing on the grand staircase, why, by all means, enjoy—just be sure to wear a proper pair of gloves to keep your hands free of dirt." But Frances loved the dirt. She loved bugs and birds and worms. Once, one of their servants had fainted when she'd poured out cold water for a ladies' luncheon and found tadpoles swimming among the ice cubes. A garden, well-ordered and contained, her mother figured, would keep unruly nature out of her house and out of her daughter.

So she smiled with approval as she watched her daughter through the back window, telling the gardeners how to place the begonias in neat rows, looking every inch a proper little girl and the future lady of the house. She did not know that Frances already had a secret garden. Out by the potting shed, where she dug holes with her bare hands, collected insects she'd unearthed, put them in jars, pinned them and labeled them, planted rhododendrons so she could hide beneath them if anyone came looking for her. She realized she was resistant to poison ivy, so she planted a wall of the stuff around her real garden so no one would ever bother her there.

Then there was the day she went to the dentist, and for a treat her governess took her to the natural history museum, and she saw all those insects and arachnids mounted and labeled with names Frances hadn't known, species she'd pinned at home but couldn't identify, and she loved it and she cried when it was time to go home, until the governess promised her she'd take her again the next time she went to the dentist. And there was the night the following week when Frances took a pencil and poked at her gums until they were gross and inflamed, and her parents were alarmed and they told her she'd have to go right back to the dentist, and then they couldn't figure out for the life of them why she was smiling.

There were all those nights when she'd wait for everyone to go to bed, and she'd slip out her bedroom window and head out across the moonlit grass and lie beneath the stars and fall asleep to the sound of the night, alive around her, until she was awoken by the dawn, and she'd hustle back home before anyone knew she'd been gone.

There was the time before that—she was about five—when her family was on a grand tour of Germany, and a famous actress, some beautiful stage star, came to visit and lit a cigarette, flouting her father's strict rules against smoking inside, and Frances was sure her father was going to go ballistic, but instead he scrambled to find an ashtray. And there was the time when she was eighty-four and looking back on her life and remembered how she became determined to be like that woman one day, so famous she could make her own rules, so she wouldn't have to hide how odd she was, how unlike other people. "Few people," she'd write, "really held my attention.

It was the birds and mammals, reptiles and insects that filled my dreams and eternally whetted my curiosity."

For nine years, on Saturdays, in the ballroom at the Milton Club, she learned to dance and all that went with it (the entrances and exits, the curtsies and steps, how to hold one's head and one's partner's hand, where to look, where not to look, how to twirl but not too fast, how to smile but not too wide) to prepare for a future of balls and cotillions, as the wife of a diplomat or a man who owned factories. But no one ever asked her to dance. There were more girls than boys, and the boys didn't quite know what to make of her. She sat by the wall and watched and waited. Then she'd go home and return to her secret garden, to be alone with all the things she kept hidden away—her sick animals, her cigarettes, her rifle and ammunition—and to lie in the grass and dream of Africa and the Amazon.

There was a night, years later, when she had to tell her father she'd flunked out of Smith College. She couldn't be bothered to be interested in things that weren't interesting, all the preliminary courses and well-mannered nonsense. Her father told her she would need to get a job, then, perhaps assuming she would repent, slink back to him asking if he knew anyone at Mount Holyoke or Vassar. She got a job. She became a model. The only marketable skill she had was wearing dresses.

There was the night she went dancing—she was twenty, and boys wanted to dance with her then, especially when she wore her red velvet dress—and one young man, tall and handsome, came up to talk to her. He told her how he wanted to be a scientist, a naturalist, and to study animals in Africa, and she asked him if he wanted to get out of there. They went down to the beach and the pier, where people like them didn't go, where there were honky-tonks and hot dog stands and the place where they spun sugar into cotton candy, and they wound up at this joint where they played jazz. They had never heard jazz before, but they soon found their rhythm, and they danced until the sun came up. Frances thanked the bandleader on her way out, saying that it had been the best night of her life. Three nights later, three nights after seeing her in her red velvet dress, Frederick Hamerstrom asked Frances to marry him. She asked what had taken him so long. And there was the time that Frederick's grad school adviser said there was a job working with animals for both him and Frances. The job wasn't in Africa or the Amazon, as they'd hoped, but in Wisconsin. They would study prairie chickens.

And then there was the day they showed up at an abandoned farmhouse on the Wisconsin prairie and her high heels clacked on the frozen ground. In the mornings, they'd start a fire and wait for the room to get above freezing and celebrate if it was warm enough that they couldn't see their breath. During the days, they'd go out looking for prairie chickens. Studying their ways. Trapping and banding them. Day after day, season after season.

Some days she would stand in front of an ornate antique mirror they'd brought with them out to the Midwest and see if she could still curtsy. Other days, she got letters from her mother reminding her how to set a table when they were entertaining guests (should she send more dessert forks?), and she'd laugh at how much her life had changed.

There was the night the pump froze and there wasn't any well water, and not enough snow to melt to drink or to wash, and they needed to light a fire to unfreeze the pipes, so she soaked her red velvet gown in kerosene and burned it and knew that her old life was over for good.

And good riddance.

There were twenty-one years in which they studied the Wisconsin prairie chicken, struggled to understand why they were dying off, why they were on the brink of extinction, when they weren't being overhunted like buffalo or the passenger pigeon. Two decades of hosting grad students and volunteers, sometimes dozens at a time, who'd marvel at Frances and Fred and how they seemed one with each other and one with the land, immune to the cold and to boredom. Their visitors would be slack-jawed when rugged Frances showed them her curtsy or recalled some cotillion or other strange story of society life that seemed to come from a whole other life entirely.

Some nights the wind would howl and scare their two children, born to a fine family but born to the prairie. Some days they couldn't believe how fast the children had grown and how happy they were out there in the wild.

There was the time Fred's doctor told Frances her husband had pancreatic cancer. And the day not long after when he died. And there were times when she read tributes to her husband and to the work they did together, how it had saved the prairie chicken, how the two of them were people who'd figured out that extinction didn't come only from overhunting, but could be caused by habitat depletion. In their decades tromping through the low grasses of Wisconsin, they developed an approach to studying animals that is common sense now, but was revolutionary then. It was interdisciplinary. Zoology needed botany, which needed meteorology, which needed limnology, and on and on. They realized you couldn't understand what was happening with the chickens that ate the seeds without understanding the plant that dropped the seeds, or the creatures who burrowed beneath the seeds, or the stream that fed the seeds. They learned that the prairie chicken needed the prairie itself to survive. They discovered that all the prairie's creatures—its bugs and its grasses, its birds and its trees and its creeks that froze over—all the countless little things combined somehow to give the species life. They were all connected.

And when she was ninety years old, a few years before she died, there were trips down the Amazon, and to Africa. Frances would listen to the night and think of her husband and their fifty-nine years together, and of her life before, and the countless moments and choices big and small and the days unmarked or wholly remarkable, times remembered and lost that combined somehow to make a life, and she would fall asleep beneath the stars.

A Timeline of the History of the Temple of Dendur

At the start of the timeline, there's a story that goes that Caesar Augustus, the first Roman emperor and the adopted son of Julius Caesar, after defeating Antony and Cleopatra and taking over Egypt, wanted to keep his new subjects in line. He built a number of temples up and down the Nile to the local gods. It was a way to show the folks there that the new boss wasn't so bad. He wasn't going to force some weird new religion down their throats. It was also a show of largesse: a splash of cash on a public-works project. He picked Dendur, or his people picked Dendur, just north of Aswân, because there was already a smaller temple in Dendur dedicated to two princes who'd drowned nearby in the Nile and had, through some mechanism of belief that held sway for a relatively brief time in ancient Egypt, become gods. And so the people of Dendur were used to going to that spot to make offerings to deities to ask for bountiful harvests and mild flooding and healthy sons who wouldn't drown, and the Romans signed off on that location for a modest structure, and a few years later, around 10 B.C.E., here was the new temple, dedicated to Isis and Osiris and the two princes. And here were the men who had cut sandstone from a cliff face in a quarry, who'd carved it into blocks, who'd dragged them across the desert, who'd hefted them on their shoulders or sat upon them, still warm, as sunset cooled the air and a breeze shook the reeds, and a flat-bottomed boat floated down the Nile to the place where two princes had once drowned and become gods. And here were the men who stacked those blocks. Who chiseled them into columns and lintels. Falcon-faced gods. Set them in place just so. Sat and ate in the shade of a wall they'd built with those blocks. Men who would see the temple as their lives went on, would watch it change colors with each change of the light, or shimmer in the heat on the horizon, or see it half-submerged by the Nile, flooded again—and think, "I built that. I was here." And they'd tell their kids, who'd say, "My father built that. He was here." Maybe their grandkids too. Until eventually the Temple of Dendur was just landmark and landscape, sandstone eroding.

At the next points on the timeline, the story goes, travelers (explorers, soldiers, wealthy dilettantes) discovered the Temple of Dendur, over and over again. Saw it in the distance as they came around a bend in the river, as their caravan crested a hill and they stopped for a spell. Watered their horses or their camels. Rested for a bit in the shade of its walls. And carved their names; you can see them there still. The first one is in an ancient script—some tagger scraped it around two thousand years ago, but you can still make it out. And then there's someone named Drovetti in 1816. And an L. Politi in 1819: Luigi? Leonardo? Leandro? We don't know, but we can almost see him there, mustachioed, sweating through wool and linen, chipping his name into the soft stone of this temple. There was an antiquities dealer, or thief, depending on how you want to look at it, from Baltimore. His name's there too. And there's a New Yorker, Luther Bradish, who came upon this minor temple on his way to see better sites, and took a few moments out of his grand tour one day in 1821 to carve his name and to say to history: "I was here."

The story goes that the Nile flooded too high, over and over again, for millennia; that was the way of the Nile. There is a point on the timeline, in about 1954, when there were twenty-three million people in Egypt and the flooding was brutal and there was only one crop that year and there was a food shortage that threatened to become a famine but didn't quite. And so the government decided to raise the height of the Aswân Dam and make a lake that could help irrigate enough land to ensure three crops a year and sufficient food for those twenty-three million people. But such a lake would drown the Temple of Dendur, and many other archaeological sites that were far more significant. Hundreds of tombs and towns and forts. Abu Simbel, the great temple of Ramses II, the one with the four seated pharaohs carved into the hillside. You know that one, I bet. And you know it because the Egyptian government went to the U.N., which was brand-new back then, and asked the nations of the world for help, and fifty countries gave money to save it, and to save as much of this history as they could. Afghanistan gave two grand. Togo, newly independent, gave $815.30 as one of its first acts on the international stage. President Kennedy went to Congress and made an impassioned speech asking it to help preserve the antiquities, and to seize that moment in history and make its mark. The United States donated twelve million dollars. And that money paid for cranes and trucks and chisels and contractors and archaeologists and day laborers to dismantle and box up and store as many tombs and temples as possible before the waters rose.

There's a point on the timeline, marked on November 22, 1963, when a young president was shot in the back, in the back of a car, and fell onto his young wife beside him, and then was shot in the head while it lay on her shoulder, and he died. And then a couple of years later—after everything; after LBJ, one hand on the Bible and one raised in the air on Air Force One with Jackie beside him in the pink Chanel, still bloodstained; after Jack Ruby and Oswald; after John-John saluting; after all of it—the Egyptian government offered the American government one of the temples as a thank-you for helping to save so much from the flood. Other countries would get things, too, but the United States gave the most, so it could have first pick. The story goes that Jackie was asked to make the choice, because saving the temples and the like had been a cause dear to her late husband. That story's not entirely accurate, but that's how the story goes. It goes on to say that she chose Dendur; she chose this temple because it was the most beautiful and Jack would have loved it the most. And what she wanted—what she wanted for this temple, what she wanted for her husband, now two years dead—was to rebuild it in Washington, D.C., amid the faux Greco-Roman temples to Jefferson and Lincoln, and the fake Egyptian obelisk that is somehow supposed to evoke George Washington. What she wanted was to use this temple to Isis and Osiris, and to two princes who'd drowned too young in the river and become gods, as a memorial to the man she'd once met at a dinner party hosted by mutual friends, and then had fallen in love with and set out to spend the rest of her life with and

The story goes that the Metropolitan Museum of Art had hired a new director. His name was Thomas Hoving. He was thirty-six, which was remarkably young to hold a job like that at a place like that, especially then, but it was 1967 (you can find it on the timeline), and he was charged, in part, with harnessing the spirit of the sixties and making the Met a little less stodgy, within reason. Certainly less sleepy. People who've been around the museum for a long time will tell you stories about going to the Met to look at art on summer afternoons, when school was out, when tourists were in town, and having whole wings to themselves. Thomas Hoving wanted to change that. He wanted crowds.

At the same time, President Johnson was deciding what to do with this gift from Egypt. He had already ruled out Jackie's idea for a memorial—he wanted no part in deifying his predecessor. Instead, he wanted a contest: He asked museums and cities to tell him why they were the best place in America for an Egyptian temple. Not much of one, admittedly. It didn't come with any mummies or anything. Wasn't even all that old. But there were proposals from all over. From the Museum of Fine Arts Boston. From the Smithsonian. Memphis, Tennessee, and Cairo, Illinois, pitched their respective downtowns because they were named after cities in Egypt and wouldn't that be cool. And from the Met in New York. Hoving made a choice: He also knew this wasn't much of a temple. That there were already dozens of objects in the museum's Egyptian art department far more important. He knew it would cost a fortune to bring it to the museum, that he would have to raise money and wrangle with the board. He knew it had questionable aesthetic and historic value. But he also knew that you or I or anyone standing in front of it wouldn't really care. And he wanted to leave his mark on the history of the Met; he wanted to say, "I was here."

There's a black stripe that stretches along a section of the timeline of the history of the Temple of Dendur. It delineates the period of protracted competition and debate over who would get to have it, and that section is super boring so we'll jump over it. But there's one part of that story worth telling. We'll mark it with its own little dot.

When Thomas Hoving ran into one particularly thorny obstacle in the process, he called Jackie Kennedy, who was just about to get remarried, and asked if she could help, if she could put in a word with President Johnson on behalf of the Met. She said, Hoving claimed, claimed he wrote it down word for word, "I want it to be built in the center of Washington as a memorial to Jack. I don't care about the Met. I don't care about New York." She said, "I don't care if the temple crumbles into sand."

The story goes that the Temple of Dendur sat in pieces on an island in the middle of the Nile for almost twenty years. Then it was packed up into 661 crates, sent up the river (tamed by the dam by then), and loaded onto a Norwegian freighter and borne across waves to New York. That was in 1968.

It sat around for nearly a decade. A plastic dome was built outside the museum, where conservators could work on it and keep it protected from the elements. They were mostly waiting for a new wing to be built, with a room—with a high ceiling and a wall of glass looking out onto the park—made especially to house the Temple of Dendur. And then curators and teamsters and laborers brought it inside and put it back together. They are still around, a lot of them. Still saying, surely, to themselves, to their kids, to their grandkids now, that they built this, that they were here.

And there's another point on the timeline, another part of the story. *The New York Times* wrote it up: One day they were rebuilding the temple (scaffolding, hard hats, ancient dust catching the light through the windows) and work just stopped: Jackie Onassis and her daughter, Caroline, who was just about to turn eighteen, came into the room. Jackie lived a block away. It was 1975. It had been twelve years since her husband had been shot in the head while it lay on her shoulder. The *Times* didn't record what she said or know what she felt, of course, just that she looked around awhile and signed autographs for the workers.

And the timeline stretches on, with a point marking the opening reception, in 1978 (champagne flutes, wide lapels). There's a point placed at Hoving's death, in 2009. Dendur is mentioned near the top of his obituary. There's a point for teachers telling school groups the story. Explaining how this minor temple comes from the tail end of what we think of as ancient Egypt, when the old gods were on their way out, and that we are closer in time to its construction right now, by almost five hundred years, than the construction of the pyramids and the sphinx were to the men who built this temple and sat in its shade. But you can just tell that when the kids get home, the story will be "Mom, I saw a place where they put the mummies." And good for them. Mark a point for the night when one of those kids sleeps and dreams of Dendur. Mark a point for the selfie taken at arm's length, a tourist saying "I was here," another for the security guard saying "No flash, please" for the gajillionth time that day. One for the toddler eyeing the pool at the foot of the temple, with his parents warning him away, lest he be drowned and deified. Mark a point for each change in the light. And how it changes how the temple looks. Changes how you feel when you come upon it. Mark a point for you, here, now.

Points Excised from the Timeline of the History of the Temple of Dendur

Thomas Hoving had set his sights on Dendur before he had a place to put it. He sold President Johnson's panel on a vision of soaring windows and shifting light. Climate control. A space where people could come and commune with the past and where this sandstone temple could stand for another two thousand years. He would need a whole new wing, so he would need a fortune to build it: $3.5 million in 1967, an astronomical ask.

It was much harder than he'd hoped. He went down the list—the brothers Lehman, the family Rockefeller, Lila Acheson Wallace—but they all rebuffed him. The price was too high. But there was another name he had heard for the first time not long before, Arthur Sackler, a doctor, he was told, who had made his fortune manufacturing disinfectant. The product itself was no more or less exciting than one could reasonably expect a medical-grade cleaning solution to be, but Sackler had sold it through a method that proved revolutionary: marketing medical products directly to doctors. The doctor had spent much of his newfound wealth amassing a collection of Asian art and antiquities and had, a few years before Hoving was hired, lent it to the Met, where it was put on display in a gallery that bore his name. Hoving asked Sackler if he would like to help build a new home for the old temple. Sackler said he would like to build the whole thing. He had been enjoying having his name on a gallery at the Met. He had grown up humbly, the child of immigrant parents, who'd never imagined their son would be the kind of man whose name would be known by a man like Thomas Hoving; Sackler liked being known.

His two younger brothers had been following in his footsteps toward their own fortunes, perfecting his marketing techniques and selling painkillers through a network of doctors. Arthur Sackler thought they should join him in spending some of that family money on burnishing the family name. Hoving could have his new wing under these conditions: The payments would be spread out to allow the brothers to save money on their taxes, and the Sackler name would be on the wall in every gallery in the wing that would itself bear the Sackler name, and it would appear in every official mention of this temple to two drowned brothers. Place twenty points on the timeline, one for each year beginning in 1974, when the Metropolitan Museum of Art received a check from three brothers in the amount of $175,000.

At some unmarked point on the timeline, Nan Goldin realized that the name of the people who made the drug that had made her an addict was the same name she had been seeing all these years. Sackler in the Met. Sackler in the Guggenheim. The Louvre. The National Gallery. The Victoria and Albert. The Sackler Museum at Harvard, down the street from her first apartment, where she started to take the photographs that would put her own name on museum walls. Nan Goldin knew addiction. She'd kicked a heroin habit in the 1980s and had survived when so many of her friends and photographic subjects had not. But when she was in her early sixties and had surgery to cure tendinitis in her wrist, she was prescribed OxyContin to manage pain during her recovery. It is likely her doctor didn't know it was addictive; a marketing plan overseen by two of the Sackler brothers went to great lengths to obscure that fact. Her life soon revolved around scoring the drug. When she couldn't, she copped heroin. One time it was laced with fentanyl and she nearly died, nearly became one of the hundreds of thousands of Americans lost to an opioid epidemic in the first quarter of the twenty-first century.

Mark another point on the timeline for a winter Sunday in 2018, when Nan Goldin stood at the edge of the pool at the foot of Dendur, determined to lay the blame for an unrelenting wave of addiction and death on the Sacklers, and to use her fame as an artist to shame the museums that bought her work while helping launder a family name. She shouted that name as though her fury could shake it free of the gallery walls. Threw empty pill bottles into the pool, the fake Nile, and lay down on its marble banks as though she were dead, surrounded by fellow activists, some recovering addicts like her, others who had lost friends to overdoses, others who were fathers and mothers who'd done everything they could to keep their children from drowning but could not save them.

There were other protests at other museums. Years of them. In the fountains at the foot of the glass Pyramid at the Louvre. Fake prescriptions snowing down in the thousands from the spiraling galleries of the Guggenheim. Letter-writing campaigns. Appearances before panels. Congressional committees. Federal investigations. And then came word that the Met would be removing the Sackler name from its galleries, a lifted curse. Mark a point on the timeline for a day in December of 2021, when people came to see Dendur and the name was gone, as if it was never there.

In 2015, I was the artist in residence at the Met. I turned in my piece with the title "A Timeline of the History of the Temple of Dendur." I was told that, per a legally binding agreement, if I mentioned Dendur in the title, I would have to add "in the Sackler Galleries for Egyptian Art." I instead called it "Temple." I am glad to be able to return it to its original name.

Dreaming Caroline

The story was old and half-remembered. About a young noble-woman, who, by the laws of fifteenth-century France, became a duchess, but who, by the customs that constricted women then, wasn't allowed control of her own life. She wielded no power and held her title for a short time before ceding it to her young son. She died at fifty-four, her memory kept only in brief references in books on French peerage and in histories chronicling the emergence of the French nation-state. But four hundred years later, a Danish writer took that obscure, real woman and molded her into the nearly purely fictional heroine of a new story he called *King Rene's Daughter.*

Our own story begins one morning in 1873 when his book finds its way into the hands of our heroine, Caroline Shawk Brooks, the wife of an Arkansas farmer, and she sits down to read it rather than go and churn butter.

What she reads is a fairy tale of sorts. In it, the French duchess is instead a beautiful princess, blinded in infancy. Her name is Iolanthe. Her parents keep her locked up within a walled garden. The people who tend to her—her handmaidens and tutors and the palace guards—have to follow one important rule: They can never let her know she is blind. They are strictly forbidden from using the language of vision, of light and form and color, in her presence. One day, as may not surprise you, a handsome duke happens upon the garden and finds Iolanthe asleep in the grass, dreaming peacefully. He falls in love at first sight with the girl who can't see. She wakes. They talk. He is falling hard, when, noticing she can't tell the difference between a red and a white rose, he realizes she's blind. Not knowing the kingdom's rules, he excitedly tries to explain sight to Iolanthe. He can't find the words to do that, but he does know how to pledge his love. He leaves her in the garden, telling her he'll return when he's won her father's permission to marry her. She is game. She loves him too. She's been in this garden her whole life, so she assumes she'll be perfectly happy waiting around until he comes back. But she isn't. She struggles in her new state of being—of being without sight while not understanding it, of suddenly knowing that she lacks something, but not knowing what it would mean to have it.

Plot convolutions follow. There are misunderstandings and reversals of fortune, there are armies and alliances, but in the end, there is love and magic and a cure for the blindness of the beautiful princess.

I can't say what this story meant to Caroline. As is true with many turning points in her life, she left no record of what she felt in this important moment. We can speculate, as some have, that she and the countless women who read Iolanthe's story when it was a literary sensation during the second half of the nineteenth century might have seen something of themselves in the princess, in the ways so many of their lives were restricted by their husbands or their fathers or the paternalism of rules and norms that kept them from experiencing fully the world beyond the home. We do not know what the story stirred in Caroline at thirty-three years old, reading a book one day on her husband's farm. But we know what it inspired her to do.

Caroline had spent her childhood in Cincinnati making art. She would dig up clay from the creek bed behind her house and sculpt flowers or try to copy a bust of Dante Alighieri that was on the cover of a book on her father's shelf. She grew up and there wasn't time for all that. She had a husband and a farm and cotton to haul and cows to milk and butter to churn. But then one day art came back into her life in the form of a friend's copy of *King Rene's Daughter*. She felt that spark of inspiration.

This is what she made.

Iolanthe, dreaming. Moments before her awakening.

There is no record of how Caroline felt in this moment either. Could she see what she had done? What she was capable of doing? Did she suspect she'd always had it in her? Had she been beating herself up for years for not working harder, for not trying harder, for being too afraid to try at all? Did she ask herself, there in the quiet farmhouse, looking at her completed sculpture for the first time in the gathering twilight, where this might take her?

Her husband came home and was astounded. He had not known she could do this. Maybe there was something here, in this thing, this dreaming woman that his wife made one day when he was out. People needed to see it.

This is the part of the story where everything changes. By this point, you have correctly understood that you are reading a tale of the woman who will have her life changed by art. But that art?

It's made of butter.

It is just lots and lots of butter. If this sculpture were in a museum (and it is not, as, again, it was made out of butter), there would be a label nearby that would look something like this:

Caroline Shawk Brooks
American, 1840–1913

Dreaming Iolanthe 1873
Butter

She was not the first person to sculpt butter. There is an ancient Tibetan tradition of carving and molding butter made from yaks' milk. In the United States, there have been many other butter sculptors. There might well have been better butter sculptors than Caroline Shawk Brooks. You might well have seen better butter sculptures by better butter sculptors on some midwestern midway, or in some gee-the-heartland-sure-is-something-isn't-it segment on a morning wake-up television show. It is a living, if melting, art form. But I don't want you to see Caroline's work in the same way that you may view sculptures of competing presidential candidates on display at the Minnesota State Fair during an election year. It may be hard to think of butter art as fine art, but you are Iolanthe; you have not yet learned to see.

Try instead to see an art show in Cincinnati in 1873. There are still lifes of fruit bowls. There are landscapes of a half-imagined American West, blades of godly sunlight cut through blue-gray clouds to shine upon buffalo grazing in a glen at the foot of the Rockies, or whatever. See a clutch of visitors, a family, a bearded father lifting his young daughter to bring her to eye level with a marble bust of Lincoln, not long dead. And then see more visitors. Dozens pressed together, jockeying for position, craning to see *The Dreaming Iolanthe*.

Somewhere in that crowd was a reporter from *The New York Times*. He wrote a rave review: "It is safe to assert that no American sculptress has made a face of such angelic gentleness as that of Iolanthe." And though the reporter, like nearly everyone who has written about Brooks, noted the peculiarity of her medium and remarked with some condescension about her homespun methods (working, as she did, with a normal butter paddle as opposed to the traditional tools of a clay sculptor), he was struck by the artistic possibilities of the material: Its "translucence gives to the complexion a richness beyond alabaster and a softness and smoothness that are very striking." Another writer assured readers that, in any gallery, you would find no medium "more graceful, or more thoroughly ideal," and that "this butter head, moulded in a milk pan, is alive in its translucent shadows. It is well named the dreaming Iolanthe, for as in dreams the pulses rise and fall, and new mysteries and meanings pass across the sleeping face, so in the twilight or beneath the shade of the student's lamp, this Iolanthe in her half-conscious sleep, seems a breathing thing."

Over the next three years, Caroline built her reputation at Ohio art fairs. Each season she debuted new sculptures brought from Arkansas in a box of ice, continually replenished on the road: a bas-relief butter bouquet of blooming geraniums; a bust of Little Nell, the heroine of Charles Dickens's *The Old Curiosity Shop,* that was so stirring that one writer lamented that the famous author hadn't had a chance to see it during his recent trip to America. She always brought

The Dreaming Iolanthe too. It wasn't the same as the one she had first sculpted back on the farm; that had long since turned. And even though she had perfected and even patented a mold that would allow her to continually replicate her original triumph, she never used one. Each year she would sculpt a new version.

She was interviewed many times about her work, but no one ever seemed to ask her why she chose to sculpt Iolanthe again and again. That photograph you saw earlier is the only known documentation of these re-creations. The written record tells of variations and improvements that suggest she was reaching for something, that she wasn't merely playing the hits for an audience that continued to adore the sleeping beauty. It might be that each new Iolanthe offered her a way to play and experiment, gauge her progress, keep in practice, or stretch herself and her art in ways that only she could see, could feel in her fingers, and in other, more abstract ways. Was there a meditative state she entered when she improvised Iolanthe? Did the butter in her fingers, the smells, the rhythm of the work, bring her back to something familiar, comfortable, even as her life was taking her to places she had never been?

Lucy Webb Hayes was a family friend from Caroline's Cincinnati girlhood, but while Caroline's marriage took her to an Arkansas dairy farm, Lucy's took her first to the governor's mansion and then to the White House as Mrs. Rutherford B. Hayes. She loved *The Dreaming Iolanthe* and pulled strings to get her friend's art exhibited at the Centennial Exhibition of 1876. That summer, some ten million people walked through the Philadelphia fair, and many found themselves in the Women's Pavilion, a soaring white mansion that occupied a full acre of the grounds. In it, they heard speeches on suffrage and equality by Elizabeth Cady Stanton and Susan B. Anthony. Lectures on the roles of women in philanthropy, philosophy, education, medicine, and literature. It housed innovations by female inventors, artists, designers, and artisans. And in the center of a Venn diagram of all of them was Caroline Shawk Brooks. A bestselling guidebook to the fair (that was a type of bestseller back then) wrote glowingly of her innovative method. With its piles of butter, its paddles and bowls and awls, and its reliance on modern refrigeration to achieve optimal plasticity, her technique seemed the perfect marriage of all the spheres of womanly activity on display in the Pavilion.

A newspaper clipping tells us about an ecstatic note she wrote to her husband back home, telling him she was "the sensation of the exhibition." There is no record of a reply. And so we are left to wonder what her husband thought as her letter arrived at the farm one summer day and he opened it to read of his wife, who was not merely *at* the Centennial Exhibition (an event that was, even on the banks of the Mississippi, the talk of the town) but *the sensation* of the Centennial Exhibition. And we can't know what it meant to his days, at work on the farm, to hold this idea, and whatever images it conjured as he tended his fields and animals: Caroline, at the fair.

His wife drew so much attention in the Women's Pavilion that she was invited to demonstrate her techniques in the Main Exhibition Hall. This was not a space for women. The only ones who were part of the Centennial Exhibition's central art show were marble nymphs and maidens, painted nudes and silk-draped odalisques, biblical queens and allegorical embodiments of various virtues and vices, and now there was Caroline Shawk Brooks. Did she belong here? The question hung over the exhibition. After all, there was a handful of women sculptors and painters whose work met the rigorous and rigid standards of the curators of the exhibition, but who were still stuck in the Women's Pavilion. These were women who'd come to art through the proper path of prestigious schools, pedigreed families, grand tours of Europe, master classes at the Uffizi and the Louvre (women who, we might add, joined the rest of the art establishment in looking down on the butter lady). How had this humble woman, wife of a farmer, churner of butter, mastered these classical forms? When they saw her work critics and curators were skeptical that she was as humble as she purported to be. There were even whispers that she might not be the artist at all. But unlike the oil painters in the exhibition, who needed to wait a week or more for a single layer of paint to dry, or the sculptors of marble cherubs, who spent countless hours chiseling and polishing, Caroline could make art on demand. So they demanded it.

She once described her private toil on the farm as "the kind . . . that you never get through with." You just keep working, "from year's end to year's end." But she spent the centennial summer of 1876 in festive Philadelphia making art in public.

Give her a lump of butter and an hour and a quarter and, as one guidebook exclaimed, "the shapeless, golden mass was transformed into the relief bust of another sleeping beauty." With each session, a new artwork. The crowds thrilled at these acts of creation. A chain of flowers. A cooing infant. Each with no model, no sketch. Each an improvisation.

And at summer's end, she didn't go home. She left the farmwork to her husband and she went on tour, making butter sculptures for paying audiences in the great American cities of her day. In a grand auditorium in Des Moines, she stood at center stage while two thousand people watched her work as a marching band played. The audience thrilled as she scooped and shaped the butter—a simple mound that looked as though it were fresh from the churn, something with which nearly all had personal experience there in farm country—and turned it into a face, a profile in bas-relief. And then, on cue, "La Marseillaise" played as she transformed that face into Napoleon; and then another martial song, an American tune, took over, and Napoleon became George Washington, all before their very eyes. (Think of the conversation with the conductor beforehand, the cues and the timing.) The crowd roared. But then wonder turned to worry as the vibrations of the bass drum and the low *whoom* of the tubas and the bleat of the high brass shook her easel and the bust began to split at the shoulder, unleashing an avalanche of sliding butter, but

Caroline was quick and caught it as it fell, and within moments the piece was repaired and completed, and the audience, relieved and astounded, applauded with a force that, if not enough to shake and rebreak the sculpture, surely stirred its creator.

She took up residency for several weeks in Boston, charging visitors to watch her at work in her studio. She sold photographs of her sculptures, permanent documents of her impermanent art. In Washington, she unveiled her most ambitious Iolanthe yet, the princess in full form, in draping garments.

At least one critic derided the work. It was lovely in its way, he couldn't argue, but its failure to conform to classical proportions still marked it as the work of an amateur lacking formal training and exposure to the great masters of Europe. But in July of 1878, two summers after her triumph in Philadelphia, that amateur was on her way to France to show her work at the world's fair in Paris, her passage paid for not by a wealthy father or through the largesse splashed upon the distinguished graduate of an eastern city's finer finishing schools by its women's art league, but with the money she'd earned making art.

Would that I had a paddle, some kitchen tools, a dozen or so pounds of butter, and the gifts of Caroline Shawk Brooks. I would create for you here, before your ever-widening eyes, an image in bas-relief. It would be partly a historical frieze in the spirit of Saint-Gaudens's monument to Robert Gould Shaw and the Massachusetts 54th Regiment marching toward war, partly an allegorical work. I would conjure a sculpture in dairy of the woman known, during the time she was known at all, as "the Centennial Butter Sculptress," and present it in a packed theater in Des Moines, Iowa, a marching band at stage left. Cue "La Marseillaise."

Picture a lively tableau set on the docks of Le Havre. Porters and stevedores scurry hither and yon. A high-toned, buttery couple, just arrived from Manhattan for their grand tour of the Continent, wobble, their land legs having yet to return; the wife holds a handkerchief to her mouth to keep out the scent of brine and diesel from the idling ships in the chaotic port at the height of summer. The keen-eyed viewer can spot butter wharf rats eating butter produce trampled on the pier. At the center of this scene find the artist, a woman in her mid-thirties in a modest dress, petticoats, and a traveling bonnet, petite but strong-shouldered. She stands beside a crate, recently pried open by one of three customs officials in tall hats. Two of the men stare in evident surprise at what has been revealed inside: a sculpture of a beautiful woman asleep on a bed, ringed by tiny flowers; a third takes notes in a book. The woman watches the three Frenchmen with what appears to be amusement.

There is only so much that any sculpture, even an imaginary one, can capture. A kitchen knife could never effectively etch what the man is writing in his book, the thing that amused Caroline: He listed *The Dreaming Iolanthe* as "118 pounds of butter."

My sculpture would capture Caroline as she had depicted Iolanthe so many times: in a suspended moment before the contours of reality are revealed. There on that dock, in that liminal space between her point of origin and her destination, between her life before and her life that was about to begin, what could we see in her face but pride and hope? She had earned her way there. She was an artist who had been called to Paris. She was on her way.

She didn't know yet that she would not make it to the exhibition on time. She had already been held up in New York for reasons now lost to history, but she was about to be further delayed by the challenge of securing passage on a train that could not only carry her and her sculpture, but accommodate enough ice to keep that sculpture from melting. When she arrived too late, she rented a storefront near the fairgrounds and got to work. She was always improvising. She would sell enough admission tickets and souvenir photographs that she could begin to reach for that thing that she was told she needed: art-world credibility. She toured Europe and saw the classical sculptures in the great European museums that American aesthetes had long deemed required viewing for the would-be serious artist. She saw them on her own dime. She bought marble from the quarries of Carrara. Paid stonecutters to fashion new works from her models, in the mode of the most renowned sculptors of her day, taking her first shot at making art that would outlive her.

Caroline Shawk Brooks died at the age of seventy-four in 1913 in St. Louis, where she appears to have lived for some time. We don't know much about what she did during the years after she returned from Europe, though that is true of so many areas of her life. We know she had a daughter named Mildred. At some point Caroline decided to live permanently apart from her husband, but we don't know when, or why, or whether their marriage came apart all at once or whether it became clear over time that it just wasn't going to work.

We know she was a working artist. That she made enough money to work and to travel but was never rich. We know that despite this, she became ensconced for many years in high society in Washington, D.C., perhaps after an introduction from her friend, the one-time First Lady. She took commissions and made frieze portraits of prominent Washingtonians. She worked in butter, her first language, then made plaster casts from which marble sculptures would be copied. She wrote proposals for at least two prominent commissions, marble monuments to Columbus and Ulysses S. Grant, but was passed over.

Her most ambitious work in marble is a group portrait of a wealthy New York family. She who could make a sleeping woman in an hour and change spent six years on this sculpture. Forming studies in butter, but learning again and again that it was difficult to find the same life when she tried to make the sculpture in marble. And so we have these four figures standing stiffly around a seated woman, a blanket of roses draped heavily over a table, and this image of Caroline standing beside it.

Her sculptor peers thought little of it, not that they ever thought of themselves as her peers. Her marble work, competent but uninspired, well rendered but lifeless, gave her critics ammunition, supposed proof that they had been right about her all along.

They were not.

Why should she be able to sculpt marble as well as the titans of her time? Those artists had trained for decades; she began with butter in her thirties. She would forever be the Centennial Butter Sculptress, derided for her medium, for the way she remade the same sculpture again and again, all while the still-young nation held up Gilbert Stuart as one of its great artists, a man who painted a clenched-jawed George Washington ad nauseam; Caroline Brooks could make Washington out of Napoleon while a marching band played. Other sculptors chipped and chiseled, plotted and planned, consulted and subcontracted and criticized, while she improvised new artworks in a new medium, inventing as she went a form of performance art and a type of life for a woman in nineteenth-century America.

A handful of her marble sculptures are scattered among various private collections and museums, though very few are on display. Her greatest works, like her fame, are long gone. And unlike a landscape painting or a bronze nude or a sideboard by some once-prominent furniture maker from the Shenandoah Valley, her work can never be reappraised. No curator can bring together several versions of Iolanthe and let us walk the marble floor among the butter princesses and trace the evolution of the art of their maker, see how the surfaces catch the light, cast a certain spell, and reignite a fame that has—as it does for all of us lucky enough to make something that people see or hear or read—all but melted away. May these words be like ice, and keep her memory a little longer.

Seven Stories

Elevators are old. They'd have to be, because it is in our nature, right? To rise? So history—even ancient history—is thick with things that lift other things: ropes and platforms and weights and pulleys, with people to pull them. When the slaves of Rome were served up to the wild beasts at the Colosseum, other slaves pushed the wheels that pulled the ropes that lifted the platforms that sent them from the darkness below ground up into the sun and the roar of the crowd and the lions. In China and Hungary and on Mont-Saint-Michel, one could find monks and kings and courtesans and construction materials and meals fit for queens and assorted consorts rising, while some slave or servant or caged animal somewhere pulled on some rope or pushed some piece of wood around and around and around. One man in France spent the year 1743 inside a chimney, waiting for a bell to ring, so he could pull a rope through a pulley and hoist King Louis XV in a flying chair from the ground to his bedroom balcony, rather than have him walk a single flight of stairs.

Elisha Otis was too sickly for the family farm. He was a good-looking kid and smart as a whip, but he was kind of a weakling. When he was nineteen he moved away from home in Vermont to figure out something else to do for a living. He wound up in a furniture factory, where he and his co-workers spent their days sanding curves and decorative knobs into bedposts. Otis spent his nights designing a better way to do this. He invented a machine, a kind of lathe, that sped up the process. It increased their output, made the men's jobs a little easier, and opened up the aesthetic possibilities of the bedpost in new, thrilling ways, knobs upon knobs upon knobs upon knobs. And his boss took him off the floor and made him head engineer of the Maize & Burns Bed Factory of Yonkers, New York. So Otis got to work trying to solve one of the biggest problems in the place.

The factory had an elevator—a lot of factories were starting to have them then. These were uncomplicated machines: just a platform that could be pulled from the ground up to a second story on a chain or a set of cables or ropes. One day in the factory, the rope snapped, and the platform plummeted fifteen feet, slamming onto the floor and onto one of the men below. Its cargo went careening, smashing into the scattering workers as they fled.

A few years later, in 1853, Elisha Otis stood on a wooden platform thirty feet off the ground. The elevator was loaded with lumber and tools and barrels—just like it had been that day in Yonkers. And down below stood hundreds of gentlemen and ladies who didn't want to spend their night out on the town being crushed by construction equipment. They had come to the New York Crystal Palace exhibition to see the wonders of the world assembled in a massive building of steel and glass, on the site of Bryant Park. It was

America's first world's fair. New York was psyched. After walking through the sculpture gardens and the art galleries, visitors found themselves in a great hall filled with industrial equipment. As they stood on the floor of this main hall, light streaming through the glass roof, craning their necks to see Otis and his elevator floating in air, they might not have known that they were looking at the future.

They had seen elevators before. They had seen one inventor after another come up with new ways to get from one floor to another, and here was one more. Admittedly, it went higher than they'd ever seen—three stories instead of two—but there was no way this thing was going to catch on. Who in their right mind was going to ride a three-story elevator? If the rope broke and the elevator fell from the second floor, you'd break a leg. If it fell from the third, you'd break your neck.

So they watched Otis. They listened to his spiel about his engineering bona fides. Listened to yet another inventor claim that yet another invention was going to change the world, and then they watched Otis raise his hand. They watched his son raise a sword and then bring it down like an executioner, slicing the rope that held up the platform. The audience screamed. And then they cheered.

Elisha Otis didn't invent the elevator: He invented the brake. The little metal piece that catches the car and stops it from plummeting if the cable stops holding it up. Elisha Otis didn't invent the elevator, but he kind of invented the modern world.

Elisha died a few years after his stunt at the Crystal Palace. He got one of those respiratory infections that would clear up in a few days with some antibiotics today, but that killed people back in the 1850s.

But he lived long enough to take advantage of the splash he'd made by not splashing onto the floor at the exhibition. He made a small fortune selling the world's first safe freight elevators. And he lived long enough to teach his two sons the business.

It was Charles and Norton Otis who realized the big business wasn't in freight elevators. The Otis brothers convinced the world to aim higher. The tallest buildings back in the nineteenth century, those that weren't churches or bell towers or lighthouses, were just a few stories tall. In part, these buildings were held down by a lack of engineering know-how. But just as much, they were held down by stairs: People could climb only so many. So the brothers Otis came up with a killer sales pitch: Higher was better.

They targeted hotels first, where more rooms meant more money. And they persuaded them to turn the idea of luxury quite literally upside down. Before the elevator, the best rooms were on the bottom floor. You didn't have to walk up. Four flights of stairs? Stick the pauper in the penthouse. But the Otis brothers persuaded hotels it should be the other way around. The first floor is by the street, with hoi polloi and their noise and their sweat and their fruit carts stinking in the sun and, worse, their horses and the things horses do. Wasn't a king's throne supposed to be higher than his servants? Wasn't a lord supposed to lord over? Why shouldn't the wealthy traveler be above it all? And the hotels bit. They built high. And the wealthy travelers liked the view. And when it came time to build their next office building, or expand their shirtwaist factory, they built higher still. And they bought elevators from the Otis Elevator Company.

Buildings grew. From three stories to four, then six. And elevators became better and faster, to the delight of their passengers, who loved the thrill of hurtling seventy feet at a speed of six hundred feet a minute to a penthouse on the seventh floor. It was like a roller coaster: Trust in the seatbelt, trust in the track, and enjoy the ride. But though the Otis safety elevator relieved them of the fear of falling to their doom, it created a new concern, one ginned up in the papers and in the esteemed pages of *Scientific American,* which warned of the horrors of something called "elevator sickness." A bout of acute dizziness and nausea, owing to the fact that when an elevator comes to a stop, not all your organs stop at the same time. The best way to combat this entirely theoretical problem was to find a way to brace your head against the ceiling of the elevator as it came to a stop, so all of you stopped at the same time.

The regional headquarters of the Otis Elevator Company in my hometown is a one-story building.

At another industrial exposition, in Chicago in 1880, a crowd gathered to watch a dramatic demonstration of the latest in elevator safety technology. Not long before, a twelve-story building in New York became the tallest office building in the world. It had every architect and every illustrator in the Sunday circulars drawing up visions of the cities of the future with gleaming towers climbing, soaring, fourteen, even seventeen stories. And though people had grown to trust the Otis brake at four and five stories, what would happen if something happened while you were up there scraping the sky?

So the fairgoers went out to a field where another inventor had constructed a temporary elevator and shaft, this one 109 feet tall, and they watched as passengers climbed to the top and stepped inside. And they watched as someone cut the rope to the elevator and it dropped, plummeting for a few exhilarating seconds before it came to a slow stop, cushioned by a pocket of compressed air. And then the crowd politely applauded, the outcome never having really been in doubt, what with the wonders American inventors were coming up with all the time, and having seen this trick at an industrial exhibition before.

They might have been more excited, however, had they known that this same technique had been tested in secret in Boston not long before: When an elevator car holding eight volunteers dropped on command, the air pressure in the shaft that was supposed to cushion its descent blew out the walls of the shaft, leaving nothing to stop the free-falling car but Massachusetts soil. Many bones were broken, lives passed before eyes. Things the eight volunteers who climbed into the elevator in Chicago hadn't been told.

The Burj Khalifa tower rises 2,722 feet above the desert in Dubai. It has history's highest and fastest elevator. An Otis. The ride takes you up 124 floors in about a minute. Reviews call the experience "mildly exhilarating."

Elizabeth

L et me get us through this quickly.

There was a girl, her name was Elizabeth, and when she was eleven, she got sick. Out of nowhere. She was a happy and bright-eyed kid, and then she wasn't. She'd go to a friend's birthday party and have some cake, and it would destroy her. She would need to drink and drink and drink afterward. She started to lose weight. She was exhausted all the time. One day she got diarrhea, and it almost killed her. Her doctor diagnosed her with diabetes and told Elizabeth's parents (he didn't tell Elizabeth) that she would probably die before the year was out, because that's what happened to kids with diabetes then. They just died.

But there was a clinic. A psychiatric hospital in farm country in New Jersey, where a doctor had figured out a way to keep diabetic people alive for two years, sometimes three. That was unheard-of. And wasn't three years better than a few months? Wasn't alive better than not?

Elizabeth's father had been a Supreme Court justice. This is important here only in that her family was the sort who could get their kid into a place that helped kids live for maybe three years instead of maybe one. So Elizabeth went under the care of Dr. Frederick Allen, the world's foremost expert in the practice of starving children so they could live.

The symptoms of type 1 diabetes are described in writings on papyrus and parchment from ancient Egypt and India. Medical historians think there were few cases to describe and record back then, because if you had the disease, you would die before having the chance to meet the kind of person who would write about it. Life with diabetes, as a Greek physician wrote in the first century, was "short and painful and disgusting." Your body can't break down sugar in your bloodstream, and so it starts to poison you. You become, like Elizabeth Hughes, insatiable, and the more you drink and the more you eat, the more your body punishes you and your nervous system rebels and your digestive system rebels and your life is painful and disgusting and, at that point, mercifully short. It took centuries for doctors to know why this was happening. The treatments doctors developed for the disease were just wishes, just failed bets placed on theories based on very little.

During the Siege of Paris in the early 1870s, when the German army cut off the city and people who were trapped inside went without food, a doctor noticed that his diabetic patients improved. The idea took hold that if glucose—the sugar in food—was poisoning diabetics when it got into their bodies, they should keep food out of their bodies. And so when Elizabeth arrived at the residential hospital in 1919 and was placed in Dr. Allen's care, he kept food from her.

He was a good man, by all accounts. He was just trying to help, and he was so good at his job—at starving diabetic children—that they stayed alive for much longer than anyone thought possible. But what was the use of that life when it was spent in bed, weak and hungry?

Elizabeth had only enough energy to read or sometimes to sew. Sometimes to write a letter to one of the other kids in another bed in another room. But no one explained to her why sometimes, why most times, the kids just stopped writing back.

One twelve-year-old patient, a boy, blinded by his disease, said he wanted a canary for company. He wanted to hear it sing. But it seemed to be a ploy. He wanted to steal its birdseed. They took away the bird and the seed. He starved to death. He died of his cure.

In another hospital, another doctor, another good man who was just trying to help, said of one of his patients that when she was placed on a scale, what registered was only the weight of her bones and the weight of her soul. And this is hard to read, I know. It is no easier to write.

But there is hope, here:

Elizabeth suffered horribly for three years. Horribly. Make no mistake. But because she lived, because she endured that suffering, she was alive when a new treatment was developed. In the 1890s two German scientists had removed the pancreas from a dog and noticed that the dog became diabetic. In 1920 a Canadian doctor named Frederick Banting removed part of the pancreas of a brown-and-white collie, making it diabetic, and there the poor thing was, lying on the table, near death, when the doctor injected her with insulin, a pancreatic hormone that Banting had identified and named, and the dog started wagging her tail and jumped off the table. Dr. Allen heard about this, made his way to Canada to get the medicine, came back to his hospital and his starving patients, and made them well.

Elizabeth was five feet tall and weighed forty-five pounds when she started her insulin treatment. She was three days shy of her fifteenth birthday. She could barely walk. That was in August 1922. That November she weighed one hundred and five pounds. She was back at home. She could eat. She could run. She could play.

This wasn't a cure. It was a treatment. It wasn't the happy ending. It was the starting line.

Here we should slow down. We should think of the relief of her parents. Of Dr. Allen. Of all the nurses. Orderlies. Groundskeepers. Everyone at the clinic. All these people who had been watching children waste away and die. That had been their job, every day. Now they got to watch resurrections.

We should think of the relief of other parents and other doctors who read about how the daughter of a former Supreme Court justice had been saved by this new treatment. And think of Elizabeth Hughes leaving the hospital behind, starting a life.

But we should think, too, of the boy with the bird. And of the other patients who didn't live long enough for the insulin treatment to be discovered. Or whose parents weren't justices of the United States Supreme Court and couldn't get insulin in those early days, before it became cheaper and then ubiquitous, and so they died when they didn't need to.

Think of the people who were born at the wrong time. And of the way one's historical moment determines who gets to live and how. Think of a man in 1980, dying of a disease with no name. Of another man in 1982, with the same symptoms, but knowing he was dying of AIDS. Of another man in 1985, who hoped that a single drug would cure him of AIDS, but it didn't. And of another man in 1996, who was told to take a cocktail of drugs and who is living with HIV today. Think of the people who were lobotomized before psychiatric drugs were developed. Or who died after surgery, because their doctors didn't know to wash their hands. Think of all the people you know who can't play that game where you pick when you'd like to live if you were given a time machine, because they know they wouldn't last long without their dialysis or their statins or their synthetic thyroid hormone or their pills or their therapy or their patented medical device. Those things that allow them to live a life.

. . .

Some forty-one thousand injections let Elizabeth Hughes live until 1981. She went to college. She got married. She had a son and two daughters of her own. She lived in the suburbs of Detroit. She volunteered. She sat on boards. She founded the Supreme Court Historical Society, but when it came time to turn over own father's papers, she removed every reference to her illness and the three years she spent starving.

Butterflies

There was a mysterious knock. It kept men in vast mansions up in the dead of night, disturbed by a sound that defied explanation and bedeviled scientists. But a man named Thomas Midgley, Jr. (who looked like a man named Thomas Midgley, Jr.: kind-eyed, balding, round face, round glasses) was on the case. I'll tell you right up front that he cracks it, for the case of the mysterious knock has a solution. As this story proceeds, Thomas Midgley will follow a series of clues and draw a conclusion, and it will be the correct one. And I'll strip out any of the red herrings and false leads he might have stumbled on during his investigation, because that part of the story, the mystery—that is the part that is knowable, with a straightforward chain of cause and effect, and you'll forgive me if I cling to that little bit of comfort.

To the beginning:

Thomas Midgley was born in Beaver Falls, Pennsylvania, in 1889, to an upper-middle-class family. There's an anecdote from the life of young Tom that I'd like to share. It seems to have some bearing on the rest of his story and how the boy makes the man, as they say. Young Thomas Midgley loved baseball and became obsessed with the spitball—how some major leaguers had taken to doctoring baseballs, smearing them with petroleum jelly or tar or tobacco spit, and how that changed the way wind resistance played upon a pitched ball. It gave it a chaotic and unpredictable trajectory on its way to the plate. Young Tom spent a summer methodically testing different substances, applying sticky thing after sticky thing, until he came upon the sap of a particular variety of North American elm tree that gave him the desired effect. He could throw the ball and have no sense of what would happen once it left his hand.

That boy grew up and went to Cornell and got a job working in a lab for General Motors, where he was put on the case of the mysterious knock. The facts were these: The internal combustion engine, which was the engine of the new, twentieth century, wasn't all it could be. Often when things were combusting internally, the tiny explosion of fuel—the spark that pushed the pistons up and down, which, in turn, moved other things to make the wheels go around—caused a loud knocking sound. Engines would break, cars would struggle, planes would sputter. And those men in their mansions were up all night because they knew the knocking was keeping the future at bay. A future with planes that flew higher and farther, cars reliable enough that the average family would be willing to buy one. Everything—vehicles, commerce, America—could be moving faster, but for the mysterious knock.

Thomas Midgley realized that he could add something to gasoline that would fix the problem and stop the knocking. It took him six years to figure out what that was, of going methodically block by block through a copy of the periodic table of the elements that he kept folded up in his wallet, until he found his proverbial elm tree sap: tetraethyl lead. The next year, the cars of the three top finishers at the Indianapolis 500 auto race ran on leaded gasoline, and Midgley's bosses started a venture called Ethyl Corporation to manufacture it. They made Thomas Midgley its vice president.

Frank Durr was twelve when he went to work at the DuPont factory on the banks of the Brandywine River in Delaware. This was about the same time that Tom Midgley, at about the same age, was perfecting a spitball. We don't know much about what Frank Durr did in that factory, only that he spent his adolescence making gunpowder for DuPont. He was just another kid in another factory. But we know the work was hard, we know it was dangerous, and we know he was still there some twenty years later, and that he did the work with enough good cheer to earn him the nickname Happy. Sometime around 1921, Happy Durr was transferred to the new Ethyl plant in Deepwater, New Jersey.

First came the butterflies flitting through the factory, catching the light that filtered in through the closed window near the roofline. They'd land on you sometimes while you worked. One would sit on your shoulder, you'd brush it away, and there it was again, balanced on the back of your hand, spreading its yellow wings. Some days they'd fill the room. It was the damnedest thing. "The House of Butterflies"—that's what they called the factory in Deepwater. Such an odd thing. Butterflies in the factory. There one second, and then gone, and then there again, but never really there at all.

A man named Harry Zanes was the first to go mad. First there were the butterfly hallucinations, then the nightmares, then he couldn't eat, then his heart started racing, and then his muscles started twitching. Then he got violent and the screaming started, and they had to put him in a straitjacket and tie him to a bed, where he flailed, teeth clenched and grinning. He survived, but never really recovered.

Happy Durr was the first to die. He started raving and twitching. He died at home in a straitjacket. The end was mercifully quick. He was thirty-three years old. He had survived a decade working in a factory making explosives, but was killed by one month in the House of Butterflies.

All told, five men died at the Ethyl plant in Deepwater; three hundred more got sick, many of whom never fully recovered. The papers were all over it. There was a big blowout in *The New York Times*. It is a heartbreaking read. There were government inquiries. Thomas Midgley spent much of 1924 speaking in front of boards of health. The Ethyl Corporation pulled the product from the market while all this was going on. And there were two questions: First, what happened to those people in Deepwater? But that was obvious to anyone who knew anything about working with lead. The men were poisoned. Get lead on your skin or breathe it in, and it gets in your blood and your chest and your bones. Too much of it, you end up like Happy Durr.

Thomas Midgley certainly knew this. There was a point during his own research when he had to stop working because it had gotten hard for him to breathe and he trembled uncontrollably. He convalesced in Miami, an option unavailable to Happy Durr. But this tragedy at Deepwater, Midgley and other industry scientists argued, while unfortunate, surely, a shame, was preventable. Mistakes were made, and they would be addressed. There was no reason to halt progress, no reason to hold back the next great American industry with pointless regulation, no reason to kowtow to the "fanatical health cranks," as Thomas Midgley called the doctors and scientists who were raising concerns about leaded gasoline. He called them that in a letter he wrote while he was still having trouble breathing and controlling the movements of his own body. The government was convinced.

The second question was about the product itself: Was leaded gasoline safe? Midgley said emphatically yes. He even poured it onto his hands and breathed in the fumes during a press conference to prove it. Other scientists were less emphatic, the scientists who didn't work for the chemical companies or the auto industry. The government took comfort in—or perhaps took cover behind—a series of studies funded by the industry that suggested that people who used leaded gas regularly over a period of months showed no ill effects. But the independent scientists said of course there weren't any effects; those effects wouldn't show up immediately, or even within the period covered by the industry's studies. The problem wasn't even the pumping of gas or the breathing of fumes coming out of the tailpipe; it was what would happen years down the road, when lead molecules expelled from those tailpipes were still floating around in the atmosphere. The government suggested they study the effects again in twenty-five years, but made no provisions to do so, and the Ethyl Corporation was back in business. So was Midgley.

Having solved the mystery of the knock and successfully fought off those who would undo his achievement, Midgley turned to another case. Not only was the profit potential huge if he solved it, but he'd be saving lives. And that must've felt good to him just then. The facts were these: The refrigerator, the modern one, dates back to about 1915, the time of the mysterious knock. They are remarkable machines, even the old ones, maybe especially the old ones. Motors and pumps and compressors had to work in intricate polyphony to keep a mixture of chemicals in perfect balance and at a precise temperature. A refrigerator could fall into disharmony very easily if it got jostled or bumped. A hose could break, a valve could slip, and the chemicals and gases could come out, each one toxic. So people had to keep their refrigerators outside for safety. And even when they were running smoothly, the temperature could easily get out of whack. So next thing you know, you're chipping away at the inside of the freezer with an ice pick, and you slip and poke a hole in the side, and you die. This was the fate of several Frigidaire customers in the 1920s. Once again, Thomas Midgley took out the periodic table from his wallet and started working his way through until he came to a compound with one carbon atom, two chlorine atoms, and four fluorine atoms that could make things cold more safely. And in April 1930, on a stage in a ballroom in Atlanta, at the annual meeting of the American Chemical Society, he lit a candle and sucked in these chlorofluorocarbons through a tube and breathed them out and blew out the candle and didn't blow up or pass out.

There is nothing in the minutes of this meeting that confirms this, but I'd imagine the crowd went nuts. Because here was the man

who had invented leaded gasoline and then fought off the health fa-
natics to keep it in the pumps, and here he was again, remaking the
world, and making possible air conditioning, shipping food, a refrigerator in every home. That summer, he was elected to the American
Chemical Society's board and to the vice presidency of yet another
new company, this one formed to market and manufacture his new
refrigerant—and the titles kept coming. He won award after award
and lived in a manner that reflected his key role in having facilitated
modern life twice over. He bought an eighty-acre farm, collected
fine wines, and invented a system that used telephone technology to
water his four-acre lawn and to inject it with pesticides and fertilizer,
and tested strain after strain of grass until the whole thing looked
like a putting green.

When war came to Europe and leaded-gas-filled RAF fighters repelled the Luftwaffe, Thomas Midgley volunteered his services to
his government, eager to tackle his next project: inventing the future
of warfare. But his own future was short. On a crisp autumn afternoon in 1940, he was having lunch with his son at a country club and
he started to feel sick. By the next morning, he was paralyzed. When
he did his own analysis of the incident sometime later, he put the
odds of a man of his age contracting polio at about the same as
those of picking a particular playing card out of a stack piled as high
as the Empire State Building. He was flabbergasted that his life had
taken such an unpredictable turn, and he doubted that even he could
find a cure, but he thought his own ingenuity could provide him
with a better life, at least. After all, he must have thought, he'd already done that for so many other people so many other times.

So he built a pulley system, an elaborate contraption of ropes and
harnesses, so he could lift himself out of bed and into his wheelchair
in the morning. And it worked, until the morning his wife came in
and found him dead, choked by the tangled threads of an invention
by Thomas Midgley.

Like the rest of us.

For the inventions for which he received those awards and that brought him acclaim and eighty acres poisoned the earth. That's what they did. The health cranks, in short, had been right, and by the 1960s it was clear that all the atoms released into the atmosphere by burning tetraethyl lead were still there. They were in the soil, they were in the water, they were in your blood. They are in my bones. If you lived near a highway, if you lived in a city, if you were a baby at the time of exposure, then more of them were in you. What scientists worried about in the 1920s, they knew for sure by the 1960s. When leaded gas was banned entirely in the United States in 1986, some seven million tons of it had already been burned.

And what of Thomas Midgley's other breakthrough, his one carbon atom, his two chlorine, four flourine? Well, although he could breathe them in and blow out a candle onstage in Atlanta with no harmful results, things were different in the upper atmosphere. Up there, especially in the polar vortex that swirls high above Antarctica, the compound broke down and released chlorine atoms until a hole opened up in the ozone layer because, decades before, two mysteries had crossed the desk of a particularly sharp in-house scientist working in R & D at a major American corporation.

Today, a century later, scientists, doctors of public health, and sociologists are still trying to understand the breadth of the havoc caused by leaded gasoline. They have tied environmental lead levels to respiratory disease and death, to learning disabilities, hyperactivity, even violence and crime. Other scientists look up to the ozone layer. They trace straight, predictable lines between the hole there and increases in skin cancer, cataracts, and blindness. They raise questions about the impact of the ozone hole on plankton, and the chemical composition of the ocean, and the climate. There are those who would lay all of it, the countless millions of health problems, the courses of lives and societies, and an altered planet, on Midgley's grave, the grave of this company man, this salaried scientist, who with two discoveries invented the way so much of the world lived for so much of the last century.

His biographer, his grandson Thomas Midgley IV, doesn't dwell on the toll. He quotes those who point out that leaded gasoline pro-vided an edge for the Allied tanks and Jeeps and planes that won the war in Europe. He proudly points out that the *Enola Gay* was fueled by leaded gas, placing Thomas Midgley, Jr., at the vanguard of a story of American might and progress that soars forever onward, never looking at what's been left behind. It is impossible to entirely untangle the chain of cause and effect, or to fully follow the chaotic path these molecules and compounds took when they left his hand. There are things he could have done, there are things he could have known—surely not all of them. One can't know what will happen to one's creation once it is free to run the countryside, or what might happen on the other side of the world when a butterfly flaps its wings.

Fifty Words Written About the Arctic Bowhead Whale After Learning That They Can Live up to Two Hundred Years

There is a whale swimming right now
who may have escaped a Nantucketer's harpoon in 1850
and a Japanese whale ship in 1950
who once heard the distant songs of 50,000 of her kind

then several thousand

then hundreds

but who can hear 25,000 again
singing in the warming water.

Peregrinar

*A postcard from the road between Parlier and
Fresno, California, March 24, 1966*

S omeone had swept the floor. Someone had collected the soda
cans from the picnic the night before. And someone had tied up
the trash bags and asked their hosts where they kept the bins and
took them out back. And then they all knelt for Mass. And then they
marched, as they had every day since they'd left Delano, for twelve,
fifteen miles a day. Onward to Sacramento. Beneath the banners of
the United States and Mexico, of the Virgin de Guadalupe and the
United Farm Workers, the black thunderbird on white on red, designed to be so simple anyone could draw it and put it on a button or
print it on a sign that you could wave while you walked.

There had been seventy-seven marchers when they left Delano.
One man, a grape picker, now a striker—*un huelguista,* like the rest
of them—had gotten the flu and gone home. He didn't want to go
home. There were a few hundred now, on this, the eighth day of a
three-hundred-mile journey up the backbone of California's Central
Valley to its state capital to demand the right to organize field-
workers as a union, to demand $1.40 an hour, to demand nothing
short of human dignity. That's how Dolores Huerta and Cesar

Chavez and Luis Valdez framed it in their "Plan of Delano," their declaration of purpose, read aloud every night in every farm town on the road, and quoted to the reporters who followed them on foot in a pack, alongside the agents from the FBI, who were there to look for subversives but who found only citizens, marching up the 9 and along the service roads, through budding orchards and tilled tomato fields.

They were marching because Chavez admired Martin Luther King and the men and women who'd marched with him from Selma to Montgomery. They were marching because Chavez admired *los peregrinos,* on the road to la Basilica de Santa Maria de Guadalupe, near where the Virgin had appeared to Juan Diego Cuauhtlatoatzin; he admired those pilgrims who journeyed sometimes hundreds of miles, the last of those miles on their knees. They were marching because Chavez, like his church, believed that pain and penitence were intertwined, and because he knew they could do it, despite the heat and the miles and the blisters—he knew the marchers would have the necessary endurance. All they had ever done was endure. They picked and planted and cut and tied and hauled. They had few worker protections, no job security, no minimum wage. They had spent their lives in the fields in the heat, in the cold, with no breaks and no bathrooms, often no trees to hide behind, just their fellow workers, walls of women who'd block the views of overseers. They had spent their lives bent, often forced to use an eighteen-inch hoe, not because it was the best tool for the job—it was not—but because they had to bend over to use it, so their supervisors could catch them stretching or slacking and could shout at them, or worse. Because they spent their lives bent, they spent their lives hurt. They knew what their body felt like after twelve hours of planting beet seeds four inches apart, row upon row upon row, or clipping thorny vines, or lugging hundred-pound sacks. They knew sexual assault. They knew skimmed wages. They knew squalid shacks. They knew waiting all morning in the hopes that they'd be picked by the foreman to be given the opportunity to spend another day bent over. And because they spent their lives bent, Chavez knew they would stand when given the chance and could march as long as required.

He also knew that marches made for good press. That they gave protesters goals: this many miles today, this town tonight, that town tomorrow. He knew they gave the press something new to report on every day, with each arrival in each new town, and gave the people in those towns warning—the churches, the charities, the farmworkers—gave them incentives and deadlines to get their act together to be ready to help, to stand up themselves when the pilgrimage came through.

Seventy-seven people marched from Delano. Men and women, old and young. Nearly all of them Mexican American grape pickers. Now there were nuns from the local parishes. There were activists from Berkeley looking for their next cause. There was a Black man and a white man who'd come all the way from Mississippi and told the paper they'd grown tired of northerners coming down south to help them; it was time for them to help up north. There were the first Protestants that many of the pilgrims had met in real life. The first Jews. The first state legislators, too, there to score points in an election year. There was a guy from Wisconsin. He managed a Finnish-language newspaper back home. He had come to California for vacation—the sun and the surf and the Sierras and all of it—but had read about the marchers in the paper and now he was one of them.

They had left Delano with sleeping bags and some clothes and signs and song sheets and no food. They trusted that there would be food in the next town. That there would be good people to take them in. And there always were. And floors to sleep on. Meals, home-cooked, brought in covered dishes. Or sent by union locals. Fraternal organizations. People lined the roads to cheer and to witness and to hand out water. The Highway Patrol was there to keep an eye on things, but by now the officers knew there wasn't going to be trouble; they just had to make sure no one wandered into traffic, and count up their overtime, as the marchers made their way through Steinbeck country. See it: the golden valley unfurling, flanked by sunburned foothills.

Kids cut school to spend the day on the road. Mothers brought little ones, for an hour, for whatever felt right, so they could tell them one day that they'd marched. Workers left the fields and joined the pilgrims, for a day, for a mile, for a block, for as long as they thought they could get away with, before heading back to their rows and their quotas while the banners disappeared over the horizon.

In sixteen more days, on Easter Sunday, the marchers would arrive in Sacramento. And they would be eight thousand strong. So many farmworkers and activists and well-wishers would join them that it would take an hour for everyone to cross the bridge over the low river at the edge of the city. By then, one of the grape producers had agreed to recognize their union. There would be other victories in the future. And losses. There would be plenty. There would be other marches. And hunger strikes when the marches stopped making headlines. There would be factions and fractures in the farmworkers' organization, and in the organizations those factions and fractures would yield. There would be steps backward and steps forward. There would be a day off from work every year for Californians for Cesar Chavez's birthday. And there would still be so much to do. But they didn't know that then, as they walked in the sun on the roads by the fields they knew so well; they just knew what they could endure, and they knew how seeds took root, and they marched on.

New England Granite

I like to think of the men in the first part of this story as just a bunch of dudes, just a bunch of dudes doing dude things. Someone has an idea (probably while drinking). The year is 1774. It is the eve of the Revolutionary War. The place is Plymouth, Massachusetts. They have recently organized a militia there. They have put up a liberty pole, which is essentially just that: a big wooden pole. But it is, of course, more than just that. It is a symbol of defiance against the Crown, a metaphoric middle finger, rising from the town green.

The liberty pole tradition traces its roots to ancient Rome, where a group of senators celebrated the emperor's assassination by sticking a red cap on top of a pole. The cap was the same type that was given to freed slaves to signal their new status; the senators, it seems, co-opted the cap to suggest that Rome, with Caesar's death, had been similarly freed. Then, during the Renaissance, when everything Ancient Rome was new again, people revived the concept and refreshed it for a new era, turning it into a more generalized symbol of liberty, one that could be carried or rallied around as necessary, eventually bringing us to the poles that popped up all over New England on the eve of the American Revolution, and from there back to the dudes in Plymouth.

They want to do the other towns with their red-floppy-cap-

capped poles one better. This is Plymouth, after all, founded 154 years earlier by people who famously fled English oppression. A regular pole isn't going to do. The next morning a "large number gathers" (that is as specific as the historical record gets on this) on the town green with oxen and the biggest cart they can find, and they head down to the shore to dig up Plymouth Rock and put it on top of the Liberty Pole. That will show them.

I like to think it wasn't just the transatlantic journey of the *Mayflower* in 1620 that led those men down to that shore with shovels in hand, but another, much shorter trip. That one took place in 1741, when a man named Thomas Faunce heard they were planning on building a new wharf on the Plymouth waterfront. Faunce was ninety-five, which is plenty old now, but which back then was truly extraordinary. And when he heard about the wharf plan, he was bereft because that wharf was going to cover up what we now know as Plymouth Rock. By all accounts, the very first time anyone mentions any rock in conjunction with the Pilgrims landing comes in 1741, 120 years after they landed, thanks to Thomas Faunce.

His father had arrived in Plymouth on a ship called the *Anne* a few years after the *Mayflower*. It being a very small community, Thomas's dad was pals with the original Pilgrims, and one day when Thomas was a little boy, twenty-some years after their arrival and after the first winter and first Thanksgiving and all that, his dad pointed out to the water's edge and said, "See that rock? That's where Miles Standish and all of them first got off the boat." Some ninety years later, when he heard about the plan to build the wharf, he says he remembered that day with his dad and it didn't seem right to build a dock over such an important piece of history. So he told someone— his kids, a neighbor, we don't know who—that he'd like to see the rock before it got covered up. But this wasn't going to be so easy. He lived outside of town and was impossibly old and not particularly mobile. So the next day he was carried in a chair for three miles to see it.

I like to think of this ninety-five-year-old man being set down in the sturdiest chair they could find, a blanket wrapped around his frail shoulders, being lofted through the woods as a crowd forms and joins them, swells as they approach town in the soft morning light, and the smell of the sea greeting them as they come up and over Cole's Hill and make their way down the grassy slope to the shore, where a witness named James Thatcher will write down that Faunce, there upon that rock, "bedewed it with his tears and bid it an everlasting adieu." And I'd like to think this actually happened that way, that a ninety-five-year-old man was so distraught that this history was being forgotten (a history that only he, apparently, knew, and thought to bring up at all only at the eleventh hour) that he wept so forcefully that tears actually splashed down onto the rock. But I doubt it. "Bedewed it with his tears and bid it an everlasting adieu" is the stuff of poetic license and bad poetry.

To this day, historians debate whether Thomas Faunce's memory, at ninety-five, was accurate. And whether that specific rock—or any rock, for that matter—played any particular role in the Pilgrims' arrival. But it is clear that it didn't hold any real significance, practical or sentimental, to the Pilgrims themselves, because they basically wrote everything down, and no one ever mentioned it.

Instead, the thing that makes this rock "Plymouth Rock" is poetry. There is something moving about this ninety-five-year-old man being moved. There's something romantic about the idea that this, right here, on this spot, this is where it all began. That is where it all began for the idea of Plymouth Rock, at least—when they built the wharf in a different spot and started to protect this rock and turn it into a relic, a symbol of freedom, a tie to a glorious past, an object worthy of veneration, and apparently of being dug up by a bunch of dudes gathered at the waterside to stick it to England. Back in 1774, our dudes set themselves to the task of removing a ten-ton boulder from the sand to get it into a cart where thirty strong oxen would haul it up Cole's Hill, and then they would place it atop the liberty pole to tell every redcoat in the area that Plymouth was ready for a fight, that the spirit of the Pilgrims, brave and defiant, still flowed through their veins.

They set at the ground with their shovels. They wedged enormous and ingenious screws beneath the corners of Plymouth Rock. It began to rise and the ox driver urged on the oxen and got the cart into position, and the gathered men put their shoulders into it, pulled at the levers, got ready to heave and push and lift this sainted stone. Maybe they agreed to push on the count of three, and they didn't even need to stop and ask whether they would push on three or say one, two, three, and then push. They were together. They were of one mind, filled with the spirit of revolution and of their ancestors, who, 120 years before, had stepped off that fabled ship after sixty-six days at sea, and as their leather shoe soles touched that New England granite, they left their lives of persecution behind. And so the men counted to three and they pushed, and Plymouth Rock sheared in half. The top just popped off like they were splitting a muffin with a co-worker at the free continental breakfast at the airport Marriott.

I like to think of those men there in the sand, having just broken Plymouth Rock, and of the shock and the finger-pointing. And the panic. And the comedy. It seems that at one point someone said some version of "Hey, hey, hey, hey! Hear me out! Hear me out: What if this is actually good?" And suggested it was a sign from God that the colonies would, like this rock, break . . . away from England. And they just went with it. They put one broken half of Plymouth Rock into the wagon, and the thirty oxen had an easier trip up Cole's Hill, and they deposited it beside the liberty pole. No effort was made to hoist it. There it lay for many years. A sturdy and symbolic soapbox for speeches on liberty. A point of pride for Plymothians.

In the 1830s Alexis de Tocqueville, the French chronicler of early

America, arrived in Plymouth. He marveled at how the young nation, this great experiment in secular democracy, had turned this
rock into a relic, had imbued it with near religious power.

He saw pilgrims (lowercase *p;* not the "Pilgrim" pilgrims, whose
own mythic power was expanding well beyond historical reality).
He saw Americans who'd come to Plymouth to see where this whole
thing began, to touch their own toes to this rock where those leg-
endary trailblazers of liberty might or might not have touched their
own two hundred years before. He saw others who wanted to take
a piece of it, who'd come to the metaphorical mountain with chisels
in hand. In his travels, Tocqueville saw pieces of the famous Plymouth Rock all over: used as doorstops, as paperweights, set in the
centers of mantles like the mandibles of sainted martyrs. What had
once been a point of local pride was being woven into the national
story.

There was a Pilgrim museum built in the middle of the nineteenth
century. They moved the rock again so it would be next to the museum. Another bunch of dudes and a bunch of oxen got it into a
cart, in one piece this time. But when they were taking it out, they
dropped it, and it split in two. I like to think of those men, who had
surely heard about the last time some dudes moved Plymouth Rock,
who'd probably joked about it, wouldn't it be kind of hilarious if
they dropped it again while doing everything they could not to drop
it again. Praying, "Please, please, please don't let me drop it again."
And then dropping it again. They put it back together this time.
They put some mortar in there and smushed it together and it was
all good.

In the 1860s, when the Pilgrim story was fully enshrined as one of
the pillars of capital-*H* History, Thanksgiving became a national
holiday. The genocide and forced removal of Indigenous peoples in
the West was in full swing, and the Thanksgiving story, in its reduc-
tive, construction-paper-Pilgrim-hat form, was offered up to soothe

the discomfort of white Americans. They built an elaborate Victorian canopy to protect the rock from relic hunters and seagulls, and they also chiseled the date 1620 into its face.

In the 1920s, they redid the waterfront, opened it up, got rid of some of the piers. It's nice. They moved the rock again, managing to keep it in one piece this time, and put it back there at the water's edge, more or less where it was when Thomas Faunce bedewed it with his tears, or didn't, and where the Pilgrims first set foot on the land that would become America, or didn't.

It is still there, still underwhelming tourists. Now it's surrounded by a fence and protected by a neoclassical structure like the Lincoln or Jefferson memorials or any of the other places where this secular country turns its recent history into Greco-Roman myths.

They've repaired the rock a number of times. A full moon or storm tide can cover it for a while, and the salt water does a number on the mortar. At some point, before too long, scientists tell us, the sea level will rise permanently above where it now rests. And perhaps we should just let it. There is so much that people have willfully gotten wrong about the story of the Pilgrims in their first years in this place, Wampanoag land, that maybe we should just let the tide wash it away. I suspect they will move Plymouth Rock again one day. The old story, true or not, right or not, is too dear to too many people. People like to think what they think. I just hope they are more careful with it next time.

1,347 Birds

Thirteen hundred and forty-seven birds in drawers and boxes, dead and labeled with paper ID tags tied to their thin ankles. They are horned larks, and grasshopper sparrows and field sparrows, red-headed woodpeckers and eastern towhees. The oldest of these (two towhees, black-winged and black-hooded with red-brown feathers flanking their white bellies, found in Kalamazoo, Michigan), as well as a lark (a brown-speckled male with streaks of bright yellow framing his face), have been in storage in natural history museums in Illinois, Michigan, Indiana, and Ohio since 1880. They have lain there flat, wings folded, chins up, beaks up, legs stretched out, each one looking as if it could be thrown like a dart, a specimen tag trailing behind it like a banner from a plane circling over a ballpark on a Memorial Day weekend. The rest were collected in various fields and forests and town greens and nature preserves and at least one shopping mall over the course of the last 135 years. Then, in 2014, a couple of PhD students—Shane DuBay, an evolutionary biologist, and Carl Fuldner, a photographer and art historian—opened those drawers and boxes.

Their theory was that these five specific species of birds could tell them about air pollution in five states between 1880 and 2015. The birds of all these species have white bellies that can become discolored by soot and other particulates. Furthermore, at least once a year, each bird molts and grows a new set of feathers. So if you looked at, say, specimen 116522, a female horned lark collected at Geddes Pond in Ann Arbor, Michigan, in 1949, you know that the soot that still clings to that dead bird, turned her white belly gray, dates to 1949.

Black carbon—put into the air by a coal plant outside Gary, Indiana, in 1899 as a lark circled the smokestacks; or by a smelting factory on the Allegheny River in 1922 as a sparrow nipped a cricket off a tall reed at the river's edge—is still there on those birds in those drawers in those museums.

The researchers used electron microscopes, but you don't need one. You can just see it: A bird, once white and black and reddish brown, is nearly solid gray from living in Ohio in 1913. You could line those birds up. Specimen after specimen, sequentially, year by year, and you could see it, see how bad the air was, and when. And get a sense for how dark the skies must have been to have darkened those birds. The radiant yellow of a male lark, enhanced over however many millennia to attract mates, hidden by black carbon particles produced in one year by the incomplete combustion of the coal that fueled the American industrial economy during its dramatic rise in a handful of decades.

But you could also see the birds lighten, see their colors shift; could chart fluctuations in gradations of gray. The researchers were able to match those changes with points on a timeline of human activity. They showed that city ordinances governing coal-fired power plants and factories—rules about where they could be, how they could operate—as well as people's choices with respect to the air over their cities, meant that those cities had prettier birds.

And they documented how the yellow of the lark, the rich red of the woodpecker, began to return during the Great Depression, when industrial production plummeted, and how the colors retreated again during the ramp-up to World War II and the postwar boom, and how the birds steadily brightened with the Air Pollution

Control Act of 1955 and the Clean Air Act of 1963 and its expansion in 1970.

The study yielded an important data set for climatologists charting atmospheric carbon and wrestling with its impact. And it gave historians points of reference from which to imagine that most elusive thing: what it was like to be someone else in some other time; what it was like to live beneath darker skies, to wonder what a woman at her window in her family's rented room in Joliet, Illinois, in 1906 thought of the smoke from the factory where her husband and father and uncles poured molten steel. How did the haze change the slant of the light and color the sunset? What did she imagine the smoke was doing to her lungs or to her daughter's ability to grow and to concentrate, never mind what she thought of the color of the birds?

Her daughter would grow up to see lighter skies dotted with brighter larks and sparrows; for her granddaughter, they were lighter and brighter still; and her great-granddaughter could go to the Field Museum in Chicago, find specimen 52780, an eastern towhee collected in Joliet in 1906, one of those 1,347 birds, and see how different the air was in her great-grandmother's time.

But what of her daughters? Of ours?

No bird's belly in Pennsylvania is flecked by the haze of Beijing or Jakarta. There is a grasshopper sparrow tagged 498413 from December of 2015. Its feathers can't tell you that the Paris climate accords agreed to carbon-emissions targets that same month. And there is no redheaded woodpecker which will allow future researchers to pinpoint the year the United States left the treaty. No horned lark whose yellow throat will tell them which year atmospheric carbon dioxide passed four hundred parts per million. No eastern towhee can tell them when carbon emissions pushed the global temperature past two degrees, or three. When there may well no longer be field sparrows in Illinois or Michigan or Indiana or Pennsylvania to collect and to catalog, to tell us how well humans have done with respect to the air.

NATURAL HABITAT

RANDOM HOUSE
PUBLISHING
New York : MMXXIV

he cable said that her husband was dead.

It had come while she was getting her hair done, shampooed, just before. Or it had come while she was walking back home in the February air, hustling to get ready for the party. The usual crew, the friends who'd kept her company all these months while her husband was away. And now there was a cable that said that Bill was dead.

There had been nothing in his letters. No reasons to worry. He'd been so upbeat. Even when the expedition got held up in Shanghai, snared in the typical tangle of permits and payoffs, Bill's letters had been so positive. He'd said they'd be leaving for the bamboo forest in no time.

The cable didn't say how her husband had died. Neither did his obituary. A big one, in *The New York Times,* befitting the scion of a wealthy family, long familiar to the readers of the paper's society pages. William Hunter Harkness was a handsome Harvard man turned explorer, which was a type of guy in the early 1930s.

Bill was famous for bringing the Komodo dragon back from the wilds of Indonesia to frighten children at the Bronx Zoo and to thrill and comfort their parents with evidence that the dark corners of the world were tamable by handsome, white Harvard men like Bill Harkness.

People had read in the papers about his wedding to Ruth McCombs, who'd arrived in New York unannounced, with no pedigree and no title, the daughter of a carpenter and a seamstress from Titusville, Pennsylvania. She'd fallen in love with the wider world through books and maps and set out to see it, first going off to college in Colorado, then teaching English in Cuba, before landing in Manhattan, with no particular plan, in the middle of the Jazz Age. She charmed her way into a job as a dress designer at one of the biggest fashion houses in the city. Made fabulous friends. She was no great beauty—she would tell you that herself—but she was brash, and whip-smart, and funny as hell. She owned every room. And one night, who should walk into one of those rooms but this Harvard man. They fell hard.

He, too, had read all the books that had helped her fall in love with the wider world. He, too, understood the magic of names on maps, cities, mountains, river valleys. They'd talk about the places they would go one day, while they went all over New York, speakeasies, wild parties, Harlem hot spots, the whole nine. It was a new world. He was rich. They were young and drunk and alive. And at night, and on mornings after, they'd read to each other from those books, trace the ribbons of rivers that rippled blue across maps unfolded on their unmade bed, and dream about where their life together would take them. The world was theirs and they would see it all.

But first Bill would see it without her: It was nothing personal; there would be time for all of it; but Bill Harkness was going to be the first person in the world to capture a live panda.

No one in the West had even known pandas existed until about 1870. A French missionary had seen a pelt on a farmer's wall. A famous naturalist had spent months in 1908 in a bamboo forest at the foot of the Himalayas where the pandas live. He found plenty of evidence that they were there, but he never actually saw one.

People started to speculate that they didn't exist at all. *The New York Times* wondered whether this was a unicorn situation. But then, in 1929, Theodore Roosevelt, Jr., and his brother Kermit (themselves mustachioed, pith-helmeted Harvard men) became the first white people to hunt and kill a panda. A dubious honor, sure, but at least people believed pandas were real now. They could go look at one at the Field Museum in Chicago, which had funded the Roosevelt boys' expedition to the tune of one hundred thousand dollars.

Ruth's husband's expedition—bolder, more audacious than the Roosevelts'—was both an adventure and a business trip. They would be separated for two years. Maybe more. But when he came back famous, and wealthier still, their adventure together would begin.

But her husband was dead. Throat cancer. It came so quick. Ruth Harkness was lost.

There is no map that can lead you out of such grief. That is the way of grief. One gropes until there is light. There is no way of knowing the territory a dream occupies within you until you feel the contours of its absence. But Ruth Harkness knew where she was: thirty-three years old, a widow, no pedigree, no title, a million miles away from Titusville, with in-laws who had no intention of continuing to fund the fabulous life she had been leading with their son. She would inherit twenty thousand dollars and that would be that.

Ruth's friends, pedigreed and titled and fabulous as a birthright, were kind. They were heartbroken for their heartbroken friend. And maybe a bit for themselves, because how long would she be able to hang? Twenty thousand dollars wouldn't keep her in her apartment, or anywhere near the life they all enjoyed together. They knew they were going to lose their lost friend one day. They just couldn't have imagined it would happen so soon.

On April 16, 1936, those friends waved from the docks as an ocean liner carried the widow Harkness away from New York. Some of them thought it was a joke. What woman in her right mind, what dress designer cum high-society party girl, with no husband and no prospects, gets on a boat to China? But there she was, on a boat disappearing over the horizon, with little more than a notion, an impulse, a thought that had come to her so bright and clear and true, in the long nights spent in a bed to which her husband was never going to return.

Her notion was this: She would finish his work. She would cross the oceans of the world to China, to a place she knew only from the books in her childhood bedroom. She would trace the Yangtze, that ribbon of river; she would stand at the foot of the Himalayas, and search the bamboo forest, and she would bring back a panda. What else was she living for? What was she living for if not to do something like this?

Ruth Harkness was the toast of the town of prewar Shanghai. This was in part because Shanghai, with its jazz and its gangsters and its opium and its rickshaw-riding colonials, was just the place for a woman like Harkness: hard-drinking and witty and worldly and up for anything. She had party invitations and dinner companions and guides, would-be suitors who were happy to help her. They liked her. And in a city internationally famous for its permissiveness, where anything could be bought for the right price, why, there are worse vices than indulging in romantic fantasy.

She was introduced to Jack Young, who was Chinese, and his wife, Su Lin, who was Chinese American. They were both adventurers. Jack had tracked the panda that the Roosevelt boys had shot. Jack and Su Lin were unavailable, booked to lead some other Harvard men in a climb up some Himalayan peak. But Jack's brother, Quentin, was available. He was only twenty-two years old. He'd just graduated from college. He'd never led an expedition before. But he'd watched his brother do it, and he was smart and brave and game. And Ruth Harkness liked the sound of that.

She liked him too. He was quick to laugh. He was almost comically handsome. Six foot and ripped. Thick black hair. He didn't condescend or patronize. And he liked—was shocked to learn, really—that she didn't either. She had none of the blithe bigotry of the other Westerners he'd known. And he readily accepted the chain of command: He was the guide, she was the boss. He walked her through options, then he accepted her decisions.

And so there in Shanghai, with a plan coming together and the days till their departure ticking away, Ruth started to feel less lost, and to feel that familiar thrill that comes with names on maps and ribbons of river.

Her husband was everywhere. In his papers, in his notes, in the shoes she'd had made for herself from an old pair of his boots. And in a cardboard box—she was unsure what to do with his ashes—but she was a bit more sure every day of what it was she was doing.

At least for right now. She was heading into the unknown, but she was heading toward the light.

From Shanghai by plane. Rolling hills. Rice paddies. Earth from above for the first time in her life. The Yangtze River, the blue ribbon on her maps, tea-colored in real life, rolled on for days on end. Past port towns and countryside. Towering gorges draped with waterfalls. To Chengdu, the walled city, and on to the foothills of the Himalayas.

Along the way, she sent letters home, letters that said she felt something miraculous happening within her. There was a feeling that she was finding herself there in China, in the landscape, with its people, in a language she was beginning to understand, meaning emerging from what had been just noise just before.

Quentin Young taught her Mandarin. Words and phrases here and there. There was something there, between the two of them. Despite the dozen-year difference in their ages, despite a fiancée he had back home, despite her grief. They'd been hiking twenty and thirty miles a day. Through swaying forests so thick there was perpetual twilight, drinking from streams fed by snowflakes that fell at the top of the world, and her body was new, strong like she'd never imagined. And when they came upon the ruins of an ancient monastery—a lamasery for Buddhist monks, a crumbling castle on a hill, fit for a woman on a quest for a unicorn—and they walked its echoing halls, watched white snow alight on green bamboo from its balconies, what else could they do but fall into each other's arms?

They camped there at the castle. Each day the party would fan out, slip off into the bamboo forest looking for pandas. Each night they'd return. Drink corn wine. Smoke cigarettes. Ruth would tap away at her typewriter, bundled in clothes of yak wool, of fox fur. She'd write letters home that spoke of joy. And one morning in the forest, one of their party heard a cry, almost human, and followed it through the fog. There was a baby panda in the crook of a hollow tree.

No one knew what to do. No one had found a baby panda in the crook of a hollow tree before. They didn't know what it ate, didn't know how much it slept, didn't know if they should keep it warm or cold, didn't really know what sex it was; they guessed it was a girl. Ruth, ecstatic, overwhelmed, held it close, called for the powdered milk and baby bottle she had thought to pack back in Shanghai, just in case. And that night, Ruth and Quentin and a baby panda slept in a tangle of bodies and blankets and furs on the floor of a thousand-year-old monastery. And the next morning, Ruth spread her husband's ashes on the twisted roots of a flowering tree.

Ruth and Quentin and their expedition, along with a panda cub they called Su Lin, headed back east, moving quickly, buoyed by success, and by the thrill of this creature who was always in Ruth's arms.

She didn't have a child. Didn't want one. Wouldn't really have known what to do with one, but the principles seemed to be the same. She kept the panda warm, she fed it milk—she wore a fur coat; the panda's real mother had had one, after all—and when they were back on a boat on the Yangtze, going with the current this time, she kept the windows open, kept it cold and Tibet-like in there.

She kept them open in her hotel room back in Shanghai, too, where it seemed like every reporter on the Pacific Rim came to snap pictures of Ruth and Su Lin. They loved the whole story. And they loved Su Lin. None of them had ever seen a baby panda. Of course they loved her. And they loved Ruth too: brave and witty Ruth, who had slipped so easily back into her urbane self.

When she said goodbye to Quentin, paid him, and sent him back to his fiancée, she gave him Bill's wedding ring. It was the only thing she could think to do to symbolize what they'd shared and the life they'd briefly lived together. This was in December 1936.

By April of the next year, Ruth and Su Lin were on a boat bound for San Francisco. And let me take a moment here, while they cross the Pacific, snuggling together in a stateroom on an ocean liner, bobbing on the waves.

It's just a moment.

We have time.

Natural Habitat

That panda shouldn't have been on that boat. I know that. She should have been with her mother until she was weaned. Or longer, usually until her mother got pregnant again, when Su Lin was about two. She shouldn't have been put on display. Shouldn't have been taken care of by a chain-smoking lady stumbling her way through exotic-animal husbandry. I know that. And my twenty-first-century brain gets caught on the whole thing: that a white, Western woman would spend an ungodly sum to command an international operation dependent on the labor of dozens of poorly compensated, non-white laborers to risk life and limb for her dream. It makes me a little queasy. But I'll say this: Her memoir and her letters home reveal someone who was ahead of her time, without the casual racism of her day, or that thing where she's projecting virtue and a kind of angelic simplicity and righteous, enviable primitivism on the people she met, the kind of stuff that makes you have to squint to block it out so you can see the person you want to see. Let's see this person there in the bed with a panda. Fumbling to find herself, and to keep this creature alive.

And so back to the boat as it pulled up to a pier in San Francisco on a morning in early spring. Strangers lined the docks, thrilled to see the famous pair. This impossibly adorable creature and the plucky gal who had risked so much to bring it back to America. And then they were back in New York, in a suite at the Biltmore, for more reporters and cameras, visitations from old friends, and meetings with zoos.

There was no way Ruth could keep Su Lin. She knew that. She had no idea how to care for an adolescent panda. And she was already scratched up by this fuzzy little thing. What would happen when Su Lin was a hundred pounds? Or two hundred and fifty? There was no way. And so she sold Su Lin to the Brookfield Zoo in Chicago.

Chicago fell in love with the panda. Three hundred and twenty-five thousand people came to see her in her first few months on display. She had twenty-four-hour care in a cage set up like a human nursery, with a playpen and a cradle, and a football to play with. And Ruth went back to New York knowing that at least Su Lin was in the best hands available. But now she was back home, back in her old apartment, back in the new version of her old life without Bill. Without Su Lin. With memories of China and of who she had been in China. She needed to get back there.

The zoo in Chicago gave her some money for a second expedition. Not a lot, but enough to get back to Shanghai. Enough to pull together a crew. She didn't need all the luxuries this time. Didn't need first-class passage. She could rough it. She had been a person who could rough it, not long ago. She wanted her body back. It had grown soft and slow with too much drink and too much sorrow. So she would go and find Quentin, and they would head west together and do it again. They would find a male, a breeding partner for Su Lin, so it could all keep going. So it didn't have to end.

She didn't find Quentin in Shanghai. She heard that he was married now and working a desk job in Hong Kong. She pressed on. Got the band back together as best she could and set out for the bamboo forest. But it was slow going. And snow was piled high by the time they arrived at the old temple.

She was sick with a flu she couldn't shake, and she stayed behind while the party fanned out each morning. She spent the days tapping away at her typewriter, drinking too much corn wine, and writing home about feelings that were nothing like joy. She wrote that she was lost and afraid she might be losing her mind a little.

It went on like this for weeks. And then one day someone came back with a panda, just a bit older than Su Lin. But it was different. It was aggressive. And Ruth couldn't get it to eat. She had to keep it in a cage. She slept on the floor beside it. It took her a while to gain its trust, and even just to get close enough to know that it wasn't a male, which she had wanted to bring back for Su Lin. The zoo took the second panda but gave her less money than before. But it could be enough. She needed to be there to get back to the place where she once was herself.

On her third trip, China had changed. Japanese warplanes shot at her hotel and killed seven hundred civilians caught out on the waterfront. She headed west as fast as she could, but the forest was changing too. Everywhere she stopped, at each of her old haunts, she heard about teams of trappers and hunters. About pandas being swept up by the score. Heard about valleys where pandas had roamed for hundreds of years, but where they didn't anymore. Ruth did find one. Brought it as far as Chengdu, where she heard that the government was cracking down. There were too many pandas being killed and exported. She could've worked the system. Could've found a way to bring it back to the States. But instead she turned around. Hiked back through the summer heat. And felt nothing but relief as she set the panda down and it ran off and disappeared into the trees.

Ruth Harkness would spend the rest of her life lost and groping. She tried India for a while. She followed a rumor of a South American panda deep into the jungles of Peru. But there was no panda. And no light. She died at forty-seven years old, of alcohol-related gastroenteritis. She was found in the bathtub of a Pittsburgh hotel.

Su Lin sits stuffed in a glass case in the Field Museum in Chicago. Her fur is a little patchy in spots. She's positioned on a rock. Her pose is awkward. She's shifted forward a bit, like she's sitting on a park bench made just a little too hot by the summer sun. She's been on that rock for eighty years, since just after her death, only a year or two after Ruth brought her back to America. They think Su Lin choked on some bamboo. Something that probably could've happened in the wild.

But it didn't.

It happened in a zoo. In a cage with a cradle and a football.

It is strange to see her in the museum today, stuffed—to see any of the taxidermied animals, really, in these old museums. Because it is such an old way of seeing animals. Usually you just click on a link. Or you catch a documentary on TV. Or you go to a zoo. Someplace that's so much nicer today than it used to be when you were a kid. With bigger enclosures, places nearly worthy of the word *habitat.* Someplace that seems, maybe even to the animals themselves, like a place they might belong. Ruth Harkness found hers, but was never able to get back to it. But these habitats, the ones that are better now than they were when you were a kid, that are so much better than when your parents were kids: Ruth had something to do with that.

In the span of five years, the world went from thrilling at the exploits of the Roosevelt brothers, and piling into the Field Museum to stare at their static trophy, to seeing the live animal itself. Watching it play. And eat. And be an animal. Zoologists started realizing they couldn't really study animal behavior without watching animals behave. Zoos realized the best way to keep crowds coming through the doors was to have zoologists figure out ways to keep animals healthy and alive. Before Ruth found Su Lin, the advertising pitch at zoos boiled down to "Come see the gorilla or the giraffe while you can; there's no way we're not going to screw this up and kill them accidentally." Ruth changed that. People all over the country were heartbroken when Su Lin died. They had fallen in love with her because Ruth had fallen in love with her and had spoken so eloquently, with such charm and wit, about Su Lin as an individual with a personality and inherent dignity. And that was new. And it helped teach people a new way to see animals. To think of them as worthy of life. Ruth changed, when she was heartbroken and fumbling to find something. She found a panda and found a fleeting light.

Crazy Bet

The guards rolled their eyes as they let the woman through the gates of Libby Prison. Elizabeth Van Lew was used to that sort of thing. Ever since she was a girl growing up in Richmond, Virginia, long before it became the capital of the Confederacy in the spring of 1861, people had called her an odd duck. They'd whispered about her and snickered. She was so headstrong and opinionated, for a girl. And when she reached marrying age, even though she was the daughter of a wealthy business owner, set to inherit a mansion in the center of town and a farm just outside, she had very few suitors. It seems her reputation kept them away. And when she was twenty-five and her father died, this strange, willful woman did something that confirmed to all of Richmond society that she was indeed nuts: She freed her slaves.

For the next eighteen years, while the country went down the road toward civil war, Elizabeth Van Lew was the neighbor the people of Richmond would cross the road to avoid. She was the peculiar spinster who lived in the crumbling mansion, just her and her mom and her Black servants, whom she paid.

. . .

The first Union POWs started showing up at Libby Prison in late spring of 1861, right after the start of the war. And Elizabeth Van Lew did too. She arrived with cakes and bread and meat wrapped in cloth, and books and Bibles for the prisoners. The guards decided to let her in. She was harmless. She was the lady they'd grown up calling Crazy Bet. She was the woman who didn't march in the torchlight parades to support the troops, the one who'd talk about her ridiculous unionist politics when others were singing the praises of their new nation's new president. For that matter, she was a woman who talked politics; she had to be crazy. As the war went on, she seemed to become even more so. She stopped brushing her hair. She didn't bother to mend her clothes. She talked to herself incessantly. She would zigzag about when she walked down the road. And the guards laughed. They called her Crazy Bet to her face, and then they waved her through the gates.

On the last day of February in 1864, three years into the war, Union forces were set to move on Richmond. Five hundred soldiers, led by a one-legged colonel named Ulric Dahlgren, were ready to free their compatriots locked up in Libby Prison, but the raid failed. The Union forces miscalculated the depth of a stream and had trouble getting their horses across. Dahlgren's men had to retreat, but he didn't make it back. Confederates shot him and stripped his body of its valuables, his wedding ring as well as the finger that wore it. Took his wooden leg too. President Davis ordered that he be buried under cover of darkness a few nights later, in an unmarked grave.

This was bad form, and President Davis knew it. So later, when Dahlgren's father, himself a rear admiral in the U.S. Navy, sent him a personal letter asking that his son's body be located and returned, the president agreed. But when the soldiers he dispatched to dig up Dahlgren opened his coffin, it was empty. The whole thing was mysterious, and not just the case of the missing colonel. Something was going on at the prison too. Some prisoners had recently escaped through a tunnel they'd dug and then poof, just vanished. And there was the failed raid itself. It had nearly succeeded. Why did the attack take place on that night? Was it a coincidence that it was the same night the guards were transferring thousands of prisoners to a facility farther south? Could they have known something?

Well, someone said, Crazy Bet was at the prison every day. Now, she was crazy, and she was always talking to herself, but she was also always talking to herself about bringing down the Confederacy. Maybe they should check that out.

Soldiers knocked on Elizabeth Van Lew's door. She let them search her house. And they didn't find anything. Just a dusty old mansion. They grumbled and walked away to follow another lead shaking their heads at the strange spinster.

A year later, in April 1865, the capital was falling. Robert E. Lee's men could no longer defend it, and fires and panic were spreading through the city. Shells exploded day and night. Union soldiers broke down the doors of Libby Prison.

Again, angry people came knocking on Elizabeth's door. Because from the top of her house, for the first time anywhere in Richmond in the four years since the war began, there flew an American flag. Elizabeth's neighbors had come to burn it, and to burn her house down while they were at it. But Crazy Bet opened the door, wild-eyed and laughing, pointing at each of them in turn. Calling them out by name. She said she was making a list that she would give to General Grant, so he could make sure his Union Army torched each one of their homes if they laid another finger on hers. And the mob dispersed. Because she just might do it. She was called Crazy Bet for a reason.

After Richmond fell, and the fires were mostly embers, and Elizabeth's American flag yet waved above her house undisturbed, there was another knock on her door. And Elizabeth Van Lew, her hair combed, her clothes proper, her manner not crazy at all, opened the door and invited Ulysses S. Grant in for tea.

The two of them, the future president and the neighborhood pariah, talked politics and swapped war stories. His tales of four years of blood and valor on the battlefields at Shiloh and Vicksburg and

Cold Harbor and Spotsylvania Court House; her tales of espionage and four years of playing crazy when really she was gathering information that she spread through a network of spies, most of whom worked in her house—the people she used to enslave. They'd take a book she'd loaned to a recent arrival at Libby Prison and that the prisoner had returned to her, having used a code she had developed, and send a secret message through imperceptible pinpricks. Then they'd pass the book from hand to hand to a Union general out in the field. She told him about having overheard the plan to bury Colonel Dahlgren in an unmarked grave, and how she sent one of her employees to follow them and mark the grave, and later to return to dig him up and transfer his body to a metal coffin and rebury him on her farm outside Richmond, so he could be given a hero's funeral after the war. She told Grant everything. He loved it.

After the war, when Grant was president, he thanked her for her service. And put her in charge of the Richmond post office. She was good at delivering messages, after all. But it was hard to work in Richmond. She wasn't well liked. Yet she lived out her life in the city, until her death in 1900, in the old mansion, just her and her niece and forty cats. The crazy lady up the street.

Enlargement

Two men on a roof in Nashville, Tennessee, the year after the Civil War. There is a third man in the picture, though it may take you a second to see him. Find his feet to the left of the seated man in the white shirt. Find his face above that man's head, poking out from the narrow opening of the large contraption.

We know his name, that of the half-hidden man, though not much else. He is James W. Braid. We know he worked for the guy on the left, the bearded man in the long coat, his hands jammed into his waistband. That man is Joseph H. Van Stavoren, whose Dutch parents, we believe, immigrated to Delaware just after the revolution, making him a member of the first generation of Americans. As far as I have been able to determine, no one now knows who the seated man is, he of the jaunty cap and the rakish vibe. I can't tell you anything about him other than that we believe he worked with the other men at Van Stavoren's Nashville photography studio. That's about the extent of the concrete information we have on the men in the picture, but I can tell you plenty about the contraption.

It is, as the lettering just above the base will tell you, the Jupiter camera. It was one of some small, unknown number of "solar cameras" built in North America and Europe during the middle of the nineteenth century. Pre-digital photography worked by pointing the camera at the subject—a vase of begonias, the pursed-lips wife of a grim-faced banker, a sailor kissing a nurse in Times Square—and letting light inside. In the cameras of the 1860s, when this trio was working in Tennessee, the light fell upon a glass plate that had been carefully treated with a wet chemical film (which is where the word *film* comes from), activating a process that yielded a negative image. You then needed to go through a whole, finicky process to get a positive image onto specially treated paper. It was delicate business, getting the chemicals and the light right. But if you nailed it and were so happy with the result that you wanted to make a copy of the picture you had just taken, you would then undertake one of a few other equally exacting methods to yield another image of the exact same size. The three men on the roof thought bigger.

As with so much of their story, we don't know where they learned about solar cameras. An art professor in Baltimore built the first one in 1857. Any of our trio could have read about it in a trade journal, or heard about it from another photographer or just someone who'd met a guy who'd met at guy during the comings and goings and chaotic disruptions of the Civil War. However the idea came to them, it seems it was irresistible. The contraption is a giant camera, used to make photographic enlargements. Sunlight comes in through the camera's lens, passes through the negative you want to make bigger, which has been positioned within the chamber, and casts a positive image onto chemically treated paper on the far end. Think of a projector on a cart wheeled into a classroom to show a film on a screen pulled down in front of a blackboard: The image on the screen will get smaller or larger as you move the projector nearer or farther from the screen. In this duplication camera, you could move the glass negative around like the projector on wheels, making the image larger or smaller. They could make an image as large they wanted. They just needed a light source strong enough to make it work.

And so we find these three men on the roof of the J. H. Van Stavoren Metropolitan Photograph Gallery, posing proudly with and within the solar camera. They didn't just build the camera but managed to do so in a city that had barely begun to recover from the trials and privations of war, where cholera was rampant, where refugees were arriving every day only to find resources as scarce as they had been wherever they fled from. Somehow these men had managed to scrounge and find wood and metal and glass and gears and chemicals and paper, and made this thing. Somehow they thought to do it at all. In a ruined place after so many brutal years, they'd dreamed big. They'd sought larger lives through larger pictures.

Those pictures were not easy to make.

Unlike a studio portrait, for which a subject might be asked to sit still for as long as a minute while the photographer exposed the film, the Jupiter's enlargements needed to be exposed to light for far longer. The enormous camera would have to be aimed directly at the sun for hours at a time. But the sun, rather famously, does not stay in the same place for hours at a time. And so in that photograph of the camera on that rooftop, we find four wheels that could rotate the camera on a circular track at its base and raise and lower the lens, aligning it with the sun as it made its way across the sky.

This was both a mechanical challenge—the Jupiter was massive and persnickety—and a mathematical one, as its movements needed to be calculated precisely each day in accordance with the calendar. The photographer also had to set and adjust the aperture depending on weather conditions and on the sun's shifting intensity. It was hard enough to make a good photograph under any conditions at that time, but blow it in the studio and you would need to ask the subject to wait a few minutes while you reset; blow it on the roof and you had lost a whole day.

Solar photography was difficult work. You were out for hours in the elements. The job was meticulous but tedious. Fall asleep out of boredom, or simply let your mind wander too long between movements of the camera, and things could get dangerous. On at least six occasions, someone failed to move the camera just the right way at just the right time, and the sun, focused by a condenser lens and a mirror, set fire to the building.

While the work of sifting through history does not carry with it the risk of accidental immolation, it does have its challenges. I cannot tell you anything definitive about the character of these men whose lives left few indelible marks on the historical record. I can only make inferences from the facts at hand. Like how, after the fun of chasing the shared dream of the solar camera ended and the boring and tedious part of making the thing work began, they showed no interest in doing it themselves. They burned through low-wage worker after low-wage worker, several of whom, in turn, almost burned them. It was a challenge to find an assistant capable of handling the boredom and misery of staying on the roof for uninterrupted hours in the sweltering Southern summer and the cold and windy winter. Eventually their prayers for a life of ease were answered when a young woman replied to an ad they'd put in the paper. She was a widow, her family was desperately poor, and she had an eight-year-old son who she swore could handle any sort of misery they wanted to throw at him. This sounded ideal. So up to the roof he went while the fellas hit the streets, showing Nashville what they could do.

The pictures were like nothing anyone had ever seen. The other photo studios in town were all turning out the same product. In any drawing room in any home of just about any American with any money at all, you could find six-by-four-and-a-half-inch studio por-traits, framed and lined up on a table in the parlor. Some were better than others, surely—proprietors of different studios had different backdrops to offer and equipment of varying quality they employed with varying levels of expertise. But each portrait, whether of a shipping magnate or of the man who spent his days shoveling coal into the furnace on one of that other man's ships, was the same humble size.

These men offered something grander. They could render the most important people in your life at life size. Larger, if you liked. In the chaos of a postwar world that was still mourning its dead, still uncertain of who was coming home and who they were all sup-posed to be now, here was something entirely new. And these pho-tos weren't merely big; they were beautiful. And a little strange. The further the photographers pushed the limits of the Jupiter—using bigger paper, a wider angle, images conjured through hours spent under the spell of the sun—the more peculiar the pictures became. Any photographer today knows (or any of us might discover when we order a poster-size print of a low-res image) that when you en-large a picture far beyond its original size, the image will distort. And so a life-size image taken with a solar camera yielded things beyond life, things not entirely within the photographer's control. Odd warping. Something shimmering in the eyes. A streak of unex-pected shadow or an odd absence. A minor accident in the process-ing of the original photo of your husband might go unnoticed, but when it was blown up, there might be a white blur where his shoulder should have been. Long hair could look like it had been sketched in gray crayon. Often photographers would have to correct and augment the images with pastels and paint, and the mixing of techniques would yield something weird and wonderful and wholly new.

I cannot show you a single one.

There are no surviving photos from solar cameras. Not from Van Stavoren's studio, or from any of the dozens of studios that operated in other cities in America and Europe during an approximately three-decade period during the latter half of the nineteenth century. The images were not particularly rare. They sold well. People seemed to love them. For a while, the three men found success by injecting novelty into a business that was marked by sameness. They made beautiful things that brought a bit of pleasure and wonder into lives that needed those things then. But the satisfaction of the customers couldn't last very long, because the pictures themselves couldn't. The paper, chemically treated to be activated by the sun in the Jupiter's darkened chamber, was also altered by the sun that passed through a dining room window. The pictures faded. The dark shadows dimmed. The family portrait at the top of the stairs rippled and tore in humid air. And now they are lost to history, like the name of the man in the white shirt. We are left to imagine what they looked like, just as we are left to guess what gives that man his seeming swagger as he stands by his creation. Maybe it's the feeling of having pulled it off, the joy of having once had an idea, of having said, "You know what might work . . ." and then doing it. That perfect, particular bliss that comes in that moment when it's all happening, when all is possibility, and life is all enlargement, before things fade.

When the success of the Jupiter did, Joseph Van Stavoren moved on. He founded a photography studio in Atlanta that was successful enough to appear in local business directories for many years. Those appearances are the final entries in what remains of his life's story. As for the white-shirted man, the photo from that day on the roof is all we have of him. For his part, Mr. Braid appears to have taken over the studio after his former colleague's departure to Georgia. He hung his own shingle with his own name and ran a reasonably successful business creating normal-sized images for many years. And thus ends the story of the three men on the roof.

But there is one person in this story who isn't in that picture.

At not quite nine years old, Edward Emerson Barnard spent his days warding off sleep and, alternately, heatstroke and frostbite, to climb the ladder he needed to reach the wheels he would turn to point the Jupiter camera sunward at strict intervals. This time in his life was just about the first good one he could remember. He was born just before the war, three months after his father died of causes history did not record. As an older man, he would recall that his earliest memories of growing up in wartime Nashville were "so sad and bitter that even now [he couldn't] look back to it without a shudder." Food was scarce. His mother made what little money they had selling flowers she shaped from wax. It seems she couldn't work outside the home; one of her only appearances in the historical record is her listing in a census document as a "confirmed invalid." So when the photographer whose ad she answered on her son's behalf asked her if she could assure him that her boy would stay awake, she answered yes. He'd better; they needed the money.

Edward never fell asleep. He learned how to operate the camera from the three men in the picture. They taught him how to use celestial charts so he'd know where the sun would go, and taught him the math required to make sure the Jupiter was following it across the sky as it went. They taught him that Jupiter was also a planet, though he later realized that was about the extent of his bosses' knowledge of the heavens. Patience, discipline, perseverance: He learned those on his own, day after day on the roof.

He was a young teenager when his bosses dismantled the contraption and he came down from the roof for good. Braid took him on as an apprentice and taught him photography. He stayed on until he was twenty-five years old, when he was accepted at Vanderbilt University. His previous academic record consisted solely of two months of elementary school, but he entered the astronomy department with years of experience tracking the movements of the heavens. He went on to discover fifteen comets (and co-discover two others). He was the first to figure out that novas are exploding stars. He discovered Amalthea, one of Jupiter's moons. Looking back on his life and his time on the roof with the Jupiter camera, he liked the symmetry of that.

Scientists do like their symmetry. The bilateral limbs of animals and insects. The spiraling forms of seashells and galaxies. Writers do, too, when they find it occurring in the otherwise unpredictable and chaotic nature of even the most disciplined of lives. So you'll forgive me if I can't resist leaving you with two images. First, we have this:

It is one of seven hundred pictures collected in Barnard's two-volume *Photographic Atlas of Selected Regions of the Milky Way*. The photos were selected from the more than thirty-five thousand he took during the 1890s and the first decade of the twentieth century. They were hailed as an astounding technical achievement in the photographic community during a time when most astronomers simply didn't have easy access to powerful telescopes and other tools to study the sky, night after night. This was an era when the imperfection and variability of human perception had people seeing oceans and canals on Mars one night and nothing the next. Barnard's heavens never changed; scientists relied on them for decades.

The second image is one that will last only as long as these words manage to stay in your head; it is less permanent, I'm afraid, even than one of the Jupiter's enlargements. It is of Edward Emerson Barnard, at forty-eight years old—though looking, as people seemed to back then, quite a bit older, stocky, his hair and thick mustache as white as the snow that hung heavy on the green boughs of the red cedars on Mount Wilson—5,700 feet above the Pacific in Southern California in late January 1905. There is a simple shack of unpainted wood, with a flat roof upon which he has set up a camera and a telescope he'd had hauled up the mountain. Bernard is on that roof, bundled against the cold in a wool coat and scarf, a cap pulled over his ears. Mittened hands hold a cup of coffee, his fourth of the night, because he has to stay up to adjust the telescope at precise intervals as the night sky moves around him, though he has known since he was not quite nine that it is he who is moving, not the sky. He does not like the hooting of the owls or the way the wind shushes through the trees. He does not like how the cold stings his eyes. But he knows he can stay up there as long as it takes.

The Surfman

You should never turn your back on the sea. Waves are unpredictable. Their size and behavior can shift abruptly, with little to no warning. If you are knocked down by a wave, the advice for anyone testing the edge of the ocean, from the novice to the strongest of swimmers, is to remain calm, hold your breath, allow the water to take you where it will, and wait until there is a lull between waves. Then rise up to draw a breath and reorient yourself, and prepare to do it again.

That was the job on the Outer Banks, the string of islands and breakwaters that runs for almost two hundred miles along the coast of North Carolina. Where Orville and Wilbur Wright first took flight. Where tourists flock each summer and mansions rise with little regard for the hurricanes that will batter them and the rising seas that will one day drown them. But this place was wild once. Before bridges and berms and federal programs came to restore the dunes and fix them in place, to keep the winds and the waves from reshaping the land with each storm and squall like they used to, when hurricanes would sweep whole islands away in an evening, or a rip current could create a channel that would turn one island into two. Hard people lived hard lives in that shifting place. People who knew how to find their way when the waves came—people like Richard Etheridge.

When he came to settle in these islands in the winter of 1867, it was a homecoming. He had been born there, enslaved, some twenty-five years before. Many of his earliest memories of life in the Outer Banks were of the waves and the winds and how they could change one's world in an instant. He was four when his first hurricane destroyed homes and warehouses just up the beach: The wind brought down walls, and then floodwaters sent those walls and floorboards and bureaus and white dresses floating past his house and created a river that cleaved the island on which he lived and taught him not to turn his back on the sea.

The lives of enslaved people were different on the Outer Banks than they were on the mainland. There wasn't much to plant or to pick or to sell, so they were put to the tasks of life in the dunes. Sailing and rowing, repairing. Clamming and fishing. Racing out toward the ships that wrecked upon the rocks to salvage what they could. Then the Civil War swept in, and the Union Army seized the islands and changed the world as Richard had known it, and that of the other enslaved people who escaped from the mainland across the sound to freedom: by boat, on rafts of bound boards, by their breath, swimming in the cold and the dark across the wide water. And when the Union general in charge of the occupied territory of the Outer Banks decided to turn some of these refugees into soldiers, Richard Etheridge enlisted.

He guarded Confederate prisoners. He made raids up the Carolina coast and into Virginia. He fought in the Battle of New Market. There is no record of what role he played in it, though there is a record of his promotion to sergeant just two days later. After the war ended, his unit was folded into what became known as the Buffalo Soldiers, the African American troops sent to assist the federal government in the subjugation of the West. He was sent to Texas to secure the road from El Paso to San Antonio and suppress Native

American resistance, while word was coming from back east about the discrimination and abuse the soldiers' loved ones were still suffering in the newly liberated South. He waited out his time until the wave passed over. He got his discharge and rode homeward from the constancy of the Texas plains to the marsh reeds and the shifting sands and the broken trees, the ghosts of forests that had once shaded and swayed, until they were snapped by some unremembered storm and washed away, save for the black and cracked trunks that would appear and then vanish with the shifting sands like the wrecks, the shattered hulls through which the ocean would rush and foam, the old ships rotting in the surf, timbers curving out of the sand like whale bones.

They call the waters off the Outer Banks the Graveyard of the Atlantic. The warm jet stream collides with Arctic currents, creating unpredictable tides, a breeding ground for storms, and sandbars that swell unseen beneath the roiling sea. More than five thousand vessels have been wrecked there in the five hundred years since people started counting. The *Monitor,* the famous ironclad, sank there in a storm during the Civil War. The pirate Blackbeard's flagship ran aground off North Carolina. Theodosia, the daughter of Aaron Burr, was lost at sea, along with the ship that bore her. The wrecks became a part of the landscape and part of life for the people who lived there, and the misfortune of those at sea led to the profit of those living on that inconstant land.

But the waters just offshore were too vital to American commerce—the currents too fast, the journey too tempting—for the government to let so many ships founder or run aground, and so much cargo float away, and so many people die. So a network of stations was established in a chain that ran the length of the coast. It was run by the United States Life-Saving Service, which would later become the Coast Guard. The mandate was in the name: Its men would keep their eyes on the sea and try to save people.

They needed men (they would all have been men back then) who knew the Outer Banks—knew how the currents could flip just like that, and the particular smell (ozone and sea grass and rain-grayed wood) that came before the worst of the storms. Men who could handle an oar and a sail, and themselves when waves knocked them down, and knew how to live in a world that could change overnight. Richard Etheridge was one of those men. He joined the Life-Saving Service, first at Bodie Island as a member of what they called a "checkerboard crew," because it was made up of both Black men and white men.

The men chosen for the crews were picked because they could do the job. They were strong and brave and skilled and deeply knowledgeable. But the African American men, who had won their freedom a decade before, were never allowed to rise in the ranks, even as they were treated as equals in the water. The strongest swimmer would be sent first into the breakers; the man who best knew how to read the currents would steer the boat pulled by the strongest rowers. But back in the barracks, the mission accomplished, it was the Black men who cooked and cleaned and did the laundry. They were given no chance to lead the station. Those jobs were political appointments, and the men who led the island outposts often ruled like local potentates, growing comfortable and soft while the men beneath them were anything but.

For several months each year, from the beginning of hurricane season in the late summer, through the cold of winter and the wet of spring, the life-savers worked around the clock. Training every day. Doing swimming drills. Building their strength and endurance, their tolerance for cold. Learning how to push the rowboats up and over the surf without getting swamped or flipped, learning to right them when they did, all while the ocean bucked and bashed around them. How to launch a rope from a gun on shore to the deck of a stranded ship to make a lifeline, which they would use to haul people back to shore and safety. And then back to the station house to seal the boats and braid the ropes, to feed the men and the horses that dragged them and their equipment through the sand. Every night each man in turn would be sent out to patrol the beach alone. Through rain and fog and sleet and whipping wind and biting cold. Looking out to the horizon. In the dark. Always the dark: A torch or a lantern could make people on a ship, lost in a storm, think they were being called to shore, to safe harbor, and could accidentally lead them to their doom.

They trained and waited and then sprang into action, out of bed, down the beach, and into the waves, into danger. They risked their lives so others could live. That's the kind of familiar phrase that gets put on plaques, made into mottos, repeated by rote at induction ceremonies and memorials, but the repetition doesn't make it any less true. As one of these surfmen, Richard Etheridge dove into the sea again and again. He saved men and women and children and ships and the things they carried more times than we can know.

But there was a night in 1879, when a ship signaled off Pea Island, where Etheridge was then stationed, and there were people who needed saving, and Etheridge's commander refused to send his crew out. We don't know why, just that he wouldn't let them do their job, and so those people died. And this was just one of a number of botched rescues and failures by the Life-Saving Service, according to the articles that appeared throughout the country that year as the nation followed the maritime disasters plaguing the Outer Banks. Almost two hundred lives were lost in two months. The government sent an inspector who found what Richard Etheridge had been seeing firsthand for years: Cronyism. Incompetence. Racism. Men in charge who couldn't be trusted. The inspector was faced with a dilemma: Many of these men had to go. They had failed. They had caused the men in their charge to fail. But who could replace them? Who knew the Outer Banks? The tides? The ways of the waves? The inspector went up and down the islands asking, Who should lead the stations? Who were the best of the surfmen? Again and again, he heard one name.

He wrote to his superiors to recommend that Richard Etheridge be placed in charge of a crew. He was told it would be impossible. It was against the law. No Black man, a decade and a half after the Civil War, was legally allowed to be the boss of a white man in the employ of the United States government. But the government needed him.

Richard Etheridge was named keeper, leading the only all-Black team of surfmen. They went to work.

For the next twenty years, he led the Pea Island station of the United States Life-Saving Service. He led it until his death of a sudden illness at the age of fifty-eight. The record he left behind was unblemished. He knew it had to be. He knew there would always be people waiting for the first crack, the first misstep, so they could step in and take his position away from him. One night during his earliest years as keeper, a white man, angry about his appointment, burned the station down. Etheridge and his men rebuilt it. Just another wave in his twenty years with those men on that island at the edge of the Atlantic. Building their lives together. Helping one another so they could help those who needed them. Twenty years of work, day in and day out, of preparation and maintenance and drudgery and manifest heroism. Twenty years of waking up to a changed world and finding their way.

Guinea Pigs

There once were some fruit flies. They were born. They mated. They ate some fruit. And they died, about thirty days later, as fruit flies do. But these particular fruit flies spent one of their thirty days, a winter's day in 1947, in space, as the first of Earth's creatures to leave its atmosphere.

There once were four monkeys named Albert—Albert I through Albert IV—who blasted forth from the New Mexico desert in four rockets to find out whether humans could survive a trip to outer space. Alberts I through III didn't survive long enough to let us know. So we strapped the fourth Albert with wires and sensors to monitor his health on the trip. He did great. Suffered no ill effects—until the landing. Which killed him on impact.

There once was a monkey named Yorick who went 236,000 feet up and 236,000 down, landing softly and safely with a parachute. But alas, poor Yorick didn't survive the wait for rescue; a metal capsule gets awfully hot in the desert sun.

There once were two monkeys, Mike and Patricia, who did everything together, we're told, including getting sent into space in May 1952. Awake and weightless in the nose cone of an Aerobee rocket, they made it back alive, and retired to the National Zoo in Washington, D.C., where Patricia died a couple of years later of natural, nonspace-related causes. She was survived by Mike, who lived until 1967. Let's spare a thought for Mike in his dotage: a widower, on display, a government worker until the end, whose memory, primatologists tell us, might well have held thoughts of Patricia and that odd adventure they took one spring day long ago.

There were once many dogs, Soviet dogs, chosen for space because they could sit and stay on command, unlike some fool American monkey. They'd go up in pairs. There was Dezik, who went up with Tsygan in the summer and then again with Lisa in the autumn but then died in the fall back to Earth. There were Smelaya and Malyshka, and Albina and Dymka, and Modnista and Kozyavka. All went up alive, not all came back that way. One dog named Bobik broke out of her cage and ran away in the middle of the night rather than fly into space the next morning.

Good girl.

And then there was Laika. Poor, famous Laika. Sent to her death by design. Sent to orbit Earth in a satellite the rocket scientists knew would burn up on reentry. For half a century the Russians maintained that they had invented a special machine that euthanized her right before her oxygen was set to run out, on her sixth day in flight. But they hadn't. In truth, she died just hours into the flight. From overheating, we think. A small favor, we fear.

They built a statue to Laika in Moscow: a stone rocket, a bronze dog. They said her death proved that humans could survive in space, though it did not. But the space flight of a monkey named Gordo successfully returned to the Earth's atmosphere did (though his capsule was lost on the bottom of the ocean; he is down there still). The lives of other monkeys and mice and street dogs and guinea pigs, one monkey named Sam, one chimp named Ham, proved we could. Some of them lived, others traded their lives for our dreams, as is so often the bargain.

Betty Robinson

She had never been tested. She knew she was fast, but what was fast? She was quicker than the other kids on the block. They couldn't catch her in tag, as they chased her through backyards, ducking under gingham tablecloths on clotheslines. She could beat all other girls in the races they held at church picnics. She had the ribbons to prove it. But they were girls in the Chicago suburbs in the 1920s, and there was so little in the culture of the time that encouraged any of those girls to try to be fast, to learn to run, or merely to want to win. Sewing, music, art, baking cakes: They could distinguish themselves with those things, sure, but they should leave sports to the boys. The roar of the twenties hadn't quite reached Riverdale, Illinois. So Betty was fast, but she was a lot of things. She was also good at sewing. And at playing guitar and piano. She was in all the plays—she had real stage presence and a smile that shone to the back of the auditorium. People called her Smiling Betty, which is a quaint, kind of corny thing to be called, but also, what could be better than being known as the kid—the teenager, no less—who just seemed to enjoy life?

She was a sophomore in high school and thinking about her future; she probably couldn't afford college on her dad's salary at the brick factory, but she could teach. Maybe not an academic subject—all those teachers were male—but maybe music, or art, or sewing. She was good at a lot of things. It would be hard to decide. She was just one of those people: the kid that parents could tell really had something, but what? Grown-ups would tell her she was talented but, like, how talented? How could she know if she had never been tested?

So one day Mr. Price, her biology teacher, is sitting on the elevated train waiting for it to take him home after school. There's a frigid wind off the lake, and he is happy to be warm inside the train car. His breath fogs up the glass. He wipes it away with his gloved hand and sees, down below, bundled-up teens trudging through the snow. From the back of the pack he notices one of his students running for the train. One of the girls. Betty, the smiling one. Nice kid. She's really going for it, but the train is already starting to rumble back to life and she's got a couple hundred yards and a staircase still to navigate. Looks like she'll be waiting for the next train; no chance she's making this one. But still, she's going for it. Gotta admire her spunk, if not her inability to solve for time by estimating her speed and the distance to the train, but not his fault; he wasn't her physics teacher. So he watches this girl make a go of it, all flailing arms, charmingly oblivious to her certain impending failure, and then he turns to his paper as the train starts to lurch away. Then something plops onto the seat beside him. A biology textbook. He looks up and there, hardly winded, is, of course, Betty, smiling. He is dumbfounded. He is also the track coach.

Betty Robinson stands in an empty school hallway after the last bell, behind a line drawn on the floor tiles in white chalk. Mr. Price stands behind another chalk line a precisely measured fifty yards away. Beside her a boy, a cute one, a senior from the track team, sighs, looking at her all-wrong shoes, at the awkward way she crouches at the starting line (she hadn't even known to crouch at the starting line).

Mr. Price holds up his stopwatch and blows a whistle and Betty runs. It isn't pretty, her form is ridiculous, but she is fast. She crosses the line 6.2 seconds after she started. It is one-tenth of a second faster than the women's indoor world record.

Mr. Price asks if he can sign her up for an amateur race; it's just a few weeks away. It's a quick ride on the L into the city. She says sure. He doesn't tell her it's one of the most prestigious competitions in America, and that the current world record holder will be there.

For the next few weeks, he and that cute senior (Betty found the cute senior to be a real sweetener in this whole deal) taught her everything they could about how to run. How to rein in those flailing arms, how to crouch low at the starting line, how to anticipate the starting gun, how to push off the blocks, how most races are won and lost in those first few seconds; they taught her about track conditions, about wind, about anything they thought they could cram into what little time they had, and then she lined up at Soldier Field in Chicago, a few steps away from the fastest woman in the world, and tried to remember all that—how was she supposed to remember all that?—and then she was running and running and running and running and running and running and it felt incredible. She came in second. It felt incredible.

She was invited to join the Illinois Woman's Athletic Club, where the victor herself trained. The place was paradise for sixteen-year-old Betty Robinson. Not only was it a kind of miraculous clubhouse with a café and a steam room and a pool and a library, but it was one filled with women, like none she had ever met, who were proud of being fast and strong. The twenties were roaring there. These were the women who were making the noise and declaring that there were new ways that women could be. They were proving it. Testing the upper limits of athletic achievement, and hemlines, and alcohol consumption. She loved training in their company. Of testing herself against the best every day.

Soon she is on a train across the country for the first time, seeing New York City for the first time. Breaking her first world record, though a too-strong wind would disqualify the race and keep her result out of the record books. Then, not even a year into her career as a real runner, on to the Olympic trials, where she doesn't win but she doesn't need to. She is plenty fast enough to qualify. And then she is on an ocean liner bound for Amsterdam, and she is just a junior in high school. And it is incredible. She meets people from all over the country. She runs in the sun on the top deck of the ship, in the middle of the Atlantic. She runs to the pool each day to see Johnny Weissmuller, the most perfect man she could even imagine, swimming laps. She swoons each time he passes by.

The games begin and the Americans start losing. If this were a movie, this would be the part where a montage would roll: America's male track stars, men she met briefly on the boat, some condescending, some even leering, start coming up short again and again. They stumble at the starting line and kick at the dirt in defeat.

A handsome, lithe sprinter, legs and arms pumping, square jaw set, eyes forward in gritty determination, American flag embroidered on his shirt, doesn't see the fleet-footed Finn coming into frame and blowing right past him. And then the women, the favorites, the ones we'd seen beat Betty back home, in Chicago and New York and at the Olympic trials—they start dropping like flies. Pushing desperately to overtake the leader, their faces falling as that woman, bigger and stronger, breaks the tape just steps ahead of them. Cut to an exhausted American with her hands on her knees, and another woman on her back in the gravel, the agony of defeat. But then there is Betty winning her first heat, and then another. And then the montage ends, and she is shaking out her arms on the track, bouncing on her heels, waiting for the starting gun for the next race. We see the faces of her competitors, grim and focused. The different flags on their shirts, none of them American. They are all grown women. And some announcer, some reporter tells the audience that sixteen-year-old Betty Robinson of Riverdale, Illinois, is her nation's last hope to salvage this disastrous meet. There's not much hope, to be honest, but let's see what the kid can do.

And what she does is get down in the blocks, and put her head down, and get to work.

I cannot tell you what it is like in that place.

That place where the elite athlete's mind goes when she is going flat out, when her body is doing what she has trained it to do, or when it can't quite.

I do not know the din of thoughts
or the quiet.

I don't know which it is, or if it is both at once. I cannot tell you if time slows down the way it sometimes does when you are truly present, when your senses are heightened, or if it is all a blur, a blink, a breath and it's done.

I can tell you she won, beating a Canadian competitor by mere inches. She became the first gold medalist in the first women's 100 meters ever held at the Olympic Games. She became the fastest woman in the world. I can tell you she was mobbed by her teammates and her coach; I can tell you she smiled. There were parties in the hotel, and on the boat back to the States. There was a crowd waiting on the docks. There was a parade in her hometown. General Douglas MacArthur, before his own star turn, gave her a gold bracelet that she would wear every day. Other admirers, before the International Olympic Committee set up rules prohibiting it, gave her diamonds, pearls, beautiful things she'd never imagined she'd own. She was an overnight celebrity, and not just the new favorite all-American girl: She was a new kind of girl. An athlete. A role model. And then the summer ended and she went back to high school.

She spent the next years preparing to defend her gold medal in Los Angeles at the 1932 Olympics. She had her first boyfriend. She enrolled at Northwestern University. She would sometimes drive out to her uncle's farm and go flying with her cousin in an old biplane. She was asked by the newspapers whether she was one of those young women who smoked and drank and went carousing till all hours, and she said of course not, while lying. She was having the time of her life. And one summer afternoon she was training, and it was just miserable. It was one of those sticky midwestern swelters. She wanted to go swimming, but her coach had banned her from swimming. He told her it would build up the wrong muscles and would hurt her running (he was wrong; people didn't know about cross-training then). So she figured she'd hit up her cousin Will for a ride in his plane: The breeze, the altitude, might break the heat.

They went up as they'd done a bunch of times before. She had even bought a helmet with goggles and a silk scarf, just like the one she knew Amelia Earhart wore, and they swooped and soared over the fields and the Calumet River. The air was cool on her face and she smiled.

I can't tell you what goes through your head when you know you are crashing.

When you don't know what's gone wrong but you know it's bad.

I don't know if time slows or rushes forward all at once.

I can tell you that the only thing she remembered was clouds. Whatever happened between that moment when she was looking at the sky and the moment when she woke up in a hospital bed with pins in her leg and her arm in a cast and her face cut up, after weeks spent in a coma: I can't tell you that.

The doctors told her she might not walk again. And, if she could walk, she wouldn't run, and if she could run, she wouldn't run like she used to; her legs were now different lengths by almost an inch. They were so sorry.

She had a favorite brother-in-law. His name was Jim. He'd fought in France in World War I, and came back kind of messed up. He had been gassed in the trenches and his lungs were never the same. This condition would kill him in the mid-1930s, but before that he helped Betty Robinson walk again.

Some days she couldn't get up at all. She couldn't straighten her legs. It hurt too much, or they just wouldn't comply. Jim would scoop her up and carry her down the stairs and out to the road and wait for the cars to pass by, the fastest woman in the world in his arms, and he'd walk across the park and put her on a bench and she'd sit for a bit. Listen to the birds, the wind in the leaves. Watch the kids playing tag. But other days he'd help get her onto her feet; he'd put her hands on his shoulders, and she'd take a step. Maybe the next day she couldn't get up at all. Maybe the next two. But then she would. And then just one hand, then with her elbow cricked in his elbow, then with his hand on her back, then just hovering above it as she took steps on her own. Her knees cracking. And it went like that. It was okay if she couldn't. She could try again tomorrow. And take more steps. And then once around the park. And then twice, let's try for twice.

She could jog, months later. After so many mornings in the park. She still couldn't bend over all the way, but she could run at a pretty good clip some days.

I've read about this part of Betty Robinson's life, when she was pushing through, and working, and working to get to half of what she once was, if that. I've read some of her recollections, written down in her old age, of that time in her life, and of how she was surprised to find just how comfortable she was in her changed body, despite the pain and her slow progress. She thought it might have been that her head was in such a different place too: She felt like a different person. Wasn't it natural that a different person should have a different body? And when I read that, I find the image I have of her in my head starts to drift. There is something in her words that sounds like something anyone who has come to terms with aging, as best they can, might say. About living in a body that is changing, that can't quite do what it used to, or at least not in the way it used to, and is realizing or wrestling with the notion that maybe the person they're becoming won't need that body to do all that, at least not in the same way, and maybe that's okay. And then I realize that the perspective of Betty Robinson looking back on her life sometime before she died, in 1999 at the age of eighty-seven, has taken me too far away from Betty Robinson as she was at twenty years old. When she had just become the fastest woman on Earth. When she had just been running in the salt air on the deck of an ocean liner in the middle of the Atlantic. Had ridden in the back of an open roadster in a parade through the streets of her hometown; had been smiling on the front pages of newspapers all over the world, had thrown her arms up in triumph, involuntarily—arms do that sometimes—had bent her head so someone could place a ribbon with a gold medal around her neck, and now she couldn't bend over. She could just sit at home and listen to the radio while another woman won gold at the Olympics in Los Angeles. Which meant she had four years to figure out how to get it all back.

If this were a movie, you'd want a scene here that takes place the next morning, after another woman had won the 100 meters, and Betty realizes how she's going to do it again. Maybe she drops the bracelet that General MacArthur had given her after her victory four years and a lifetime before, the one she'd worn every day since, the one that had survived the plane crash that almost killed her, and it's lying on the floor of her childhood bedroom amid all those reminders of the girl she used to be, the ribbons from her church-picnic victories, the program from the school play, a book about how to play guitar—reminders of the roads not taken—and the gold bracelet is there on the floor in a golden blade of light that comes through the curtains, dust motes shimmering, and she cannot bend over to pick it up. She just can't do it. And what should be her lowest moment gives her the idea that will bring her back to the Olympic podium. The idea is real, even if how she came to it is imagined, made clean and clear for this movie in our heads. She would never be able to win the 100 meters again, even if she could run fast enough, even if she could find the right training method, the right shoes that could somehow correct for the ineluctable fact that her legs were now two different lengths, and she would never be able to leap out of the blocks. She couldn't even get down near the ground to do it, because she couldn't bend over. But what if she didn't have to?

Imagine Betty Robinson. Find her on the track at the Olympic Stadium in Berlin in 1936. Find Hitler in the stands, find Jesse Owens stretching somewhere on the sidelines. He looks up to watch Betty. All eyes are on Betty. The comeback story. One of the first. She is standing on the oval with her hand stretched out, waiting to take the baton from another American woman. She is the third leg of a four-person relay. It is her only event, and it is the only one she can run, because it is the only one that won't require her to bend at the waist. Stay with Betty as her teammate charges toward her, arms pumping—her form is perfect, majestic. She is running neck and neck with a German woman. She stretches out her arm and the baton is in Betty's hand. And she is off. She is running. All effort. There is nothing easy in her stride but there is joy. She keeps pace with the woman beside her, who is pushing to seize this leg of the race to put distance between the Germans and the Americans. The German runner beats her to the next relay but only by a step. Betty has done what she needed to do, done all that she could have hoped to do. She watches as her teammate tries to make up that lost step and as the German woman, still that step ahead, drops the baton.

The rest is inevitable, and yet nothing about it was inevitable at all: The tape breaks and Betty runs, as best she can, to join her team-mates at the finish line. They run into one another's arms, and the camera finds the faces of the people Betty loves most. Her parents. Her doctors. Her brother-in-law Jim, who never let her give up, be-cause he never did. Her coaches who didn't believe she could do it until she proved them wrong. It is the Hollywood ending she de-served. It is improbable but is true. It is that cinematic. She is that heroic. Tape a photo of Betty Robinson above your workstation. You could do worse for inspiration.

I'd like you to take out your phone. If you wear a watch with a sec-ond hand, that will work too; unstrap it and hold it. Feel its weight there. Set a timer for twelve seconds, or be ready to look at your watch tick twelve seconds away: That is the shortest time Betty Rob-inson ever took to run one hundred meters in a competition. The time will go very fast. And since we have no idea what filled her mind during that time, we are free to fill it with what we will. We can think of her at sixteen, in a body just figuring out what it was capable of doing and where it was capable of bringing her; or at twenty-five, in a changed body, trying to figure out just how far it might still take her, and how fast. Was she focused on her breath, or the fall of her feet, or merely on not falling? Were there voices in her head—of her coach, or her own? Voices of doubt, or of elation that this is happening, that this is working—"I am winning, I am win-ning, I am winning"—and she is sixteen and this is the first time; or she is twenty-five and this is the last time and it is fine, she knows what she is capable of. She has been tested.

Set the time.

Ready.

Set.

Go.

A Washington Monument

et's build a monument, you and I, conjured from nothing but words, written here, and we'll pledge to hold it, at least for a time, pretending it's normal and fine that there's nothing here to actually hold or touch, to run a finger across, warm in the summer sun, or cold as winter seems to drag on into spring, fine that there's nothing to pose in front of on a Washington field trip.

First we will need to get rid of what's already there. So let's try to tear down the Washington Monument, try to wipe it from the landscape, erase it from the postcards in our minds, from the backdrops of photographs we've seen all our lives, or maybe even taken ourselves while on vacation—pretend it isn't a hard thing to do.

And we'll build a new monument, using plans proposed long ago, submitted for some formal approval, back when they were soliciting public input for what would eventually be chosen: the white obelisk we are trying to forget about.

I remember some story about how they were looking for ideas. I don't remember when or where I heard about it, but I don't think that should stop us from making our memorial, even though I'm sure I'm not getting all the details right. People had been talking about building a monument to Washington since before he became president, but it wasn't until the 1830s that they really got serious about it. They asked for ideas from Americans, the public, regular folks; that's how I remember it. The ideas were what you'd expect, nothing too crazy. A marble man on a marble steed. A Pantheon rip-off. A tower surrounded by thirteen columns, one for each of the original colonies, with a crypt beneath it to house Washington's remains, assuming his family would sign off on the plan. All very straightforward and stately and dignified in a familiar nineteenth-century way. But there was one idea that was proposed and rejected, if I remember correctly, and I want to build it here with you now anyway. If only in our heads, if only for these few pages, and for however long it hangs in the air or stays with you after you finish the story.

This was the idea, I believe.

Veterans of the Revolutionary War—each of them, all of them—who were still alive and still ambulatory in 1837, let's say, would converge on the capital. They would come in from the countryside—get up from their porches, put down their plowshares, and make the journey to Washington. These men would be old, a half century after the war, but there would still be many thousands hale enough to make the trip, though probably not for much longer. And each of the men—stooped and arthritic, milky-eyed, shrunken in their old uniforms now stiff and faded with age, smelling of cedar and home-made moth repellent—would come to the spot at the center of the Mall, where the monument now stands. Let's see these men, these veterans, in their thousands, and their bodies, however altered, that had once fought under Washington's command, and that had marched and eaten bad food and worn bad shoes and gotten eaten alive by mosquitoes and fleas. These men who may have desperately missed their beds and their spouses and their children, or maybe didn't at all, maybe had no idea what they were really fighting for, or they knew with every fiber, knew in their souls, knew with every step, that they were making history, that they were making a new nation, that they were ready to die for it, whatever that means. These men would assemble in the capital, men who'd made whatever they could of their lives in the new nation, who had planted fields, sold dry goods, loaded ships, mined coal, chiseled names into headstones, shoed horses, hung a swing from a branch of the elm in their yard for their sons and daughters and pushed them gently,

then higher,

then not at all.

All these men would come to the city named Washington, and each would scoop up a shovelful of dirt and toss it onto a pile. One by one. In their thousands. Until the dirt made a mound. Made a berm. Maybe a small hill. There in the center of the Mall. And someone would throw down seed and the small hill would green and become a part of the landscape.

And that is all.

That would be it. That was the idea. A Washington Monument. See it there. See it now, between the Lincoln Memorial and the Capitol. By the National Museum of African American History and Culture. See it in 1939, filled with people lifted up to try and see Marian Anderson sing; see them in 1963, trying to hear Martin Luther King. See it draped with the AIDS quilt in 1981; see women in January 2017, rising up and over it.

Just a hill. Made by men. To remember a man.

See it.

And hold it there for a moment.

George Meléndez Wright

The old woman told him to go play outside. Not that she wasn't happy to take care of her nephew's son. The poor kid was an orphan—eight years old, and he had lost two parents to two different illnesses. She loved him, but she was in her seventies; she couldn't keep up. So George Meléndez Wright explored San Francisco, heading off alone toward the gray breakers at North Beach, to the Presidio above the bay in the cool of the fog-hung hills and the Monterey pines. Golden Gate Park was new then and it was beautiful, and he liked to learn the names of the flowers placed just so to decorate the well-kept lawn, and of the trees that were allowed to grow in their well-ordered groves. He'd climb to the city's highest point, acres of woods poking out above the houses and apartments, from which George could see redwood forests, the ocean unfolding, hills that rolled beyond his vision to all the places he wanted to see, where the woods weren't penned in by houses, where the flowers grew wherever they could.

He spent the next years of his young life seeing those places. As a Boy Scout, as a teenage guide for the Audubon Society and the Sierra Club, and on his own during the summer before he headed off to study forestry and biology at Berkeley at only sixteen, when he took a ferry across the bay to Marin County and hiked all the way from there to Oregon. He found himself while exploring. At age twenty, in Glacier National Park, he wrote in his journal: "Is there anything on this earth that approaches the heavenly state more closely than a night spent at the foot of a noble pine beside a beautiful lake?" At twenty-four he went to work as a naturalist in Yosemite National Park, hoping to help tourists find their own heavenly state.

The people came before nightfall, on new roads cut through the wilderness, stretched over prairies, laid out in routes of least resistance, governed by convenience, sure, by ease of construction, by proximity to existing amenities, all those things, and by aesthetics too: stirring scenery, the soaring mountains' majesty through the windshield as the people came around the bends in the road. The people came before nightfall in cars when cars were still new, when any landscape flickering out the passenger window could still thrill, but here on these new roads there were vistas, right on cue. There was El Capitan, plum purple in the fading light; there were the Tetons, as grand as advertised; and when these people arrived at Yosemite or Yellowstone or Bryce Canyon, or any of the national parks in the American West in the 1920s and '30s, they drove right to the trash dump.

Because if you had made the journey all the way there, to the places America had pledged to keep wild, you wanted to see some wild animals. And if you made it by sunset, you could watch noble bears eating garbage. Every single night. The park rangers would toss the trash out for them, and they'd come out of the forest for a dinner of garbage. There were bleachers set up to accommodate the tourists.

The novelist Wallace Stegner called the national parks the best idea the United States ever had. He has been quoted often. The National Parks Service uses that line all the time. Ken Burns used it in the title of his documentary series about the parks system. And it has to be up there, idea-wise. What could be more in line with a particularly romantic, particularly democratic vision of America than its decision to set aside vast portions of its territory for preservation and protection from economic exploitation? Considering other competing visions of America at this late hour, the national parks can seem less an idea than a minor miracle.

You are welcome to quibble with the late Mr. Stegner, but I will ask you to grant me this: The best idea within that idea came from George Meléndez Wright. He knew the wilderness. And he knew that tourists in their fedoras and flowered dresses, sitting in bleachers watching bears growing fat on half-eaten hamburgers, wasn't wilderness.

He knew that the parks, and the nature they sought to preserve, had fallen out of balance. Yosemite was overrun by elk because the rangers had driven out the wolves and coyotes. Creeks overflowed with fish because they'd killed off birds that ought to be eating them. And some of those bears weren't hibernating. Why would they? There was food year-round at sunset. And so two years into the job with the Parks Service, at twenty-six years old, he set out to study the parks of the West and catalog their flora and fauna, talking to ranchers and hunters and the Indigenous people who lived on the land, filling notebooks with observations and tally marks. It took him three years. From his home base in Yosemite down to Sequoia and up to Glacier, up to Yellowstone, where he saw the real Old Faithful, to the Grand Canyon, which no canvas could capture, and with the data he gathered he was able to convince the stewards of America's best idea of his own best idea: The wilderness should be wild. He told them that a forest wasn't a zoo, that not every fire should be prevented, that predators should be repopulated, that the trash-heap shows should be closed, that if we were going to set aside corners of the continent for nature, then they should be natural.

This idea is the foundation of the parks we see today, though George Meléndez Wright didn't live to see any of it: He was killed in a car crash in New Mexico, at only thirty-three, while surveying what would become Big Bend National Park. But you can think of him, if you are lucky enough to visit Yosemite, or Denali, or Zion, or any national park, and come upon a bear or an elk or a wolf or any other wild animal that's allowed to be wild.

Né Weinberg

et me introduce you to Ethan Weinberg.

And to Dr. Clifford Weyman.

And Royal St-Cyr.

And Rodney Weyman.

And C. Sterling Weyman.

But first let me introduce you to Stanley Clifford Weyman. Seventy years old. Working the front desk at the Dunwoodie Motel in Yonkers, New York, just up Route 9 from the Bronx, in the middle of the night on August 27, 1960. Right before the two gunmen walked in.

He had been working the motel's graveyard shift for a year, which was longer than he had spent at nearly any job he'd ever had. He liked it. He liked the quiet. It gave him time to think and to remember the people he had known in his life. And the people he had been.

Stanley Clifford Weyman was born Stephen Jacob Weinberg in Brooklyn, New York, in 1890. His parents encouraged their boy to dream big, but they couldn't afford to send him off to the schools he'd have to attend if he wanted to achieve his particular dream of overseas adventure and white-tie luxury as a diplomat. So after high school, Stephen got a job in lower Manhattan assisting a portrait photographer with an upper-crust clientele. The men who came to the studio to sit weren't Astors or Rockefellers; they weren't the men atop the pyramids of capital and government and public works. They were the men who held those pyramids up. And as Stephen smoothed an unruly epaulet on a dress uniform, applied powder to rein in an obstinate glare, he would listen to these attachés, vice chairs, assistants to this, special deputies for that. Through their blustering and name-dropping, Stephen not only got a window into a world of power he'd never known, he got a schematic of the world as it really worked. He studied its titles and trappings. He mastered its body language and its bons mots. And then he put his education to good use.

Stephen Jacob Weinberg's twentieth birthday party was attended by more than seventy-five of the highest, falutin-est New Yorkers. They arrived in top hats and tails, in pearls and peacock feathers. They enjoyed cocktails and hors d'oeuvres while listening to speeches by their fellow luminaries, including at least one justice of the New York State Supreme Court, who toasted bon voyage to the event's honoree: S. Clifford Weinberg, the United States' newly appointed consul general to Algeria.

It was a night to remember, and a night he could still remember fifty years later, at half past two in the morning at the front desk of a midpriced motel just off Route 9.

And no one would've been the wiser to his elaborate charade back in 1910, except that a week later, the Supreme Court justice— who, like all the guests, had been taken in by Stephen's sham invitation and rented tux, and by the faux consul general's gracious manner and boyish charm—invited Stephen down to the courthouse for lunch. However, he also invited Stephen's boss to take a photograph to commemorate the visit. Even though his exposure as a fraud landed Stephen in a psychiatric hospital for six months, it taught him two things: First, if you look the part and talk the talk and look people in the eye and tell them you are someone you are not, they will believe you. And, second: Doing that was incredibly fun.

And so in 1960, while tallying the nightly take from the cashbox of the Dunwoodie Motel, he could also do an accounting of how he'd spent his seventy years. Of the day he told the head-shrinkers at the asylum that he was done with imposture for good and they recommended him for parole. Of the two and a half years he spent in a prison upstate for skipping out on that parole. And of all the times during those two and a half years when he'd thought about the night of the twentieth birthday party, and the banquet, and the toasts, and about how every night should be like that.

Stanley Clifford Weyman was the name he chose for his workaday life, the one he'd answer to while he plotted out his grander impersonations. It was the name he used in the phone book, the one reporters used when they called him for comment after one of his many elaborate scams was exposed. He was always happy to talk to them.

He'd tell them about the day he bought a used naval dress uniform, swapped out the U.S. insignia for decorations of his own design, and declared himself the consul general of Romania. He hired a boat, came up alongside the flagship of the United States' naval fleet, and asked permission to come aboard, and then spent the day touring the ship alongside an admiral, who was so pleased by the foreign dignitary's visit that he honored him with a twenty-one-gun salute.

He'd be happy to tell them about the time he read in the paper that the princess of Afghanistan was in town, so he showed up at her door and declared himself a State Department official charged with making her visit a pleasant one, and then took her down to Washington, D.C., and introduced her to President Harding.

He seemed to welcome any chance to regale reporters with details about how he pulled scam after scam, year after year. Sure, he wound up in jail a lot. But he always got out. What was six months here, a year and a half there? He told the papers he was "an American boy, imbued with a go-get-'em spirit. One man's life is boring. I have lived many lives. I'm never bored."

The people who read about those lives loved it. They loved how this average Joe kept going out and getting 'em. How he'd wind up landing jobs he was in no way qualified for—as a sanitation engineer from Peru, a lecturer on prison reform, the assistant to the world's most famous surgeon—and then do a good job. He kept getting exposed, and then the people he'd scammed kept asking him to stay on.

In 1926 a New York funeral home became the center of the world for a week as it prepared for the interment of Rudolph Valentino, the world's biggest movie star. Stanley Weyman was at the center of it—posing as Valentino's head PR man. He ran the funeral. And during the event, he convinced the silent-film star Pola Negri to hire him as her personal physician. Even when the papers noticed that the PR guy was the same guy as the personal physician, and was also that same guy from Brooklyn who kept scamming everybody, Pola Negri came to his defense. She said she'd never had better medical care.

People ate it up. They loved Stanley Clifford Weyman, serial pretender. At least until he was thrown into federal prison for teaching people how to pretend they were crazy to avoid serving in World War II; they were less psyched about that. And when they read about him next, a decade later, on trial for taking a loan on a house that didn't exist? That seemed beneath him. He couldn't even convince the judge he had been temporarily insane. Other men his age were starting their retirements; he was starting another jail term.

That was 1955, five years before that night in August at the Dunwoodie Motel. He'd gone to work to find peace and quiet and time to think about the days behind him. His best nights might not have been the ones that landed him in the papers: There were also times like that perfect summer night when he made up yet another name and arranged a full police escort as he picked up a friend from the train station, and they drove the length of Manhattan in a borrowed Mercedes convertible without needing to stop for a single light.

And there was the day he met a pretty young woman while walking through Brooklyn's Prospect Park and dazzled her with his naval uniform and tales of overseas adventure, and that night he turned to her and admitted that none of what he had been telling her was true. He was just a kid from Brooklyn with no job and no money, who'd never been anywhere. Or the night a few weeks later when they were married. Or all the nights during the next forty-five years

when the two of them would get dressed up, pretend to be people they were not, and eat and dance at the best joints in the city.

Those were the nights that tied the whole story together, this whole crazy plot, with all these characters he'd been making up for the past fifty years. All the adventures he'd had while pretending to be people who had adventures.

One man's life is boring. He had lived many lives, and he was never bored.

He could tell himself that at the front desk of the Dunwoodie Motel, when two burglars came in through the front door with guns drawn and yelled at this seventy-year-old man to hand over the cash box and assumed that a seventy-year-old man was just going to hand over the cash box, because that's what any seventy-year-old man would do.

Stanley Clifford Weyman was shot and killed on August 27, 1960, when he threw the cash box down and leaped over the counter and ran straight at the two gunmen. Which is exactly what any of the men he had ever been would have done in his shoes.

Below from Above

I f you want to build a bridge, a long one, over a large body of water or some other formidable expanse, you'll want to build a suspension bridge. One of those bridges with the towers on either side and the cables swooping down and up and down and up between them. And if you want that bridge to work—to hold the cars and the trucks and the SUVs and the U-Hauls, to withstand high winds, to remain standing during an earthquake or a tsunami—those towers need to stay still so the rest of the bridge can move just a little bit (it's physics; trust me). They need to be anchored deep within the ground, and you'll need to dig holes. This is hard enough to do in some rocky chasms in the Pyrenees or the Poconos, but in water it's a whole other thing.

So let's say you want to build a bridge over the East River in New York, between Manhattan and Brooklyn. And let's say it's 1870 and your options for working underwater are limited.

Fill a bathtub. Take an empty glass and flip it over, then push the glass to the bottom of the tub. There's air in the glass. There's water in the tub, but it can't get into the glass. You get it. You've made a diving bell.

Now picture tiny people in the glass. Chipping away at the porcelain or the fiberglass at their feet. Tiny picks and wee shovels. The oxygen will soon run out in the glass, so you'll need a tube or a straw poking through the top of the glass and through the surface of the water to let the good air in and the bad air out while they tap away, those tiny people with their tiny tools, digging at the bottom of your tub. And that's the idea: You build a watertight chamber, find a way to keep the air circulating within that chamber, and push it down to the bottom. Then you start building a tower, called a caisson, on top of the chamber. The increasing pressure caused by the weight of the growing tower helps push the caisson deeper and deeper into the hole. You keep going.

Now, looking out beyond the rim of your bathtub, if you are going to build a bridge over the East River in 1870, if you are going to physically connect the island of Manhattan with Brooklyn for the first time since the Pleistocene, if you are going to open up a path for travel and trade and commuters and tourists and joggers and stroller-pushing Park Slope parents, you will need a caisson, built of wood and metal and tar, an overturned box, one hundred and seventy feet long and a hundred feet wide, a capsized ship. You will need to float it out into the middle of the river and sink it to the bottom, some eighty feet down. Then you will need to start digging down into the riverbed, a full forty-four feet on the Brooklyn side, seventy-eight feet on the Manhattan side, through mud and silt and stone until you hit bedrock. And you will need people to get you there.

They were Irishmen and Italians and Germans, mostly: new arrivals, new Americans who would pile into boats before dawn for the first shift on some January morning, or just before dark for the second shift, or just before midnight for the third. They would set out for the construction site, a few hundred feet from shore, where the stone tower was beginning to rise from the water. They'd step off the boat and onto the rough boards of the pier, and descend one by one into a hole, into the darkness, a blast of hot air coming up from below. There were iron ladder rungs beneath their boots and lunch pails clacking against the walls, men below and men above coughing and cursing, cracking jokes in unfamiliar tongues. Then they'd come to a hatch, turn a wheel, and descend into an iron chamber. And be sealed within.

Down below this chamber, farther still, on the river bottom, five thousand pounds of pressure pushed on every square foot of the timber caisson. That external pressure would have crushed it and the workers, were it not for the pressurized air that was pumped in. This balanced the forces and kept the walls from blowing out and letting the river water in. It kept the men alive. But those men needed to be acclimated to the conditions they would find below, so first they were sealed in this iron chamber.

In came the pressurized air from a hole in the floor, and with it, the pain. This pushing, deep in their ears. Excruciating. And then slowly releasing. Though sometimes it wouldn't release and they'd be dogged by it all day, throbbing in their heads. They called it "being stuck in the lock." Even after they'd heard a tapping at the bottom of the metal cell and the trapdoor at their feet had opened up, and a man streaked with grime and mud and sweat poked his head up into the chamber and beckoned them down into the caisson, into another world at the bottom of the river.

In the gloaming, blue limelight flickered along the walls, and reflections rippled in the water that pooled in the mud and the muck between the boards and planks that crisscrossed the river bottom. They creaked and splintered and sank beneath the feet of the 225 men in the caisson. The roof was a few feet above their heads, pine beams sealed with tar to keep the water out and to prevent the sixty thousand pounds of rock, the Brooklyn tower, from crushing them while they worked.

It was hot. Eighty degrees at least, even in January. And wet. They'd sweat through their shirts before they'd barely started swinging a pick or lifting a shovel. Scooping up silt and sediment. Chipping at boulders, left there by receding glaciers millennia before. They'd dig up fossils—ferns and shells and strange things long gone from Earth.

There was a strange smell, which was kind of no smell. Something to do with the pressure and the air and their brains in that atmosphere seemed to trick their noses, which might have been for the best, what with the sweating men, and the smoke and the slime and the mud. And no bathrooms. Just a dark corner. Or a bucket. Or this box where they'd relieve themselves in a trough and every now and then whatever was inside would get whooshed up by a pneumatic tube and rocket the hundred-odd feet to the surface, where it would aspirate in a foul cloud above the river. And their voices didn't work right either. Words came out thin and high. Their ears worked well enough to hear the unrelenting clang of metal on rock, the grunts and lamentations of laboring men. Digging away at the river bottom. Helping the caisson sink deeper and deeper, which pushed down into the earth with the ever-growing weight of the ever-growing tower, reaching ever higher into the open air—the air that felt right in their ears, that smelled right in their noses. The air was cool. And not ungodly humid. And less like a circle of hell designed for petty sinners who prefer a dry heat.

Weeks would go by, and they'd barely sunk the thing six inches. All that digging, all that drilling, all that chipping, kicking up sparks. All those times they'd hit a stone and had not known what lay below, if it was as big as a melon or a mammoth, if it would take them an hour to clear, or if this is what a dozen of them would be doing for the next week, or six. Diving down blind into black pools, feeling around for dropped tools. Eating their lunch from a tin. On a rock. In a box a hundred feet—more—below the surface of the East River.

Sometimes a big boat, a steamer, a freighter, would pass by, and the displaced water would push against the sides of the caisson, or the tides would shift and the boards would snap and water would jet in and the chamber would start to fill until men with hammers and pitch tar could plug it. Sometimes things would catch fire. Sometimes they'd be sure the roof was caving in. Sometimes they would pass out. Or cry out at the pain in their ears, or at the pressure in their heads or their chests that just wouldn't go away. Sometimes they would rise to the surface, out of the heat and into the cold, but too fast, without being properly decompressed, and get the bends—air bubbles, nitrogen bubbles, in their blood—which is as painful as it sounds. Sometimes they wouldn't recover.

One day a fire broke out and it looked like the sides of the caisson were going to blow in and the roof would cave in and the tower would fall down and crush everyone inside, everyone fighting the fire, everyone fighting to stay alive. But it didn't. And the men came back the next day. Went back down into the hole. Into that alien world. And they came again the next day.

Think of a man who dug, who swung a pick, who bent to hoist a shovelful of river bottom, hefted buckets of stone. Think of his shoulders and chest, his triceps, his lats, like stone. Think of his head on a pillow packed with straw, in a boardinghouse at the end of the night. No aspirin or ibuprofen or Vicodin or heating pads, just pain. Think of those shoulders and arms and the joints within, of bursitis and micro-tears, frayed tendons, torn rotator cuffs—no good treatments, no insurance. Think of years spent living in that body after months in the caisson.

And think of a day in 1871, the Brooklyn tower done, when that man steps up through the hatch and into the air, cold on his skin, air he can smell, and knows that the job is done. That he is done with the river bottom.

There was a big to-do when they opened the bridge on a spring day in 1883. A perfect day, they say. Blue sky. Wisping clouds. Shirt-sleeves. Floral dresses. Fourteen years after they'd started construction. Fourteen years after the first men had gone down into the

Brooklyn caisson. Eight years after the last men climbed out of the caisson on the Manhattan side. And they'd poured concrete down into the hole and sealed it up. Fifty thousand people came from out of town. Came off boats from Connecticut and Massachusetts and New Jersey. The president came up from D.C. People sold souvenirs. Bands played. There was bunting; it was a day for bunting. And little flags in little kids' hands. There were speeches. Photographs. Fireworks. And a quarter of a million people walked the bridge in its first twenty-four hours. Marveling at the thing. This thing they'd watched grow for years, for half their lives, for all their lives, depending. They could walk from Manhattan to Brooklyn. Could see those towers up close. See their city from high up, higher than most of them had ever been. See seagulls and seabirds and terns turning beneath their feet. The governor. The mayor. Various dignitaries. Prominent business owners. A who's who of people no one remembers now. Marveling at the thing, and at the river, so far below their feet, and with them, men who knew what lay beneath it.

Stories About the *St. Louis*

The story was already familiar by the time the passengers could see the lights of Miami Beach. The first article about the *St. Louis,* an ocean liner owned by the Hamburg-American Line, and the more than nine hundred Jewish refugees it bore, appeared in American papers in May 1939, not long after the ship left Germany for Cuba.

The Cuban papers had printed the story even earlier. That country's right-wing press had warned of an invasion. It printed the same sorts of anti-Semitic screeds and cartoons that had been weaponized by the German state, whose program of terror in the previous year alone had burned synagogues, looted Jewish homes, invalidated Jewish passports, closed all Jewish-owned business, forced Jewish men and women to change their names and removed their children from German schools, removed Polish Jews from Germany and stripped them of the right to own property—all of which laid the groundwork for their forced removal. The Nazis had already built Buchenwald and Ravensbrück and more camps and were already killing Jews there, and dissidents and homosexuals, and disabled people, and African Germans, too, but they had not yet industrialized the process. They still did it with forced labor and beatings and pistols and firing squads. Heinrich Himmler hadn't yet mechanized operations for maximum efficiency in order to protect German soldiers from the mental toll of having to kill people one by one.

People knew those stories. Many thousands of Cubans embraced them, even, and they rallied in Havana against the looming arrival of the *St. Louis* and two smaller boats, cheered as a spokesman for the country's former president pledged to fight the Jews until the last one was driven out. The more sober press didn't focus on the Jewish people onboard, but they railed against the *St. Louis* with reasoning that would be considered more polite. They weren't anti-refugee, of course not: They were pro-Cuba. The island was still mired in the Great Depression, and it was small, the job market was tight. Setting aside jobs for the moment, if the state allowed a sudden influx of any population—setting aside the question of Jews for the moment, merely any population who didn't speak Spanish or share Cuba's customs and traditions—wouldn't that change the character of the country?

That whole story was familiar to Americans, too, who had been following how their own government had spent recent months debating marginal adjustments to existing immigration quotas. Refugees were always in the news. Everyone knew someone would have to do something. War was coming, maybe not to America, but Europe was on the brink. There would be more refugees. So many more. Maybe millions of migrants, looking for safety, and then after safety, jobs, social services, and this was 1939, and America wasn't entirely out of its own economic struggles, either, and all those arguments the polite Cuban papers made could be adapted for the United States. So the papers were filled with stories about the progress of various committees and commissions. A senator from New York and a congresswoman from Massachusetts had a bill that would allow twenty thousand German Jewish children to immigrate to the United States. That was in the news all the time. The big editorial boards came out in favor of it, as did prominent churches, but it got saddled with amendment after amendment in the House. Then it got blocked from reaching the Senate floor by a North Carolina Democrat who was an avowed anti-Semite but was also a key vote that FDR knew he'd need for the war effort. So Roosevelt dropped it. Still, there was this sense that things were happening that would solve this complex problem, that all the politicking and horse trading and trial-balloon-floating would add up to something. It was all sort of abstract at that point. Easy to lose the thread. But things were happening. The papers said so.

But the *St. Louis* wasn't complicated. It was nine hundred people on a boat. The average reader could get their head around that. There was drama playing out in the papers, a new development each day. There were characters—real people with clear motivations and the highest of stakes, and there was a story arc built into the journey, a destination, and a question hanging over it all. Would those people get to safety? Would those people survive?

Everyone knew about the *St. Louis*. They followed the story as Cuba rejected all but a handful of its passengers. They read about a New York lawyer named Lawrence Berenson who was sent from an American Jewish organization to lobby Havana to accept the passengers' visas—almost all the refugees had them in hand—and about how, when his pleas were rejected, he tried to get Cuba to agree to put them in what they called a concentration camp, a temporary holding facility, a place for them to stay apart from the general population while they applied for asylum and their permanent status was determined. They read how the government demanded $435,500 to do so, to cover the refugees' care, to keep them from being a drain on the average Cuban. Berenson asked for more time and managed to raise $500,000, had it sitting in an escrow account at Chase National Bank in Manhattan, but the Cuban government said it was too late.

Then came stories about two other boats that would have followed the *St. Louis* to Havana but were turned back to Germany. There were stories of failed attempts to resettle the refugees in Mexico and the Dominican Republic, and stories about how relatives of the passengers made their way to Havana to save them, including a man who brought an engagement ring from New York to give to his fiancée when she got off the boat. There were many people who'd hired boats from a Florida marina and piloted them to Cuba and alongside the *St. Louis* to get close to their families and friends, whom they hoped to take home. Instead, the passengers stayed on the decks of the ship, shouting down to their relatives from the rail, close enough to talk to them, close enough to hear sobbing over the sound of their idling engines, the slap of waves on the hull. The boats were close enough to see a man named Max Lowe, a lawyer, a father of two, leap from the ship. The blue water purpled with the blood from the slits he'd cut into his wrists, while he flailed as he tried to will himself to drown before he was pulled ashore.

The American papers were sympathetic. The American people were sympathetic. They were a sympathetic people. But few papers called on the U.S. government to take the refugees in. The president didn't respond to a cable sent by passengers on the *St. Louis* asking for him to intervene. A bureaucrat from the State Department pointed out that if they let in these particular nine hundred German Jews, they were going to have to lower the official quota by nine hundred other German Jews, and those people were already in the queue. There could be an executive order, of course, but the idea was slapped back by isolationist Republicans during the midterm elections, and with his own reelection bid around the corner, saving the people on the *St. Louis* wasn't where FDR was prepared to spend his political capital. Instead, the federal government sent a Coast Guard patrol boat to sidle up to the ship where it sat, three miles offshore from Miami Beach. Just in case anyone got any ideas about jumping in and swimming for shore. Or to respond if the captain ignored orders. He'd been cooperative so far but had been on edge since Max Lowe's death and was worried about more suicides, maybe even a mutiny.

Everyone knew what was happening. They read about it and wrung their hands. Nodded gravely as they read *The Washington Post*'s plea for sympathy for the plight of the passengers, without actually calling on the United States to take them in. It laid the blame on the shipping company, which, the paper said, should have made sure the Cubans would take them in before they took off across the Atlantic, and on the German government. "Were the Hitler Regime," the *Post*'s editorial board wrote, "more generous in the treatment of the unwanted element of the population, they would not be forced to flee as frequently as they are."

And so the *St. Louis* returned to Europe.

The final articles, the end of the story everyone had followed so closely, were datelined Antwerp, Belgium. They told of a pact among hundreds of the passengers to kill themselves before they reached shore, if they were sent back to Germany. Instead, Jewish organizations negotiated to send the passengers to four different countries. Two hundred and eighty-eight were sent to Great Britain. One hundred and eighty-one were sent to the Netherlands. Two hundred and twenty-four found temporary refuge in France. Two hundred and fourteen were allowed to stay in Belgium.

A few years ago (you may be familiar with this story already) the United States Holocaust Memorial Museum in Washington, D.C., undertook a massive project to determine what happened to the passengers of the *St. Louis* after they walked down the gangplank in Antwerp. The museum found that all the passengers who were sent to England survived the war, except one, who died in an air raid the following year. But nearly all who found refuge on the Continent were trapped, and nearly all were sent to camps. Two hundred and seventy-eight of those survived the Holocaust. Two hundred and fifty-four did not. Because the boat was turned back. Because the politics of the day were challenging and complicated, and refugees were caught in the middle. But you are familiar with that story already.

Full Circle

The nation was brand-new. It needed new everything, essentially: an army, a navy, an economic system, mottos, symbols, letterhead. And it needed artists to celebrate and articulate Americanness to its citizens and to the world beyond, whatever Americanness turned out to be. Now, artists are not a navy, or even letterhead, when you get right down to it, but at the beginning of the republic, at a moment of boundless possibility and youthful idealism, they were a nagging, unchecked box on the Founding Fathers' to-do list.

John Vanderlyn was born the year before the Declaration of Independence, in 1775, in Kingston, New York. His father was a painter, though he could never quite make a living at it; he installed windows and sold paint and brushes to get by. And his son was determined to become more. More than his dad, sure. That's the normal order of things. But John wanted to be more than just a painter. He wanted to be a great American artist, a great man of his age. And why couldn't he be? What wasn't possible for a young, white man in this young country led by young, white men, at that moment?

He was a teenager when he convinced Gilbert Stuart to take him on as an apprentice. You know Stuart's work from the dollar bill in your wallet. The classic George Washington portrait with the sour grimace of a man with the world on his shoulders and terrible dentures in his mouth. Vanderlyn copied Stuart's portraits for practice, and one day the subject of one of those portraits stopped by the studio. It was Aaron Burr. You know him too: third vice president and the first ex–vice president to shoot an ex–treasury secretary.

Burr thought the kid had talent and maybe he was just what the country needed. He paid to send Vanderlyn to Europe to study with the greatest painters of the Old World, so he could come back to the New World and harness the spirit of these recently united states— their plainspoken republicanism, pluralism, embrace of the individual citizen, self-determination, aesthetic simplicity, and rejection of kings and queens and European opulence—on canvas.

So John Vanderlyn went to France in 1796. He studied with venerated masters. He was hailed at Parisian salons. He won medals. But he also got stranded. He ran into money trouble; Burr killed Hamilton, and that was a whole thing, and then other patrons were hard to come by, and France in those years was pretty much going bananas. During the nearly twenty years Vanderlyn spent there, he saw the tail end of the French Revolution, the rise of Napoleon, the fall of Napoleon, and the restoration of the monarchy. John Vanderlyn took it all in. When the dust cleared, he was ready to show America what he'd learned. It was 1815. He was still young, but he was a man of the world, at the height of his artistic powers. He set sail for home, determined to become America's greatest painter.

He arrived in New York to find that the position had already been filled.

John Trumbull had studied overseas too. First in England, then in France. Trumbull had beaten Vanderlyn home and was already thrilling audiences with his sweeping paintings of the recent past— the surrenders of Cornwallis and Burgoyne, the Battles of Princeton and Trenton and Bunker Hill. And the paintings were . . . pretty good? They had some scale. They had a sort of, if not quite majesty, an oomph?

Vanderlyn knew he had Trumbull beat.

In a barn in Kingston, John Vanderlyn was hard at work on a project of undeniable scale that oozed oomph. In France, he had seen panoramic paintings, circular landscapes so massive they literally surrounded viewers and immersed them within the scene—a battle-field, an Alpine valley, wherever. At their best, they gave people the illusion of travel. A feeling that they'd been transported out of their own lives. Now at home, Vanderlyn knew exactly where he wanted to send them.

While he was in his studio in his barn, month after month, with rain rapping on the roof or the cold winter wind whistling, Vander-lyn was thinking back to a day not long before: late summer, just outside Paris, in the gardens of Versailles, then newly restored, when he'd stood in the sun, mist from a burbling fountain, the perfume of flowers, September sounds of buzzing dragonflies and birdsong, gravel crunching beneath the feet of running children, laughter aloft on the warm air. A perfect day that he had spent making meticulous sketches, using an optical device that allowed him to trace the scene onto linen and capture every detail and angle, all while thinking of home and imagining how he would share this perfect moment with America, and begin his inevitable rise.

It took him more than a year to finish his panorama. When it was done, he needed a place to hang it, so he built one.

On a June afternoon in New York City in 1819, visitors walked between the neoclassical columns of Vanderlyn's Rotunda, a two-story brick building, cylindrical like the Pantheon, and capped with a thirty-foot-tall zinc-plated dome that changed color with the shifting angle of the sunlight, and flashed bright as clouds broke above the park downtown where it stood by City Hall. For a dollar, New Yorkers could ascend spiral stairs at the center of the building and emerge onto a circular platform beneath the dome and marvel at Vanderlyn's painting. Here was Versailles, on a lovely late afternoon on the verge of autumn. Men in high hats and spats and lacquered canes. Fine ladies strolling arm in arm. A boy chasing a butterfly as the shadows grew long. And there in the Rotunda, light streamed through a hole cut in the glinting dome and shifted with the clouds, shifted with the seasons, and brought his painting to life. And brought Americans, for a moment, to Versailles.

But Versailles wasn't a place Americans wanted to be. In the first year the Rotunda was open, the panorama brought in a mere $1,200. The painting alone had cost him two grand, not to mention the cost of the whole building he'd constructed to show it in. Some critics were impressed with what Vanderlyn had achieved. But they had to ask: Why, of all things, was this what he wanted to achieve? The

panorama was cool, don't get them wrong, but Versailles? In America? When there were mountains upstate? Why French royalty? Why aristocratic excess? Why not minutemen at Lexington, or citizen farmers tilling the Shenandoah Valley? Why not transport people to Liberty Hall or Plymouth Rock or Valley Forge? John Trumbull was out there creating grand paintings that folded recent American history into the classical tradition of "history paintings," showing every other American artist how it was done. But Vanderlyn?

Vanderlyn was out of step with the American character. He had missed a thing or two while he was off in Paris for so long. But rather than taking the hint, or at least another crack at a different panorama, he dug in. He took Versailles on tour. First to Philadelphia, where no one really came either, and where the gallery's roof leaked and soaked the painting through.

He spent forever fixing it. And forever again trying to make it a success, but it was never a success. He tried for decades. He even went on a misguided and doomed quest to get Congress to buy his Versailles. He kept scheming and holding out hope, despite all evidence to the contrary that his country would recognize his genius, and in that, at least, he wasn't entirely out of step with the American character. But he had certainly fallen well behind his peers.

And he was crestfallen and more than a little bitter when John Trumbull was commissioned to paint patriotic murals in the Capitol rotunda. And when Congress asked Vanderlyn to take some of the load off an overworked Trumbull and paint a small panel of Columbus landing in San Salvador, it was little consolation. But it was work, at least.

It was 1839. He was sixty-four. During all the years he'd spent dragging Versailles around, trying to convince America that he was its greatest painter, he'd barely painted. He was rusty. And he knew it. So he went back to France, thinking that being there would inspire him, would help get him back to where he'd been before, to when he was young and everything felt so full of promise.

He found that Versailles hadn't changed. The same mist from the same fountains in the same breeze, the same long shadows as the day grew late. But he had changed. As one does. He was heartbroken, he wrote, to be reminded of who he'd been those years before. A young American, standing in this garden, imagining painting this garden and all that painting this garden was going to bring.

His Columbus painting was kind of a flop. And Vanderlyn's story ends not long after, in the place where so many true tales of dashed dreams end: in a small rented room, where he died alone.

People die and their descendants are left to sort through their stuff—expired bus passes, insurance policies, weird figurines none of the kids want but don't have the heart to throw away. Vanderlyn left behind a 165-foot-long painting; his sister didn't have the heart to throw it away. But she didn't have enough room for it either, so she cut it with a knife into seven strips, rolled them up, and squirreled them away in her basement. Then, a hundred years later, a new owner of the home was poking around, found the canvases, and donated them to the Metropolitan Museum of Art, which didn't have anywhere to put them either, and rolled them up and squirreled them away in its basement, where they lay for the next thirty years. And then, in the 1980s, the Met was renovating the building and needed a gallery to double as a multipurpose room. Somewhere they could hold the occasional cocktail reception or symposium on the future of the American museum and whatnot. The people at the Met realized they had a perfect backdrop already. I'd like to think Vanderlyn would have been pleased. But he was never pleased.

In order to fit Versailles into the room, the Met had to lop the top off the painting. So where there once was sky, there is now acoustic tile. And what was once a perfect circle that would surround you and transport you is now two curved canvases split by doors at each end of the room to provide exits in case of fire and passage for people on their way to something they'd rather see, like a Trumbull, maybe. So it takes a bit of imagination on our part to see Vanderlyn's Versailles. As it always has.

Looking Up

A Postcard from the Waldorf-Astoria, May 19, 1910

They started crowding into the express elevator at ten o'clock. Bundled in their topcoats, puffed in their furs. Friends who had been up there earlier in the week had warned them about how cold it gets on the roof, and besides, a little extra protection might be useful on a night when there was a chance they might all die.

Astronomers were in heaven. They'd trained their telescopes on Halley's Comet as soon as it rounded the bend on its seventy-six-year circuit of the solar system. They had learned so much about it—its relative velocity, its eccentricity, its aphelion, its perihelion—and they had discovered two things that had made headlines beyond the academy. First, the comet's twenty-four-million-mile-long tail was composed, in part, of cyanide gas; and second, for six hours in 1910, when the comet would be at its brightest in the night sky, that tail would envelop the Earth.

Those things were in all the papers. That neither the cyanide nor the comet's tail posed any but the very slightest, barely calculable danger to anyone at all was less widely covered. Instead, there were stories of panic in every corner of the soon-to-be-destroyed globe. Many were overblown: supposed mass suicides in Hungary, riots over the exorbitant costs of voodoo protections in Haiti. Others were true: the Florida man selling space on his submarine where people could be safe from the comet's rays. The miner in California who crucified himself, convinced that the end-times were nigh.

But here were well-bred and well-read Manhattanites, stepping off the elevator and into the most exclusive party in the world, knowing that the chances that that world would end were incredibly small, but still big enough to make the whole thing extra fun. So onto the roof of the Waldorf-Astoria and into the crisp night air. Into music and French perfume and cigarette smoke. The women compared their silver comet pins and their gold comet-tail charms and their diamond fireballs. The men fetched them comet cocktails from the bar. They smiled at friends, at people they'd run into now and then at the symphony or in the men's lounge after a squash game, smiling at anyone, because to be here at all was to be someone worth smiling at.

Just before midnight, when the planet first became enwrapped in the comet's tail, they could look out across the rooftops of their city and know there was nowhere else on Earth they would rather be. They could see the lights from other parties on other rooftops: the Plaza and the Gotham and the Knickerbocker and the St. Regis and the Astor and the Belmont and the Majestic. They could make out people standing on the observation decks of steamships churning the Hudson. They could see the construction site of the Woolworth Building, which someday soon would rise higher than they were right now, but not tonight. They could look out to New Jersey, where the mayor of Woodbury had ordered the police department to make wake-up calls to make sure no one slept through the big moment. They could look down on tenement roofs, down on the people who lived there, the people who read the rags that sold fear to sell papers. Some of whom had bought so-called comet pills or sucked on comet inhalers in the hopes that when morning came, if morning came at all, they'd be the smart ones, left to rebuild the ruined world. They could look out over the whole city, awake and alive. Leaning out of windows. Craning their necks. Playing the this-could-be-our-last-night-on-Earth card on reluctant lovers. Passing bottles between neighbors on stoops and fire escapes. Dancing like there was no tomorrow. Letting the kids stay up late. Talking to strangers on the street. They could look out and see the whole world looking up.

As They Were in Life

Did he know what he had done? We have no way of knowing if he did at first, despite his claim that he wrote down the unvarnished truth for posterity, and despite the fact that he told his story at least once under oath. I have read those accounts and read the attempts of historians to answer the many questions that still hover over the life of William Mumler, and I will tell you up front that I do not believe him. And I don't think you should either. So many of the people who saw the pictures when he was alive didn't believe him, and, looking back now, you can immediately see it's all a trick, even if you don't know exactly how he pulled it off.

The consensus among historians is that he stumbled onto the photographic process that would make him infamous. It was the summer of 1862. He was a thirtysomething bachelor with a steady job working for an engraving company in Boston. He had been spending his weekends dabbling in photography at a friend's studio by the Old State House. One afternoon he was practicing making portraits, using himself as the model. Setting up a backdrop. Futzing with the curtains to get the lighting just so. Draping a cloth over his arm to hide the mechanism with which he would operate the shutter. He opened the aperture, held still for the minute or so that was required back then, closed it, and then took the photoplate over to the window to wait while the sun activated the chemicals. But as the image began to materialize, there was something that shouldn't have been there. It looked like a ghost.

It couldn't be a ghost, he thought. He went off to a bar to show the image to some of his photographer friends. They passed the photo around, cracked some jokes at Mumler's expense, and offered their best guesses as to what he'd done wrong. They couldn't agree on whether he'd screwed up while taking the picture or while developing it, but they all figured he'd somehow made a double exposure. When he took the self-portrait, they said, he must have accidentally added an unprocessed image from an earlier photo shoot. So when he developed it, there he was—coming up on middle-age, bushy whiskers, a bit of a paunch—in a well-lit, standard, professional-quality studio portrait, but there was someone else in the picture too: a remnant from another image taken at another time that revealed itself only when processed simultaneously with this one. It probably looked as it did—mostly transparent, shimmery, and poltergeisty—because the chemical residue on the glass plate had partly evaporated. That's what his friends figured. But there was another person whose opinion mattered more.

William Mumler was in love with a woman who worked a couple of doors down from his friend's studio. We don't know how it started, who approached whom first, but either one would've had an opening: They were both into photography. Hannah Green was a single mother; her husband had skipped out on her and the kids a few years back. She'd started her own business braiding hair, specializing in a type of traditional plaiting done for bereaved women. She would sit with her customers and weave in beads and silver pins and small mementos of the person they'd lost. At some point she wanted to be able to offer an upsell, braiding in photographic lockets, so she'd learned how to take pictures. The braiding business was successful, but she was best known around town for other services she was performing for mourning customers: Hannah had become one of the most sought-after mediums in Boston's then blossoming spiritualist community. She was very good, it was said, at talking to the dead.

Mumler had never met anyone like her. He was not a spiritualist at this point in his life, and perhaps not ever. Spiritualism was still new. It was a religious movement, a new cultural current, a trend, an engine of economic and personal empowerment for women like Hannah Green, all that. It directly challenged the hierarchies that had defined faith in America since Plymouth. It created a new geography of the afterlife: The dead weren't above in heaven or down below. They were all around us, occupying a liminal space overlaid on our own: the spirit world. It must have been thrilling. And thrilling for William Mumler to meet Hannah Green, the charismatic, worldly woman at the center of the Boston spiritualist scene.

He was smitten. When he showed her his picture and she told him that the person in it who looked like a ghost was indeed a ghost, who was he to argue?

Years later, he wrote that he felt ambivalent when his name and a

description of his photograph first appeared in Boston's spiritualist newspaper, *The Banner of Light,* one of the growing faith's primary evangelical organs. He didn't feel comfortable calling himself a photographer, never mind a medium. He did not write about how he felt when, the very next day, dozens of spiritualists arrived at Hannah's door wanting to pay to sit for the amazing Mr. Mumler, and when this woman he loved looked at him, beaming. But we know what it made him do.

In the first months that William Mumler worked as a professional spirit photographer, he told customers up front that there was no guarantee that anyone would be in their picture other than themselves. He claimed his photographic technique merely opened a pathway between this world and the world of the spirits; he didn't claim to control what happened there. When your picture was developed, your mother might appear beside you, just as you had

hoped she would, and just as you remembered her. Or there might be a presence, a woman who was maybe not quite like your mother. Wasn't she a bit smaller? Was her posture the same? You might turn to Mr. Mumler and object, but he would demur, leave it to you to decide. Maybe you didn't remember her so well, all these years later. Maybe bodies changed in the next world. Maybe your faith wasn't strong enough to allow you to see the truth before your eyes. Or there might be another family member. Maybe you had come to Mumler's studio hoping to see your mother, but instead you saw another woman, perhaps her sister, the one you had met only on that half-remembered day when you were young.

One afternoon when William Mumler was still in the swirl of early fame, a woman came into his studio having just lost her son. She did not give him her name but he knew her immediately. She was the president's wife. Mary Todd Lincoln was a spiritualist. She had brought mediums into the White House to try to contact her boy Willie, who had died of typhoid at eleven years old. It was no

surprise that she had arrived at his door in her grief and desperation, hoping for a photograph with her boy. Instead, she was given a picture of herself and a Confederate soldier that she assumed to be her half brother Samuel, who had died at Shiloh on the other side of the war. Historians have suggested that Mumler chose not to give her what she wanted, because he was afraid she would take the picture straight to the press, which would hurt her husband's chances for reelection. Mrs. Lincoln left heartbroken but didn't complain: She was a believer. Mr. Mumler had never said he could command spirits. Sometimes they didn't come at all. He took your money all the same.

Let's be direct: William Mumler was a con artist. His wife was his accomplice (one scholar even makes a compelling case that she was the inventor of spirit photography and used her husband, and his maleness, as a front for an operation that was all her own). His skills

were improving, and his promises grew more bold. If you sent him $7.50—which would be a couple hundred bucks today—along with a picture of yourself and a note describing which deceased loved one you were hoping to conjure, he would take a photograph *of that photograph* in the presence of the spirit of your desired departed.

It seems preposterous. A century and a half later, it is easy to see that these images are fake. With a couple of touches and swipes, the phones in our pockets can make something far more convincing than Mumler's spirits. But it wasn't so clear then.

Mumler was doing something new with a technology that was itself still new. There is that quote from Arthur C. Clarke, the science fiction writer: "Any sufficiently advanced technology is indistinguishable from magic." This idea applies here, I think. It was the middle of the nineteenth century. People were reading in the papers about waves of sound, about magnetic fields, about invisible things all around them that scientists were just beginning to understand and to develop techniques and technologies to detect and visualize and manipulate. What if the souls of the dead were made of the same stuff? Invisible frequencies. Fields heretofore undetected. Not long before, cameras had done the seemingly impossible and captured images, had frozen time with lenses and tinctures, with physics and chemistry. Why wouldn't they believe?

And why wouldn't they want to?

Your parents would die, your child would grow, your wedding day would come and go, as well as your home, your dearest friend, that person you loved but were never quite brave enough to tell, and all the places and people you left behind as you lived your life—and for all of human history, the only lifelike images you would have had of them would have been in your head, and for only as long as you were able to hold them there. And then you could take a picture.

For the people who were alive during photography's earliest years, who experienced that trick of time that turns the new from magic to mundane, happenstance divided their loved ones into two categories: those who had died before the invention of photography, and those who would die after. Here was Mumler, promising to give them something they thought they had lost forever. And when they had paid their money and waited while this man did whatever it was that he did with those chemicals and plates of glass, and then he showed them a picture of themselves when maybe they hadn't seen that many pictures of themselves—and maybe they hadn't yet gotten past the disconnect between the way they felt they looked and what the camera showed them—and there they were, along with someone he said was their sister, fifteen years gone. They might not question whether that was really the way she wore her hair, or held her chin. It was a scam. These weren't spirits. But the customers paid for comfort; he gave them comfort.

Not everyone believed, of course. From the moment he first handed that picture to his friends at the bar, there were people trying to figure out how he did it. As his business boomed in Boston, skeptics kept coming to his studio to try and catch him in the con. Sometimes they came unannounced. They would pose as a simple mourner, naïve to the ways of photographic science, when they were in fact experts. Or they would send $7.50 and a photo and a description of a dead relative who didn't exist. Other times, Mumler would go directly to them to pick up a gauntlet they had thrown in public to prove, once and for all, that he was the real deal. He would conjure spirits in these photographers' studios, or invite them to his studio, where they would observe every step of his process. They would look for tricks. Sleight of hand. Moments when one lens or photographic plate was swapped in for another. And they would see none, and then they would see a person in the picture who Mumler maintained was a ghost. They were baffled, but few walked away convinced. They didn't know how he was fooling them, but they knew he was fooling them. They would go to the papers to say so. As did one man after Mumler showed him examples of his spirit photography and he recognized one of the supposed apparitions as his own wife, who had come in sometime before to get a traditional, ghost-free portrait taken, and who remained very much alive.

The criticism of the skeptics grew so loud and so common that Mumler moved out of Boston and set up shop in New York, where he was an instant sensation. Spiritualists flooded into his studio, eager to see their lost loved ones again. But so did a policeman, who arrested Mumler for fraud. The subsequent case was front-page news around the nation and in Europe. Expert witnesses were called in by the prosecution who offered up nine methods that Mumler might have used to make his pictures. P. T. Barnum was brought in to testify against Mumler as an expert on scam artists, and presented as evidence an image he'd commissioned from another photographer in which Barnum was joined by Abraham Lincoln, then four years dead. The press and much of the public expected Mumler to crack, but he didn't. His defense argued that just because there were other, non-supernatural ways to create photographs that looked like their client's, no one had ever seen him use any of those methods. It was not the defense's job to prove that spirits existed. And no one could prove that Mumler himself didn't believe in them. The judge agreed. They hadn't proved fraud. He was free to go.

William Mumler lived and worked for another fifteen years; he died in 1884, a few days before what would have been his fifty-second birthday. He spent much of that time perfecting a method that made it possible for images to be reprinted in newspapers for the first time, but he never stopped taking spirit photographs, and he never explained how he made them. Historians and researchers who specialize in nineteenth-century photographic techniques think it is likely there is no single answer. They figure he probably alternated between several methods, depending on the tools he had on hand and how closely he was being observed and by whom. They say he was a gifted inventor and must have mastered at least a few tricks of sleight of hand to pull off his con for so long.

His real power, though, came from understanding belief itself: that as long as he never wavered, never winked or hinted that he was anything other than a faithful spiritualist, he created a space in which faith and possibility could take root. Belief itself is a suspended state, and his customers kept coming to find comfort there.

There is a Boston address on the back of his most famous photograph. He was more or less run out of New York after the trial. He had won in court but had lost the press and public opinion. He was arrested again in Massachusetts a few years later. The charges didn't stick and the case fell apart, but he was dogged for the rest of his life by accusations of fraud. Still, people came to his door.

One day a woman came to his studio on Springfield Street. She did not give her real name but he knew her immediately; he had seen her before. Since Mary Todd Lincoln had last been in front of his camera, she had sat next to her husband while he was shot in the head; she had lost another son to illness; she had been pilloried in the press for her spiritualist beliefs; she had struggled to make ends meet and had suffered ridicule from all quarters as she sold off her dresses to pay her bills. She had never been well. She came to Mumler and said she had lost her husband. She did not name him. She paid him up front, knowing that he would not guarantee the appearance of the spirit she sought, knowing the pain she felt. She prepared herself to feel that same pain again. Mumler gave her what she wanted.

Six Scenes from the Life of William James Sidis, Wonderful Boy

1.

If you lived in a one-dimensional world, you'd be a single point. You could move in a straight line, forward or backward, and that's it. If you were walking down that straight line and there was someone in your way, you'd be stuck. You couldn't walk around them, because there'd be no left or right in a one-dimensional world.

But there would be left and right in a two-dimensional world. If you lived in a two-dimensional world, you would be a flat object on a flat plane, but if you were walking around and you ran into a wall, once again you'd be stuck, because there is no up or down in a two-dimensional world.

Now, of course, in our three-dimensional world, up and down exist. You can climb over walls; you can tunnel beneath them. But if you were trapped in a box, in a room, in a cell (there are so many ways to be trapped in a three-dimensional world), with no windows or doors, you'd be stuck again.

Not so in a four-dimensional world. In a four-dimensional world, you could step right out of the box. No walls could hold you in. The rules of our three-dimensional world that say you can move only in variations of up and down, forward and back, and left and right—these rules wouldn't apply to you. This is hard for most of us to conceptualize. Here in our three-dimensional world, four-dimensional space is a theoretical abstraction that mathematicians and physicists find useful in ways that go over the heads of most nonmathematicians, like me.

On a snowy night in January 1910, a lecturer spoke at Harvard on fourth-dimensional space, a concept that had once been defined as "a speculative realm of incomprehensibly involved relationships." But he did his best to make that and other multidimensional realms comprehensible. He used diagrams. He coined words like *paralleloppedon* and *hecatonicsoheridon*.

At the end of the talk, a distinguished professor from MIT stood around answering questions from a klatch of reporters. The professor predicted that the lecturer, William James Sidis, would become one of the greatest scientists of the twentieth century. But Sidis wasn't there to answer the reporters' questions or hear the professor's praise. He was already on his way home. It was past his bedtime. He was eleven years old.

2.

Boris Sidis was on a trip to Chicago for a symposium. He was a renowned Harvard psychologist and he had been away from his wife, Sarah, and his son, William James, for about a week. He came home on the boy's birthday just in time for a celebratory dinner with family and friends. It was young Bill, now three years old, however, who had a gift for his dad.

Bill walked into the dining room and presented his father with a copy of Caesar's account of the Gallic Wars, in the original Latin. But the book wasn't the gift. The gift was that Bill could read it. The gift was that in the week while his father had been away in Chicago, toddler Bill had taken his mother's old high school Latin textbook off the shelf and taught himself Latin.

His father was pleased.

But not necessarily surprised.

He had been training Bill—training his mind to be the kind of mind that could do that sort of thing—from birth. Little Bill was both a beloved son and a guinea pig in his father's psychological experiments. There was no doubt the boy was exceptionally bright— his parents were; their parents were—but Boris Sidis believed he possessed extraordinary genius. He believed if his son drilled enough, and if he answered the boy's every question, encouraged his every interest, he could unleash an unparalleled intellect. And the people who had gathered to celebrate Bill's birthday, the people who heard three-year-old Bill read about the power struggle between the Arverni and Sequani tribes of Gaul in the first century B.C.E., congratulated Boris on having done just that.

3.

A reporter knocked on Bill's door. Bill Sidis had graduated cum laude from Harvard at the age of sixteen, making him the school's youngest graduate at the time. The reporter wanted to know about his plans for the future.

Sidis had already spent years in the public eye. Newspapers had charted his exploits and readers could rattle off his achievements like baseball statistics: the nine languages he knew by the time he was eight, and the other one he invented, with its eight verb tenses. The three months it took him to blow through four years' worth of high school instruction. They knew he'd passed the Harvard and MIT entrance exams before he turned ten, and that he'd been reading *The New York Times* every day since he was one and a half. They'd followed the debates between psychologists who wrung their hands over the intensity of his studies, and between educators who argued over whether genius could be taught, and between the theosophists who wondered if Bill Sidis was the Greek mathematician Euclid reincarnated.

So when the reporter sat down with the young graduate, he knew readers wanted to know how Bill Sidis planned to make his mark on the world. Which of the universe's great secrets did the boy plan to unlock first? Which pervasive human misery would he endeavor to alleviate? But at sixteen, weary and wary of the spotlight, Bill Sidis answered that he wanted to be left alone. He said he wanted to live the perfect life, which he defined as a life of seclusion. A life devoted only to the mind.

4.

Bill Sidis, now in his twenties, walked into the office of the Eastern Massachusetts Street Railway Company in downtown Boston. It was his first day of work.

He had held many jobs since graduating from Harvard. First, he taught math and science at Rice University in Texas. He quit after a year. He didn't like being ridiculed by his students, who were all older than their professor. After that, academic job offers stopped coming, but the reporters did not. How did he plan to get back on track? they asked. Was he squandering his talents? He had such incredible gifts, such limitless promise—did he realize he was letting people down? In 1919, after he was arrested for marching during a socialist May Day parade that had turned violent, the questions came laced with venom: Just who did he think he was? Where did he get off? How could that wonderful boy have grown into this strange young man?

By the time he walked into the office of the Eastern Massachusetts Street Railway Company, Sidis had stopped answering questions.

He had stopped doing much of anything, as far as anyone knew. He had lived under a series of assumed names. He took menial jobs where no one expected anything of him except to punch in, work an honest day, and punch out. But inevitably, someone would figure out he was the wonderful boy they'd read about all those years ago. Or some reporter would come snooping around. Bill would slip away again, make up another name, find another job.

The job at the Eastern Massachusetts Street Railway Company looked ideal. The ad said they were looking for someone to run an adding machine. He could do that. He could do that well. You had to be focused and detail-oriented. There wouldn't be time for distractions or chitchat. He could turn off his mind and just work. And the job was in an industry he loved. Since he was a boy, Sidis had collected the tickets they gave you when you transferred from one streetcar to another. He was fascinated by streetcar maps. By how the routes were organized. By how the systems of fares and departure times and rules of the road differed from town to town and state to state. He found as much beauty and fascination in transportation routes as he did in the movements of celestial objects. So the chance to run these particular numbers and keep these particular books—all while keeping to himself and escaping the questions and expectations that haunted and held him in their grasp—felt like a dream.

But when he reported to work on the first day, the office manager told him they knew who he was and were delighted to have a famous genius on the Eastern Massachusetts Street Railway Company team. They didn't want him to run an adding machine; they wanted him to run the whole thing: to do for their systems and profits and bookkeeping and strategic planning what other people wanted him to do for medicine or physics or chemistry or higher mathematics. All Bill wanted was to be invisible.

He quit on the spot. He stepped out onto a streetcar and cried all the way home.

5.

A reporter knocked on Bill's door. Bill Sidis was thirty-nine years old. He invited her in. She worked for a local paper, though an account of her interview with Sidis made it into a "Where Are They Now?" article by Jared L. Manley and James Thurber in *The New Yorker.* She found him living alone (he had never married, likely had never been kissed) in a clean but threadbare efficiency apartment in South Boston. He worked as a clerk for the city's unemployment office. At night he worked on a history of a Native American tribe he called the Okamakammessett, which purported to be a hundred-thousand-year history of the native peoples of North America. It was one of several books he had written under pseudonyms, in lieu of the scientific treatises that his admirers long before had predicted he'd produce. He had already finished a manuscript, now lost, on the lost city of Atlantis. He had written an article on the importance of Jersey City, New Jersey, in the historical development of the United States. He had translated Chekhov's play *A Reluctant Tragic Hero.* He penned works on a political philosophy he called libertarianism, a word he might well have coined. He wrote a three-hundred-page argument for banning two-way streets, called "Collisions in Street and Highway Transportation." And finally, he completed his defining work: a book that the *New Yorker* article holds up as evidence that Sidis had, after all, totally lost it. A book that even a staunch Sidis defender, decades later, called, "quite possibly the most boring book ever written."

The book is *Notes on the Collection of Transfers,* a 306-page heavily illustrated guide for people who enjoy collecting streetcar transfer tickets. In his introduction, he admitted he might be the only person who did, but he thought his book might inspire others to take up the hobby.

If someone were so inspired, the book would provide everything they needed. Here was a near-complete taxonomy of streetcar transfers, from the unique streetcar-to-ferry transfer that could take you from Portsmouth, New Hampshire, to Badger's Island in Kittery, Maine; to the complex dance of repeat- and exchange-transfers that could take you along East Fourteenth Street to Fourth Avenue in New York City, northbound to Twenty-third Street, westbound to Broadway, then northbound and, finally, westbound on Thirty-fourth Street. Sidis claimed it was one of only two cases in the whole New York Rail System in which a traveler could enjoy the special thrill of what he called "the triple-repeat transfer," a thrill that was likely lost on the readers of *The New Yorker*, who, like the rest of America, either laughed at or pitied the strange man that the wonderful boy had become.

Sidis spent the next several years suing the magazine for invasion of privacy. He took it all the way to the Supreme Court, with newspaper reporters following the story, and Sidis, all the way too. He lost his case and died not long after from a cerebral hemorrhage at forty-six years old.

6.

On a summer afternoon in 1926, several children and their parents went to a garden party in the backyard of a private home in Tuckahoe, New York. It was organized by a group called the League for Fostering Genius. The kids were prodigies, at least in the eyes of their parents. And everyone ate canapés and stood up straight, put their best feet forward, and watched performances of precocity from the gathered geniuses. The ten-year-old composer. The nine-year-old orator. The three-year-old opera expert. And the twenty-eight-year-old streetcar transfer ticket collector.

Seventeen years after his speech at Harvard that made him famous, in which he explained esoteric mathematics that charted the ineffable architecture of fourth-dimensional space and enumerated its properties and theoretical implications, Bill Sidis spoke about the theoretical implications of streetcar transfers. He said that if someone knew, as he did, the routes of the nation's streetcar systems, knew the fare structures in every municipality, knew the rules and formulas that governed the use of transfer tickets, it was possible to ride from one point on any streetcar line to any other point on any other line. If you understood the system in its entirety, a single fare could take you anywhere. You could hop on a streetcar in Cambridge, Massachusetts, buy a single fare, and then transfer to a streetcar in Boston's Back Bay; and then to one in Dorchester or Worcester or Poughkeepsie; or Baltimore; or Philadelphia; or New Haven, or West Point or Columbus or Fort Wayne or Virginia Beach or New Orleans or Jersey City or Detroit; or Gary or Rehoboth Beach or Buffalo, New York; or St. Louis or Houston; or Providence—riding forever on cars where no one knew or cared who you were, completely free, and you could go anywhere you wanted, just go and go and go and go and go and go and go.

Alexander Graham Bell . . .

. . . invented the telephone; patented his idea; successfully converted it from theory to physical object; chose partners who built a business that put that object into homes and offices and installed the poles and wires that connected those objects to those homes and offices; and dominated, for decades, the industry that his invention enabled. It made him rich, though not nearly as rich as he could have been; he sold his shares early, left the work to others, and moved on.

You can trace the path of his meandering attention by the inventions he left behind: You can start with the years he spent on the Graphophone, for instance, an important technology in the history of recorded sound, and move on to the period when he worked on the hydrofoil, a boat that rises above the surface of the water.

There are other, fainter paths, but you can find them if you know where to look. One can trace the invention of the metal detector back to a handful of days Bell spent in the summer of 1881, when he rushed to Washington, D.C., from Boston, having learned that President Garfield had been shot there. On the train, he worked furiously on a device he hoped would locate the bullet lodged in the president's body. It didn't work. His machine was too sensitive, and was triggered by the springs in the president's bed.

There was also one path that he laid that people have spent decades trying to untangle. He worked for years developing pedagog-
ical techniques for deaf students that history has proved were
misguided and even harmful, that held back the proliferation of sign
language and kept deaf people isolated from one another and from
society at large.

Often, though, the paths he went down didn't lead much of anywhere. He spent a long time trying to figure out a way to use mag-
nets to record sound, but never did. He attempted to build a machine
that would extract water from the ambient atmosphere, but that
idea dried up. Much of his later years were spent trying to invent
the airplane. He was convinced the key was tetrahedrons—three-
dimensional objects made of four connected triangles. He designed
kites of different configurations, thinking their shapes would yield
lighter, more stable wings, but he could never crack it. The kites
were just one of his many ideas, spread out over countless hours
spent chasing some thought or theory that didn't go anywhere,
some dream that swept him up, floated there in the sun for a bit, and
then fluttered down. They were just one of a million things. But
they were the most beautiful.

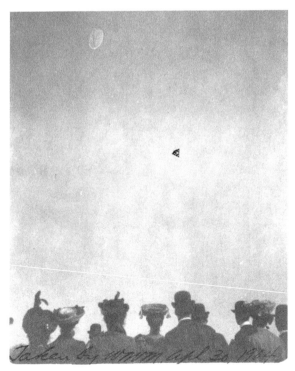

Four Hundred Words
for 79th Street

Has anyone ever been farther from home than Minik Wallace?

He was seven years old in the summer of 1897. One morning he left his family's igloo and ran to the edge of the water where he watched his father and a few other men paddle through the channels that the August sun had opened up in the ice. When they came back hours later, they weren't alone. White men had rowed ashore from a ship that appeared on the horizon. At least one of them had dealt with Inuit people in northern Greenland before. Robert Peary had been coming up here for years, trading guns and biscuits and sewing needles for sled dogs and information that could help him find a route to the North Pole. He was obsessed with being the first person to reach it. A lot of people back then were obsessed with being the first person to reach it. Not the Inuit. They hadn't heard of the North Pole before people like Peary started showing up. When they did, they weren't impressed. But back at home in the United States, between voyages, Peary spent his time impressing New York's idle rich with his stories. Impressing them with his calloused hands and his weathered face, and with the artifacts he brought back. In the fall of 1897, Minik, his father, and four other people from their village were those artifacts.

They weren't kidnapped. The Inuit were told they would see unimaginable wonders—lights, streets, sidewalks, stores, trains, smokestacks, restaurants, trees, crowds. And they did. Minik came from a tribal community of fewer than two hundred people who lived spread out over dozens of miles. And to meet their boat at the dock in Brooklyn, New York, there were thirty thousand people. They arrived on bicycles. Or in carriages pulled by animals he had never seen. And they paid a quarter each just to get a look at "the Eskimos."

Minik's father and the other adults were also told they would go back home the next year. They would be studied by scientists at the American Museum of Natural History. They would be measured and weighed and asked about their cultural practices and their diets and their family lives, and then they would return to those families bearing things—technologies, provisions—that would make things better for them.

But they didn't go home.

They got sick. They had no defense against tuberculosis. Minik's father died. Minik was inconsolable. And two other adults and one child, a girl a little older than Minik, died too. Another adult was sent home to Greenland, in the hopes that the change of scenery would cure him. Minik was alone.

He asked the people at the museum—people who were nice to him, people who felt terrible about what had happened to this boy in their care in New York—to let him give his father a proper burial. So one night, Minik and his caretakers performed an Inuit burial on the Upper West Side of Manhattan.

Seven years old and fatherless, Minik moved in with William Wallace, the museum's superintendent. He was raised as the man's son. At fifteen years old, Minik asked Wallace why the kids at school were suddenly making fun of him. And William had to tell Minik the truth: Those kids had heard about the articles in the paper, the ones that had come out revealing that Minik's father wasn't actually buried that night eight years before. That seven-year-old Minik had performed a sacred Inuit ceremony over a bag of rocks, hadn't known that that was a secret. But Minik had never been told, as these children now seemed to take a wicked glee in informing him, that his father had been dissected. That one of the museum's young scholars had won an academic prize for his study of the man's brain. That Minik's father's bones were on display.

Minik asked for his father's bones back. William Wallace asked for them, too, though he never told Minik that he had known all along what had happened to his son's real father. Never told him that he had decided which lab would be used to remove his father's flesh and organs so the museum could have an "Eskimo" skeleton in its collection. People wrote letters and wired the museum, people who remembered reading about the sad little boy years ago, strangers who were outraged to learn what had befallen him.

The museum refused to hand over the bones. Minik asked Robert Peary, the man who had brought him and his father to New York, to help get his father's bones and bring them back to Greenland. The best Peary could offer Minik was a lift back home.

There are two natural endings to the story: You'll find one at a moment in 1918, at the end of Minik's life, when he dies in New Hampshire at the age of twenty-eight, as one of the 675,000 people killed in the United States by the global flu pandemic. He is surrounded by the new family who took him in after he wandered around North America for years, going from odd job to odd job.

You'll find the other ending at a moment in 1993, when Minik's father's bones, finally released by the museum, are given the Inuit burial they deserved, nearly a hundred years after Robert Peary's ship brought the man and his son to that strange place a world away.

But I'd like to finish this story at a different place. At some undocumented moment. In 1913 or 1915, during the period he spent back in Greenland. A young man. Alone, briefly, out on a hunt, feeding his dogs, but alone. Out in the perpetual darkness of the Arctic winter. Out on the ice. Under stars he could never truly see in Manhattan. With thoughts coming to him in two languages, the one he'd spent the last two decades speaking, and the one he'd had to relearn after returning home. Nagging thoughts that would eventually lead him to decide that he didn't belong in Greenland either.

Has anyone ever been farther from home than Minik Wallace?

Snakes!

What happened with the second one was there were these kids playing in the backyard in August 1953 in Springfield, Missouri. Maybe they were playing catch, pretending to be Stan Musial, or—better yet—there's a sprinkler sweeping lazy arcs, the sun making rainbows in the spray as the kids jump through it, getting soaked, laughing. And their dog, some bulldog mix, is rooting something out in the shrubs by the fence that separates their house from Mr. Mowrer's, and then the dog's going crazy. He's got ahold of something. He's thrashing his head. Then a black snake flies through the air and lands in the grass and the kids start screaming and their father bursts through the screen door and bounds down the back steps. These are the foothills of the Ozarks, and snakes here can kill you—cottonmouths, rattlers—but Dad's lived here his whole life and he knows what to do with a snake, so he grabs a hoe, swings it up, swings it down, and that's that.

The kids head back into the house. The dog calms down. And the dad goes to clean up the bloody mess and he stops in his tracks: He's never seen a snake like that before. He calls his neighbor over, and the guy looks at the body and says, "Huh, I killed one of those with a hoe last week too" (that's what happened with the first one). Next thing you know, the cops are there. And they put the severed snake in a big jar and bring it to a professor at the local college, who peers at the creature through his horn-rimmed glasses, and it is just about the damnedest thing he ever did see: There are Indian cobras in Springfield, Missouri.

So everyone in town starts talking. Turns out there had been a third one in the same neighborhood: A woman was weeding her garden when a deadly viper native to a land nine thousand miles away crawled out of the bushes. She screamed. Her husband ran. Another hoe came down on another cobra.

And a fourth, just a few days later: Some teenagers were out driving. Their headlights caught something slithering across the road. They ran it over. Finished it off with a tire iron.

There was a scarlet macaw on the front porch of the small house on the tree-lined street. It would say hello, delighting the kids who came to the pet shop that Reo Mowrer ran out of his front parlor, and it greeted the cops when they came looking for Mr. Mowrer.

They had reason to suspect he was responsible for the deadly cobras crawling around town: All of them had been found within a block or two of his house, and he had been known to keep exotic animals, like the boa constrictors that sometimes shared his front porch with the talking bird, or the alligators he kept tied up in his garage, or the penguin he sometimes hosed down in the backyard. Suspicious, too, was the fact that his animals often broke out, leaving his neighbors to complain about six-foot-long iguanas on their roofs or monkeys in their oak trees. Also, Mowrer had several wooden crates filled with live cobras in his basement. That seemed like a clue.

But when the cops suggested that he—a man who had dozens of deadly vipers in his house, a man who was known primarily to his neighbors as the weird guy with all the exotic animals that kept escaping into people's yards—was somehow responsible for the deadly vipers that had escaped into people's yards, Reo Mowrer said nope. Not my deadly vipers.

The cops were incredulous, all sputtering disbelief. But Mowrer was firm. Sure, he had cobras, but none of his cobras were missing. Must be someone else's cobras, which was preposterous. Reo Mowrer was the only importer of Indian cobras in the United States. He got them through a dealer who worked out of Thailand, and then flew them to Kansas City, Missouri, where he loaded them into his station wagon and brought them home, before selling the snakes and shipping them to zoos and reptile parks around North America. But none of those zoos or reptile parks were in the southwestern Missouri area. It was just Mowrer. But he knew that, according to state and local statutes, he hadn't done anything illegal. He knew, too, that, in the absence of laws, and in the absence of shame, you can just lie and lie and lie.

Meanwhile, a fifth cobra was killed when a little girl was sent to the garage to fetch something for her mom and found herself face-to-face with it, hood opened wide, hissing, and she screamed, and her mom rushed in and took it out with one of Springfield's apparently ubiquitous hoes.

Police Chief Frank Pike's phone was ringing off the hook. Citizens were freaking out that there were freaking cobras crawling around. Other people were calling for Reo Mowrer's head. The chief got a call from one of Mowrer's neighbors saying he'd seen a cobra crawl into a crevice in the concrete steps to his house, and then Mowrer ran over and grabbed the snake by the head and ran off with it, saying some version of "Nothing to see here, just a regular snake, no cobras here, you thought you saw a hood but it wasn't a hood, totally not a cobra," while hiding it in his arms, making sure no one could see it. That was probably the sixth cobra. But the sixth dead cobra? Chief Pike saw to that one himself. Some men had found the cobra under a house around the corner from the pet shop. Cops show up. Smoke it out with tear gas. Then Pike's men shoot the thing six times, somehow don't kill it, so Pike snares the snake with a makeshift snake-snaring pole-and-lasso contraption, and then finishes the job himself with the by-then time-honored Missouri tradition of whacking the cobra with a hoe.

And now the phone calls are coming in from all over. The national newspapers. International herpetologists, to whom Pike surely said, "Herp-uh-what?" and they said, "Snake experts," and he said, "Why didn't you just say that in the first place?" And then he's getting antivenom shipped in from a zoo in Florida, and a mail-order copy of Ditmar's *Snakes of the World,* which he reads from cover to cover and keeps in his back pocket.

Pike has men stationed around the clock on the porch of Mowrer's shop (the macaw must have driven them crazy). They were there less to keep an eye out for snakes (at this point, Mowrer had bent to pressure and shipped all his remaining cobras to a roadside snake show in Kentucky) than to keep scared Springfieldians from burning the place down.

Mowrer wasn't helping Pike's case at all. When reporters showed up on his porch to grill him about the cobras (the seventh one died just down the road; more teenagers, another car, another squished snake), Mowrer would repeat his firm statement that no cobras ever went missing from his shop. He'd say he thought maybe a circus train had stopped in Springfield and some snakes had slithered out and just happened to wind up in his neighborhood. And then he'd go on and on about how cobras weren't all that dangerous. They injected their venom only after they had completely clamped onto you. It wasn't just a quick-bite-and-you're-dead thing. So the key was: Just don't let them completely clamp onto you. And besides, there were deadly snakes all over the Ozarks. There were rattlesnakes and cottonmouths and copperheads and coral snakes; a cobra was hardly any more dangerous than any of those. People just thought they were because of movies and dime-store adventure novels. The whole thing was silly, really.

No one in town wanted to hear that, of course. They were rounding up a posse. Taking to the streets with shotguns and hatchets and hoes—of course there were hoes—and baseball bats, that most American of weapons. And they *were* afraid: These were cobras.

The town's director of health and safety got a recording that some Missourian missionary had made of authentic snake-charming music, straight from the streets of Calcutta, India. Cops rigged up a flatbed truck with a PA system and speakers and drove around the streets of Springfield, hoping to draw out the cobras. Reo Mowrer told another reporter that this was the most ridiculous thing he'd ever heard; snake charming was a total scam. Cobras didn't even have ears. He went on and on about their anatomies and their habits, their diets. He claimed to know a ton about cobras, just absolutely nothing about where these particular ones had come from.

And on it went, the time that Springfield, Missouri, was beset by Indian cobras.

The police chief, half-crazed by the whole thing, half kind of loving the attention, the break from small-time crime in a midsize town, the break from break-ins.

The spooked kids who couldn't sleep. The parents who broke down and let them crawl into bed with them.

The good ol' boys rolling out of the bar at closing and keeping things rolling with a carry-out bottle and an impromptu snake hunt, prowling the back streets, laughing in the last warm night air of late September.

All the bad pranks played.

All the conversations started at the bank, and the feed store, the VFW hall.

And the snakes: The eighth cobra was smashed with a boulder.

The ninth was cut in two (another advertisement for off-label hoe usage). The tenth was found in a plumbing-supply shop, where there were plenty of pipes on hand with which to whack it. The eleventh was caught alive and taken to a zoo.

And that was the last cobra they found in Springfield, Missouri, during those strange months of 1953. Some folks figured the rest of the snakes froze to death when winter came. The winters are mild in that corner of the state, but still a lot colder than in Calcutta. Chief Pike figured they were probably done with the whole thing before winter anyway; there were only ten or twelve to each box Reo Mowrer had kept in his basement. Folks still worried they'd come back. Maybe they were off breeding? People told the teenagers who liked to swim in the old quarry to watch out. The cobras probably took to the caves for shelter and would go after the first warm body they found, a pointed warning to the young couples who went there to fool around.

As for Reo Mowrer, he moved on. It's tough to sell pets when you are the town pariah. He moved down to Florida. He popped up again in the papers in the mid-sixties when he tried to mail a Galápagos tortoise to his father back home in Missouri. He settled near St. Pete, renting out exotic animals for commercials and birthday parties and the like. It was good business for a while, but then Busch Gardens wild animal park opened up in Tampa and he just couldn't compete.

He died in 1970 and never copped to the fact that the cobras had been his, though they certainly were.

But here's the thing:

They were his. But he didn't let them out.

Thirty-five years after those strange days and sleepless nights in 1953, a man named Carl Barnett came clean. He told his story to a columnist at the *Springfield News-Leader.* Barnett had been fourteen that summer. And he'd loved hanging out at the pet shop. Loved saying hello to the macaw. Loved how you never knew what kind of creature you were going to see there. He saved up his lawnmowing money to buy a tropical fish and brought it home in a little jar. But when he put it in his fishbowl at home, it died. And when he went back the next day looking to get his money back and instead got some know-it-all lecture from Reo Mowrer, it made him mad. And then when he found some boxes of snakes stacked up in the back of the shop, he opened one as revenge. He had no idea they were cobras. The next weeks for Carl were just fear: that someone might get bitten, that *he* might get bitten, that he might deserve to get bitten, and months and years, it turned out, of living with the fear of being caught. Which is just a terrible way to live, with this secret out there, like a deadly viper slithered free from your neighbor's in-home pet store.

The Wheel

What if they just took the boat?

They could do it. It would be dangerous, but what if they just took the boat?

They had the men—there were seven who were solid. They were good sailors, and they could keep their mouths shut. They had the men. And, truth be told, Robert could probably handle it all on his own. He worked on all sorts of ships. Schooners and slips, side-wheel steamers like the *Planter*. Just let him get his hands on the wheel. Robert Smalls knew these waters; he'd been sailing them for years. Knew every inlet, every island. He could read the tides, intuit the shifts in the currents.

He'd been piloting the *Planter* for months, moving Confederate soldiers and supplies up and down the coast. He knew where all the mines were around the channel out of Charleston, South Carolina. Hell, he'd been there when they'd laid them down. He could do it.

He could.

What if they just took the boat?

It had started as a joke from one of the other enslaved men who worked on the *Planter,* but the joke stopped being funny. They started talking about it at night, started making plans. They were a year into the war. A year since Fort Sumter—just two miles across the harbor—put up Jeff Davis's flag. But the Yankees were closing in. They'd taken back Beaufort, on Port Royal Island, just up the coast.

Robert's mother was there now. He was born there, and she had been too. Two generations born into slavery on that island. She'd be safe there. Free, even, if the Yankees stuck to their word, but who could say? He couldn't control what Abe Lincoln did. He couldn't control much. He wasn't the man at the wheel.

But what if they took the boat?

They could go straight to Beaufort, but they wouldn't even need to. If they took the boat, they'd just have to make it to the blockade not far off the coast, where the Union gunboats lay in wait. They'd have to pick their moment. They'd have to put enough distance between the *Planter* and the shore before anyone raised the alarm. They'd go right by Fort Johnson, and right by Fort Sumter itself. They'd have to get there before dawn, or else someone would notice there weren't any white faces on board and that would be that. If they got caught—

They couldn't get caught.

They would blow up the *Planter* and themselves before they got caught.

Robert talked to Hannah, his wife, a hotel maid he'd met when his owner, Mr. McKee, brought him to work in his house in Charleston. Robert's mother had convinced the man to let her then twelve-year-old boy get a side job on the docks. He made sixteen dollars a month. The man who owned him let him keep just one, but he saved for years. And when he met Hannah and they had a baby named Eliza, he was able to buy his own wife and child from their owner for eight hundred dollars. But he knew that did nothing to ensure their safety.

His mother made sure he knew that their life of relative ease in their master's house was nothing like freedom. It was an impermanent thing. She took him to watch men and women and girls and boys his age and younger sold at auction. Prodded, humiliated, distributed. She sent him into the fields to the whipping post to see and to understand that his life was not his own. Not here. So Robert told his wife his plan would be dangerous. But there were seven men who'd agreed to go with him, who'd placed their faith in him. Who would leave at a moment's notice. Who wouldn't tell a soul. Who awaited his command. He told Hannah that she and their two daughters would have to be on that boat.

The crew of the *Planter* spent the afternoon of May 12, 1862, loading cargo at a dock in front of the Confederate headquarters and its two dozen armed guards. By the end of the workday, the *Planter* was loaded with six heavy cannons and nearly a thousand pounds of ammunition. The work had been exhausting, and the ship's captain, its first mate, and its engineer wanted to kick back and head into town. They left Robert, capable Robert, dutiful Robert, in charge in their absence. Told him to make sure the *Planter* was ready to cast off the next morning at six for a routine run. And the three Confederate seamen went off to the bar or the brothel or wherever the night would take them.

At 3 A.M., Robert broke into the captain's quarters and stole his uniform, his pistols, and the broad straw hat he always wore to keep the sun from his eyes. By 3:30, his co-conspirators were aboard, stoking the fire and building up steam. The engine was loud, would certainly wake the watchmen, but 3:30 was a reasonable hour if the captain wanted to get an early start. Robert dressed in the captain's uniform, hat pulled down low despite the darkness, raised the Confederate flag, and then they took the boat.

They rendezvoused with friends waiting in a small ship bobbing in the harbor, and Robert's family and the families of four other sailors boarded the *Planter*. And off they went into the night. At Fort Johnson on James Island, the lookouts trained their guns on the boat, but Robert whistled a signal. He knew all the codes, and the fort let the *Planter* pass, but the tide conspired against them. It was dawn when they came upon Fort Sumter. Light enough that they could make out the men with their guns, ready to sink the ship if anything was amiss.

From that distance, in that light, the fort's watchmen would have been able to make out the race of Robert Smalls. But with the captain's hat pulled low over his face and his collar up high, and mimicking the same peculiar bearing that the *Planter*'s usual captain was known for, they didn't notice. He pulled the cord on the whistle, sounding out the code. Two long. One short.

And waited.

And the men at the battlement held their fire.

And by the time anyone at Fort Sumter noticed that the *Planter* didn't turn down the coast as usual, that it was heading straight out to sea, they were out of range.

Robert Smalls held the wheel and pressed on toward the blockade with a gift—that's what he would later call the *Planter* as he presented it to the Union captain who spotted the boat as it charged out of the fog, who trained his own guns on this renegade ship that seemed poised to run through the line, until he saw the white flag of surrender and the damnedest thing: a handsome twenty-three-year-old Black man, in a Confederate captain's coat and a crisp white shirt, with sixteen men, women, and children jumping, dancing, and shouting on the deck.

And it was quite a gift. There was the boat itself, a useful addition to the thin Union fleet, and the guns, some of which were Union cannons stolen after the fall of Fort Sumter the year before. But the real prize was Robert Smalls himself. While his family went off to join his mother in Beaufort, Robert became a sailor for the United States military. He could not be a sailor *in* the United States military, for he might have been free, might have freed himself, but he was still Black, and there were no Black sailors in the United States military. Not officially. But still, he took all the knowledge he had gained while under the yoke of the Confederates—of troop positions and gun placement and codes and supply routes and schedules, of methods and mines and torpedoes—and turned it against them.

He helped plan attack routes. He piloted the *Planter* through the inlets, around the islands he knew so well. Pointed out enemy positions, and points of entry and attack, on maps he had taught himself to read. His commander called him a hero. He also called him "a pleasant-looking darkie," but he gave him the wheel. Robert Smalls was famous among the furious rebels and fearful slaveholders and Southerners who were looking at the enslaved in their midst, wondering which among them might just take a boat of their own or grab the whip or burn the house down.

While a four-thousand-dollar bounty was put on Robert Smalls's head by the Confederacy, the U.S. Congress gave him a five-thousand-dollar reward. And another fifteen thousand to be split among the band of thieves that joined him on the boat. Abolitionists brought him to New York and put him in front of rapturous crowds. The secretary of war brought him to Washington, D.C., where he was a member of a delegation that met with President Lincoln to argue for freeing and arming the slaves. There are people who said that Smalls swayed the president. That his passion and his heroism changed Abe's mind, and changed the course of the war. And there are others who seem to be right—who pointed out that Lincoln had already made up his mind at that point. That he had already presented the Emancipation Proclamation to his cabinet a month or so before.

But, whatever the result, there was an August day in 1862 when a twenty-three-year-old former slave met the president of the United States, and each man knew the other by reputation. There must have been a moment when each internally assessed the other in the flesh against the man they had seen in some crosshatched drawings in *Harper's Weekly*. By the war's end, Smalls had been in seventeen battles. He had piloted an ironclad, which took ninety shells in an assault on Fort Sumter. He was awarded for his heroism. He was given formal command of the *Planter* and a rank and a pension. And when Charleston surrendered, he was at the wheel again, bringing the *Planter* back to that dock in front of Confederate headquarters. He was mobbed, hailed as the conquering hero.

He returned home to Beaufort, where his mother had been born a slave. Where he had been born a slave in a cabin behind their master's house.

And then he bought that house.

He bought the whole plantation with the money he'd gotten for taking the boat. He lived there with his family until his death in 1915. But before he died, during the fifty-four years after he passed Fort Sumter in the shimmer of dawn and headed out to the open ocean, Robert Smalls fought to keep hold of the wheel.

They call it Reconstruction, though the name has never sat right. It wasn't rebuilding. It wasn't merely a clearing of rubble, a patching of fences, or painting a new coat of whitewash on a neoclassical plantation pillar. The order of things had been upended. And there were no charts to follow. No way to know what lay ahead. Robert Smalls tried to do his part to lead the people of Beaufort through the fog. He had learned to read. He founded the first public school in South Carolina. He negotiated for better working conditions and fairer labor practices for former slaves.

He was elected to the South Carolina legislature and made the conditions he had negotiated into state law. He went on to serve five terms in the United States Congress, where he fought to try to desegregate public transportation and the military; to stop the tax code from favoring the wealthy and punishing the poor; to give women the right to vote. He was one of the most powerful and effective Black politicians of the nineteenth century—in that brief period before the Ku Klux Klan and its conspirators, and the state governors and their conspirators, defrauded and threatened and lynched votes away from men like him. Who stuffed ballot boxes and shot Black men. "We are not ashamed of it." That's what South Carolina's governor and later senator said in 1900, looking back fondly on what he achieved during that time. While Robert Smalls was trying to keep his hands on the wheel.

I'll tell you this last part of the story, but I'm not entirely sure what it means. There was a day sometime in there, after the world had been undone, when it should have been remade but instead it got reconstructed. There was a day, let's say it was in the summer; somehow that's when I picture Robert and his family living in that plantation house. It is still there. White paint. Porches and pillars. I picture summer, a sea breeze taking the edge off the swelter. And this woman, an old white woman, walked up the path toward the house, past the empty slave quarters, the overgrown lawn flecked with wildflowers, and came up the front stairs. Maybe the kids were reading on the porch. Maybe Hannah Smalls was playing the piano inside by the open window. And the woman was acting strangely. She had dementia. Robert was the one to recognize her. She was the wife of the man who'd once owned him. Her husband had died some years before and here she was, confused. She said this was her home, but it was different somehow. So different now. Smalls took her in and she lived there comfortably until her death.

AKA Leo

They took a lion cub from the Nubian Desert and they put it in the movies.

They called him Jackie. Trained him to sit. To rear up. To look fierce but not be fierce. Kept him well fed so he wouldn't eat anyone. And Jackie chased Tarzan through the jungles of the Los Angeles Arboretum. He menaced Jane from the edge of the shallow concrete pond that had been dressed with palm fronds and ferns, around the corner from the ersatz suburbs on the MGM back lot until some director called "Cut," having filmed sufficient footage to make it appear that Jackie was chasing Laurel and/or Hardy. And one morning in 1927 Jackie was let out of his cage, was led through a back lot where showgirls in sequins shuffled off to their 7 A.M. call, and walked amid extras in togas and spurs and chaps to a soundstage, where he hopped up onto two crates—one for his back paws, one for his front paws—looked into a camera, leaned into a microphone, and roared. And then he probably took a nap on a pile of straw.

That roar would be heard hundreds of times a day in thousands of theaters across the movie-mad world. It was the late 1920s and the movies were everything. There were twenty thousand theaters in the United States alone. Vast movie palaces in every city, with velvet curtains and gilt ceilings, balconies and orchestras and loges

and tuxedoed ushers. And silver screens and folding chairs in storefronts and old vaudeville halls in just about every hill and holler. A nickel. A dime. A feature or two. A newsreel. Shorts. Cartoons. A couple of coins for a whole evening's entertainment. A whole afternoon's childcare. Now with sound. There was sound now! Broadway melodies. Thundering cavalry. Clanging swords. Tapping shoes. Sighing lovers. All captured forever like Jackie, roaring at the beginning of every MGM picture.

Ten seconds in time, relived again and again and again. Duplicated. Spliced onto reel after reel, film after film. Ten seconds of sound and movement preserved on celluloid. Familiar to just about every man, woman, and child in the United States and beyond for decades.

Professionally, Jackie was Leo. That's the MGM lion's name, its nom du marketing. Jackie was the second Leo. The first was named Slats. He was born at the Dublin Zoo. He didn't roar, but he didn't need to in the silent era. He just looked around. Jackie roared, and people loved him for it.

The idea was rock-solid. People loved Leo and people loved planes. It was the summer of 1927. Charles Lindbergh had landed in Paris in May, and everyone flipped out. Aviators were in the paper all the time setting new speed records. Endurance records. Altitude records. Some guy flew from point A to point B for the first time. From A to B at night. From A to B nonstop.

So it's July or August, and someone in the publicity office at MGM said, "What if we put Leo in a plane?" It was basically the best idea anyone had ever heard. He'd be the first animal, in the nonhuman category, to fly nonstop across the country. So they found a pilot, a famous one, who'd just come in second in a race from California to Honolulu, which was a thing that could make you famous in 1927. They found a plane, which was the same model as Lindbergh's *Spirit of St. Louis,* and they tricked it out. Put in state-of-the-art navigation systems. Built a special cage for Leo. He wouldn't be able to turn around because any shift in weight could disrupt the flight. He would be fed a liquid diet of milk from a tube that went to the cockpit. But he could handle it for the twenty hours or so it would take to fly from San Diego to New York. Not that anyone asked Jackie.

The press and the public ate it up. They descended on a Southern California airfield to wish their beloved Leo bon voyage. And the voyage was going perfectly bon until they flew over Arizona and the famous pilot dipped down to wave to one of his relatives as he passed near her house. He couldn't regain altitude. He clipped a tree and the plane went down in the middle of the Sonoran Desert.

Jackie survived. You can breathe easy.

The plane broke up, but the cage stayed intact, and the pilot left Jackie some sandwiches and water and walked off to find help. Four days later he came back with some cowboys and some raw beef. They found Jackie hungry but healthy.

It was a bad look for MGM, nearly killing its mascot. Nearly breaking the hearts of the Leo-loving public. But there is, we are told, no bad publicity, and so Leo the lion became Leo the Lucky. Jackie went on tour—no plane this time.

He was driven in a custom-made, twenty-four-foot-long car, outfitted with a gilded cage with room enough to turn around. At one hundred thousand dollars, it was said to be the most expensive automobile yet built. But those publicity men said a lot of things. He traveled in a three-car caravan, with a fifty-four-note circus calliope and a trainer and a manager and valets, it was said, to attend to his needs. He ate fine cuts of meat. He wanted for nothing, they said. They knew they had nearly killed him in that plane crash; they were going to do right by him from here on out.

Doing right by him, it seems, included taking him on a forty-two-thousand-mile journey through thirty-eight states for three years straight. Doing right by him, it seems, meant he rode in an open cage on state roads at speeds that, though safe for humans, were not speeds a lion was born to travel. Doing right by him, it seems, was making stops in 1,418 cities and towns, where he did more things he was not born to do.

There was nothing instinctual, nothing lionlike, about being made to roar on command. Or about being asked not to roar, despite his desires. To offer his big paw to small-town bigwigs. To entertain at orphanages. To attend ribbon cuttings. To bring an odd joy to thousands upon thousands of human beings who flocked to town squares and village greens to see this celebrity from the silver screen, this lion they knew from those ten seconds captured forever some years before, while he sat like a dog, when he was not a dog. He wasn't bred to want human companionship. To want to be petted. To feel pleased by pleasing people.

I'm sure some of these people were cruel. They are people, after all. I don't trust a boy standing on a roadside in Michigan in 1929 or 1930 not to see what happens when you throw a rock at the only lion you're ever going to see in your town. I'm sure there were times when the nights were cold. When the crosswinds were strong on some county road out of Eau Claire, Wisconsin, or Coeur d'Alene, Idaho. When he had to sit too long while the mayor of Waxahachie, Texas, or Carpenteria, California, asked for a retake of his big photo op with the famous Leo, because he was sure he'd blinked. But Jackie was well fed and well cared for. His handlers treated him kindly, within limits set by their historical moment. It would have been bad for business to do otherwise. He spent his retirement at the Philadelphia Zoo, where he died young of a bad heart, they say. There have been far worse lives led by African lions in North America.

There were other Leos after Jackie. They were all made to do things they weren't born to do. But Jackie is still captured forever. You can see him in the old movies, flip past him on TV, search for him on YouTube. That's Jackie in semitone at the start of *The Wizard of Oz*. It's nice to see him there.

But see him, too, in a cage by the wreckage of a single-engine monoplane in the middle of the Arizona desert. And I don't ask you to ignore the bars. See the bars—he was captured forever. But see him in the desert. Not the Nubian Desert, but a desert still. Breathing its air. Scanning the horizon and the scrub brush for movement. For prey. Looking out at the stars, at the low, rolling hills, no streetlights, no Hollywood sign.

Dreamland

You could go to Dreamland. You could catch the ferry at Twenty-third Street or the Battery, or slog your way through the slow crawl of horse carts and motorcars heading south on Shell Road in the golden light of an August afternoon, down to the edge of the Atlantic, where a white city rose up above the brick and ash of Brooklyn, and you could walk through the fake marble gates as the sun went down and the sea flashed amber and then gray, and Staten Island disappeared into the shadows, and the light grew dim enough for you to fool yourself into thinking the marble wasn't fake at all.

And then the bulbs blinked on. A million of them. Lighting up the night and the largest amusement park in the world. It was a hell of a thing to see, just a few years after you'd seen your first electric light. And after you'd spent a twelve-hour day in some basement room or on some windowless factory floor, stitching sleeves or packing boxes, fitting fingers to gloves by gaslight. It would be a hell of a thing even now to see dozens of white buildings made to look like French pavilions, Roman villas, Florentine towers aglow at the edge of the ocean.

You could dance in history's largest ballroom. You could drink tea in a Japanese garden. You could sit in an auditorium on bleachers surrounding a vast pool of salt water and watch submarines fight a fake battle beneath a scale model of San Francisco.

You could buy your ticket to Dreamland and take a gondola ride through the canals of a replica Venice, past the Piazza San Marco, and the Doges' Palace, steal a kiss beneath the Bridge of Sighs. You could ride your first escalator to the top of a giant slide which would send you down, caroming off obstacles like the Plinko board on *The Price Is Right;* if you landed on the right spot, you won a prize. You could take a miniature train through a fake Switzerland. Or another from New York to California. Or walk the streets of Cairo. Or Paris. Or other places you were never going to go otherwise.

Or you could sit on a swing with your friends inside a tiny house and feel the swing move and feel yourself flip end over end, and figure out only later on when you were all laughing over beers, sitting under the string lights in the salt air, that you hadn't moved at all, that it was the tiny house that had flipped end over end around you.

You could gawk at freak shows. And at premature babies in a hospital ward, which was a freak show, too, but one that happened to be the only place in the world equipped to keep premature babies alive. You could sit and watch them through the glass, alongside their anxious parents.

You could watch a cast of two thousand people setting fire to a six-story hotel and watch firefighters put it out, scaling ladders to rescue actors from real danger, and catch them in nets as they made panicked leaps from four-story windows, so they could make panicked leaps again tomorrow night, and the next night, and the next.

You could tour the Lilliputian Village, where dozens of little people lived full-time in a half-sized model of a fifteenth-century French village—because living in a human zoo with modern amenities wasn't indignity enough.

You could fly over it all in a hot-air balloon. You could sink below it in a diving bell. You could watch a magician make a woman float right over your head. You could eat a hot dog. They'd just invented hot dogs. You could see a one-handed lion tamer. And chariot races.

And whirling dervishes. And snake dancers. And you could take a boat ride called Hell Gate, until one night one of those million light-bulbs blew and sent a spark that flitted onto papier-mâché and sent all of Dreamland up in flames. And two thousand firefighters, all of them pretend, couldn't put Dreamland back together again.

Origin Stories

Or Six Pieces Drawn from the
Author's Life as a Younger Person,
That, in the Aggregate, Could Have
Served as an Introduction of Sorts to
This Book, but That Would've Been Weird,
and So They Are Presented Here,
on Page 245,
Near the End

The Pierce Street House

spent my twenties in Providence. I lived on the bottom floor of a two-family house on the west side of the city, on the other side of the highway from downtown, and the other side of the tracks from Brown University and the Rhode Island School of Design and the homes of people who raised their kids to assume they could go to places like Brown or RISD. My mom grew up in that house. Her father did too. And when my grandfather died at eighty-six years old, his widow couldn't take living there anymore. She couldn't take sharing her space with the ghosts of days spent with her husband and their daughters, and with her husband's family, and with herself as a young woman, ghosts that would appear in every corner. At the top of the stairs. At the sink by the window. In the empty side of the bed. So my grandmother moved out and I moved in.

I loved it. And not just because I was twenty-three and aimless and underemployed and got to live rent-free. I loved the house itself. When I was growing up, it had echoed with stories, endlessly repeated at big Italian family dinners, and during the tail ends of Christmases, with the dying embers and the embarrassing uncle passed out on the maroon velour chair. For new audiences, the stories were stretched and embellished; for close family they were invoked, compressed like Mandarin proverbs until they could be summoned by a couple of brushstrokes: "Dad and the Studebaker," "Mom's Broken Finger," "Janice Through the Bathroom Window."

I loved those stories. Surely the reason I tell stories for a living is because I loved those stories. And despite the sheer volume and breadth of the memories that accumulate in a house in which one family had lived since 1914, most of the stories, and the ones retold most often, were drawn from a single era.

For several years, from the late 1930s until not long after the end of World War II, my grandfather ran a nightclub on the banks of the Pawtuxet River in Rhode Island. It started out as the Hi-Ho and was eventually rebranded as the Club Baghdad, complete with an oasis painted on the wall and a general *Casablanca,* certainly-offensive-today, Edward Said–y "Orientalism" vibe. They did a full revue: crooners, comedians, a midsize big band, showgirls, national touring acts, regional mob bosses. My grandfather was the MC. One night a few of the dancers got the flu and my grandfather called a talent agency up in Boston for some fill-in showgirls. One of them would turn out to be my grandmother.

And so there are reasons these were the stories I heard the most. They are the origin story of the family. My mom and her three sisters loved to hear about their mom and dad falling in love. The stories were glamorous and dramatic. "Dad and the Studebaker" and "Mom's Broken Finger" are solid. But the club stories were things like "The Day the Bear Got Loose," "Dad's Three Girlfriends," "The Russian [forgive me] Midgets Get Stuck in the Snow," "The Night the Great Dane Danced with the Stickup Man," "The Night My Grandmother Climbed Up the Ladder Where My Grandfather Stood Hanging the Star on the Christmas Tree by the Coat Check and Surprised Him with Their First Kiss." And "The Day They Piled into the Back Seat of a Friend's Car on the Way Back from the Beach and She Sat on My Grandfather's Lap and He Held Her Hand and She Had Never Noticed Her Hand Was So Small Before and She Knew That She Loved Him."

I heard that story a hundred times. The last time my grandmother told it to me was the night my grandfather lay dying in an adjustable bed at Rhode Island Hospital. Her hand was in mine. It was so small.

Not long after, I moved in.

The house of stories was also a house of stuff. Eighty-something years of stuff. In closets and crawl spaces and crumbling cardboard boxes stacked in locked rooms. The cigarette cases and tiepins and Bakelite clocks and the roller skate keys—all of it.

My mom and her sisters, no longer needing to ask their parents' permission to poke around in the basement, would send me on missions. One of them would call me up and say things like "There's this big Coke sign, I think, from when Uncle Leo ran that concessions stand in Narragansett in the fifties. It would look amazing over my new stove." And I'd go digging.

There was one artifact they all wanted more than any other. The holy grail of family ephemera was a record. The Baghdad had a record-pressing machine. It was a bread-box-sized device into which you plugged a microphone, and it would record whatever it heard by carving it into an acetate disk. There was a promotion at the club where you could pay a buck and then sing with the band and take your record home, like karaoke for keeps. Somewhere in the house, they all swore, was a recording of the floor show at the Baghdad. If I could find it, they could hear the Club Baghdad. Could hear Dad sing. Hear him banter. Hear him introduce the showgirls. Picture their mother high-kicking in the center of the line. I just had to keep digging.

I lived in the house for seven years. Every now and then, the sisters would check in and ask about the record. I'd tell them about other stuff I'd found. Wonderful things from that golden era of the nightclub. Pictures of the chorus girls, of the dance floor, of the bear, before he got loose. Old menus: thirty-five cents for a boilermaker, a buck ten for the Clams Casino. But no record. They'd be disappointed, but I didn't care. Because I found letters. And diary entries. And pictures of my nana's cousin Amy, the flapper, who she'd once told me had opened her world up and made it seem possible to do things like become a showgirl and cool to try smoking weed in the back of a Lindy Hop hall with two of the Mills Brothers. Okay to climb up the ladder and make the first move. I found union cards. Streetcar transfers. The ID bracelet from the trip to the hospital when my grandparents had the baby who never came home. The stuff of lives. Of raising kids. Of doing the work to sustain a marriage for fifty years after a kiss in the red-green glow of a Christmas tree by the coat check. Of my grandfather, in the years after the nightclub, putting a family on his back while working decades of double shifts as a steam fitter. Putting pipes into buildings, building boilers, when he used to sing and tell jokes and juggle dates with showgirls. So his four daughters could go to college. So I could write this for you now.

The Beach

My mom and her sisters sold the family house in 2004. Their father had died several years before (he went quickly, fading suddenly at home and then spending a couple of days in the hospital, where he was peaceful and sweet, though sometimes he'd speak to my aunt, sotto voce, about the old-fashioned numbers racket he was convinced the nurses were running, memories of days of the Club Baghdad seeming to overlay the present in his dying brain). After his death, my grandmother moved into a whitewashed shack not far from the beach in Narragansett, the only good investment her husband ever made. His union pension went toward winterizing it. There was a bird sanctuary over the stone wall behind the narrow back lawn. She loved to watch the cardinals. She would entertain, and go to the discount store and buy presents for babies, and pretty jars for seashells, and knickknacks emblazoned with sunny aphorisms. By the door to the small deck where she'd drink her coffee in the ocean breeze, she put up a little sign that said, "If you are lucky to live by the beach you are lucky enough," and most times you'd believe it. But it got lonely.

She volunteered at a nursing home, playing cards with people in the memory ward who were just a bit older than her, if that; it always seemed so brave to me. That wasn't too long before the end;

she spent her last months rather contentedly in an assisted-living facility in Providence; she liked people and seemed to enjoy the general bustle of cafeteria trips and nurse check-ins and visits from her daughters, who were now closer than they had been when she was down at the beach. The facility was just up the road from where the club used to be.

Meanwhile, I had moved on from the house and went to Los Angeles to figure out if a long-distance relationship I was in was a real thing (she is now my wife). Soon came the moment when the Mancini sisters were putting the Pierce Street house up for sale, and I wondered if I should buy it. It was so important to me. It felt urgent, like not buying it was something I would regret, surely, but I didn't really have the money, and there was this thing with this girl, so I didn't.

I do regret it.

I don't regret it at all.

That is how life goes.

On the last day I lived in the old house, before my move west, I took a final dive into its darker corners. Once more up into the attic. A last venture down into the dungeon-gray basement, which had terrified me as a kid, and from which I took the stairs two at a time, as though I were outrunning a ghost, even in adulthood. I had gone scavenging so many times in the previous few years that I wasn't expecting any treasures. By the dryer, there was a teetering tower of cardboard boxes that had repelled my previous approaches, sending me reeling, red-eyed with allergies. This time, I held my breath and jumped in.

My great-uncle had lived in the apartment upstairs with my grandfather's sister. He had been a traveling salesman, and almost all the boxes turned out to be stuffed with brochures for a cosmetics line and with perfume samples that didn't smell like anything other than basement. The rest were filled primarily with yellowed documents no one was ever going to need again. But I did find one folder of pictures. So I fled the basement one last time, excited to flip through them. I was mostly disappointed; I'd seen almost all of them before, on the fireplace mantel of one aunt or another. Over the years, my mom and Linda and Jan and Rae had curated their own collections, accumulated on earlier expeditions to the old house.

There is one, though, that they all have:

I have never had to ask why they'd all wanted a copy. Here are their parents, young and in what can only be love. His strong arms. Her dancer's frame. My grandfather's smile. A look on my grandmother's face that always seemed like certainty to me.

I have assumed that it was taken on a day my grandmother had told me about: One summer afternoon they went to the beach, took this photo, and on the way home, they squeezed into the back of their friend's car, where she sat in his lap in the back, sandy and sunkissed, and she knew for sure that she loved him. If this photograph is, in fact, from that day, what a thing it is—taken at a time when cameras weren't ubiquitous, when their successful operation wasn't guaranteed, when each picture cost money that maybe you didn't have. How remarkable to have a document of this particular day, one that would be recalled and treasured out of thousands. The start of decades of love, whatever that meant, however it changed over time, however compromised it may have been, however long-suffering or not, however simply true. What are the odds?

Or maybe it wasn't quite like that. Maybe she remembered it this way because she had this photograph. Maybe it represented some warm, half-recalled feeling from a time long ago and the photo crystallized it, turned it into a story. I never asked her about it. I don't think it matters. Growing up, that picture looked like love itself to me.

In the folder from the box in the basement, I also found this:

An alternative version of the same scene.

It raised questions. Which photo was taken first? Was this "new" photo taken just before the one we all knew? Was the "original" photo possibly a second take to correct something the photographer (I had never even thought of the third person inherent in the scene) didn't like about this one? Looking at it, looking at the two of them as they sit side by side but not embracing, it's possible to read into it a coldness or discomfort that the original photo doesn't readily suggest. Which of these photos is more representative of the state of their relationship at that moment in their lives? If this newly discovered picture was taken first, is it possible that my grandparents were cajoled or even coerced into the closeness they seem to exhibit in the original photo? ("C'mon, throw your arm around her, Ray.") Had I always been seeing a joy that wasn't really there? Or perhaps they eased into the closeness we see in the original photo, having needed that first take to warm up to each other? Does the long-beloved image on everyone's mantels project a happiness and comfort with each other that they didn't yet feel during that day on the beach?

Maybe the photographer, asking for a second pose, coaxed something out of them that perhaps they didn't even know was there. Maybe my grandparents were one of those couples that had been hooking up in what they thought was secret but everyone was on to them, and maybe what the photographer said after the first take was something like "C'mon, you two, you're not fooling anyone," and that smile on my grandfather's face is one of relief.

If this new photo was the first of two taken that day, one can interpret the space between them as positively charged: two people whose mutual attraction is just about to draw them together forever. In that scenario, the original photo might hold even more power: Could it be that this photo isn't just a document of the cherished day my grandmother would name, decades later, as the one when she realized she loved the man who would be her husband, but also might well document their very first public display of affection? I don't know. If this alternate take is the second one, maybe she pulled away. Maybe someone said something wrong or went too far. Or maybe it just got cold on the beach and they'd been sitting for too long. I never imagined that day as cold.

I like the new picture more. My grandparents as just two people figuring it out.

It isn't the cover photo for some classic love story. It isn't love itself, but it may be life itself: one of those in-between moments you don't remember later. The in-between feelings you can't quite put a name to. The space between the story of our lives and those lives as we live them. I love that space and the magic that seems to exist in a place between and beyond concrete facts and the well-worn language of familiar stories. I love the spark that is kindled there, to flare just long enough to help us remember that life, in the present as in the past, is more complicated and more interesting and more beautiful and more improbable and more alive than we'd realized the moment before. That notion animates every story I try to write. I want to conjure the magic that lies in the liminal spaces between the plot points in people's lives.

I love these photographs. But there is one more picture from that day that I may love even more, and I would like to share it with you now.

This is another photo from that roll of film, taken that same day on the beach. Maybe it's of the guy who took the photos of my grandparents. What could be more real than having the one friend who pretends his lunch is his balls? I find it incredibly moving.

On Dimes

nearly died in the best way possible. I don't mean that I nearly
died, and that that death, had it taken place, would have been the
best type of death (which, feeling no need to overthink this, is
surely some variation on "at a ripe old age in one's sleep, surrounded
by loved ones"). I mean that I had the best kind of near-death experience, and it came at just about the best time I can imagine.

The state of Massachusetts mandated that all public school students had to have a physical before the beginning of their junior year
of high school. I was nervous about my junior year. My sophomore
year had been rough. After spending elementary and middle school
just rolling along—always near the top of my class, killing it in the
humanities, a bit less in math and science, but still: killing it—
everything started to fall apart in the second half of my freshman
year. By sophomore year, I was getting booted from honors chemistry. My dad was working with me for an hour every night on geometry, the teachers' edition of the textbook in hand, and I just could
not get it. Proofs felt like they'd be the end of me. I had staked much
of my young identity on being an A student and now I was working
harder than I ever had before just to eke out a gentleman's D-plus.
And now, junior year? With SATs and college stuff? A physical was
the last thing I was worried about. But then something popped up in

my bloodwork. We got a call that said I had to go to the hospital as quickly as possible, where I was told I had nearly died. In fact, I had been nearly dying every day for quite some time.

I was diagnosed with Graves' disease, an autoimmune disorder in which your thyroid gets out of whack and produces more hormones than your body can handle. My case was historically bad. According to the various numbers with which endocrinologists chart thyroid function, I had the worst case of the disease in New England in over a decade. Graves' and other thyroid diseases disproportionately affect women; I was told I had the worst case for a male on record. My resting heart rate was 170 beats a minute, which was neither normal nor sustainable; they told me that if, instead of going to the hospital, I had instead gone to school, gym class could've given me a heart attack. Same for having sex or smoking pot or just having gotten really worked up over having to figure out the volume of a sphere on a quiz or something. Those 170 beats were too many, generally, but I also had a heart murmur and arrhythmia. I was a time bomb that couldn't tick right. And then there was something else that stunned them, had med students crowding into the room to gawk: It turned out that, even though I had managed to walk around for at least a year with this condition, narrowly avoiding catastrophic cardiac events as though I were sidestepping pianos crashing to the sidewalk all around me, I shouldn't have been able to walk around at all. They had never seen anyone with this amount of thyroid hormone coursing through their body whose brain simply didn't shut down and slip into a coma-like state known, rather dramatically, as a "thyroid storm." In countries with access to modern healthcare, things just never get that far. It did make sense to them why my Graves' hadn't been caught, though. I didn't have most of the telltale signs of the disease, like a large goiter or bugged-out eyes. This was so rare that I was later photographed as an example in a medical text of another way the disease could present, making me a literal textbook case for not being a metaphorical textbook case.

But the doctors made sure to lead with the good news: I would be fine. They had any number of straightforward ways to treat the disease. It might take a little while to sort out a few things, but, starting at that moment, with me in the hospital under their care and supervision, I was safe and was going to remain so from then on.

This was the best way to nearly die. I was in mortal danger but survived. I was in constant risk of death but never afraid. Not only was I told that my life was going to go on, I was told it was going to get better: Your thyroid plays a big part in regulating your metabolism. I was just shy of five foot eleven, I weighed 115 pounds. The doctor told me that would change. I'd put on weight. I'd get cute. The thyroid also does something I've never entirely understood that basically means it controls how chemical messages go to and from the brain. That D-plus in geometry? The nights at the kitchen table with my dad, who had always been a model of patience and kind attention, suddenly standing up from his chair to go pace and mutter in the hallway because he had no idea why this kid he'd known for the past sixteen years, whom he loved beyond measure, just could not get the simplest thing about congruent angles—they were over.

I was sixteen years old. My thyroid was working again. It was so good to be able to think again. It was fun to turn cute. And I was watching *Harold and Maude* for the first time, reading, like, *On the Road,* listening to music being made right then, while having the ecstatic conviction that these were the best songs that had ever been made, experiencing all these artworks that were telling me, each in their own way, to *live,* man. It felt profoundly useful to feel as if my near-death experience had left me knowing a little bit about what that really meant.

But also, I had almost died.

I had spent a year falling apart without knowing why. A year that, due to the cognitive effects of my disease, I could barely remember. That might have been for the best. The recent past was all fragments: the day I tried out for the baseball team at the end of my freshman year and I could not for the life of me hit a ball off a tee and I went to the coach and quit and couldn't tell my parents why, because I was ashamed and afraid. The day I tried out for the JV basketball team and couldn't make it through the first drill, had to walk off the court and lie down on the locker room floor for what seemed like forever as the world spun around me. Probably had a cardiac incident. Didn't tell anyone. The times this one senior would call me a freak in the hall; I didn't realize I was so skinny or that my hands shook all the time.

My academic record was shot. My college options had shifted. The National Honor Society was off the table. I knew those things mattered to my future and my prospects but also knew now that they didn't matter at all.

And I knew that lives turn on dimes. Mine had. It could again. It could happen to anyone. It was happening all around me. It was there in the family stories, had been there all the time. They just weren't the ones we told over and over. They hooked into me now.

My father's father had a stroke in 1969. It changed him. Meant that he couldn't work. Made him very quiet and very gentle in ways he'd never been before, which was strange for my dad and his brothers, but was the only way I'd ever known him.

My mother's mother, the grandmother whose life had changed when she decided to kiss a man as he stood on a ladder hanging lights on a Christmas tree, became a dancer as a teenager because she needed to work. Her father was walking home one day from his job driving a streetcar in Boston, and as he walked up the three steps to their back door, he slipped on the ice and fell backward and hit his head and died. That man's own father had been coming home after work from his own job twenty years earlier, and had decided to stop off for a beer, and then a fight broke out and he stepped in to break it up but caught a punch and got knocked to the ground and hit his head and died. My grandmother lost her father and grandfather because lives turn on dimes.

I remembered a story my grandmother once told me about a relative, a great-aunt, who was shopping one night before Christmas at the Peerless department store in downtown Providence. It was the late 1950s. I could see her so clearly. Her hair pinned up under a hat. A fake fur collar on her woolen winter coat. A handbag, maybe with a bottle of perfume wrapped up as a present inside. She is riding the escalator and I can see a kitten heel catch in the slats of the steps and she goes tumbling. And I can feel her embarrassment, to be falling like that. But she lands hard and is injured and her life is changed negatively and permanently, though I don't remember how.

I recently asked my mom and her sisters which relative this was. They couldn't remember. They weren't sure they remembered hearing it at all. It's possible the story never hooked into them the way it did with me; they hadn't been looking for dimes at the time.

This Thing My Mom Once Saw on TV

There was a hurricane. A minor one. Maybe Bob. It blew anti-climactically through our corner of southeastern New England, leaving us with a few downed tree limbs and a couple extra loaves of bread bought as provisions in case things went worse. We did lose power, though no one was concerned it would be out for long. So night fell and my father put the Red Sox game on the portable radio and I grabbed a flashlight and whatever I was reading in AP English at the time and settled in for the evening. There was a knock at the door. Some friends of mine had driven over and wanted to know if I could hang out. My folks invited them in and we went to the finished basement in our raised ranch and played cards by candlelight.

The next morning my mom asked how my night was; she said it sounded like we had been having the best time. I said it was fun, nice to have the company. "But you guys were roaring with laughter," she said. Something like that. I told her that was pretty standard; we were all pretty funny. She shook her head and looked at me like she had to tell me something serious.

She told me she was lucky if she laughed like that once a year, and that she also had funny friends. She told me some people never get to. What happened downstairs in the half-dark during the half-hearted hurricane was rare in life, even if it happened to be a regular thing right now. I needed to know that.

Then she told me about how Paul Simon, the singer, had been on the *Today* show or *Good Morning America* or *Regis* or whatnot the other morning, and how, as they wrapped up the segment, the interviewer said something like "Paul Simon. You have sold millions of albums, you have written beloved songs, you have performed all over the world, you have sung in front of hundreds of thousands of people at your famous concert in Central Park. What was your best moment?"

My mom told me he didn't hesitate to answer. Paul Simon said the best thing he ever did was steal home in a Little League game. The host—Matt Lauer, Katie Couric, whoever—was baffled. Paul Simon explained that it was the best moment in his life because as he ran toward home, he started realizing he was going to make it, that the pitcher and catcher had been caught completely off guard. He was going to steal home, and he thought, "This is the best moment of my life."

And this thing my mom once saw on TV snapped something into place for me. I had spent so much of the however many months since I'd gotten out of the hospital looking for the dimes upon which life turns, finding them in its traumas and terrors and times when things fall apart. And here I was having my life changed—in a real way that has stayed with me to this day, and that has, if not set the course of my life, set a lens through which I have seen life as I have moved through it—by a conversation with my mom about a morning show segment I didn't even watch. It made me feel like there were dimes all around us. Some of them are marked by joy, or deep comfort—not just trauma. We just weren't seeing them for what they were. There are moments as good as any other—that it might just be that there were limits to delight, that the literal feeling of singing "Cecilia" to a sea of people who are singing it back to you in Central Park might in fact be no more pleasurable or invigorating or enriching than stealing home in a Little League game or, for that matter, laughing with your friends, or having a great kiss, or any number of life's quotidian joys, these things that are happening all around us, all the time, if we just stopped to notice them as they happened and remember them when they were done. I set out to do that: to notice and to remember. And to remember, you need a story.

Here's one:

Other Families

Aaron told me I should just hang out. He was going to hop in the shower, out in a few. And so, tired from the drive from Providence to Greenpoint in Brooklyn, I flopped down on the couch where I'd sleep that night, and sifted through the CDs on his glass coffee table to pick something to play through his schmancy new stereo, my friend's first adult purchase. But there was something under the jumble of CD jewel cases that caught my eye: a faded *Playboy* from the 1970s, which was entirely out of character for my friend and stuck out in his grad student's apartment among issues of *The Nation, Art in America,* and dog-eared books by Foucault and Deleuze. Poking out of the *Playboy* was a photocopy of a newspaper article stuck with a neon-pink Post-it, upon which was written, "Your family is insane."

I met Aaron during the second semester of my freshman year at Dighton-Rehoboth, a public high school drawn from two small towns in Massachusetts, about a fifteen-minute drive from Providence. Mr. Driscoll, who was its football coach and my world history teacher, introduced a new student who had just moved from New Mexico. The kid's mustard-yellow shirt with the New Mexico flag on it was a clue. He had unfashionably long hair that he absent-mindedly twisted around the end of his nose, and glasses so thick the lenses would refract afternoon sunlight through the window and splash rainbows across neighboring desks. He was a total dork. I liked him immediately. He would, a few years later, pop over to our house during a hurricane with his brother and a couple of friends.

Our parents had a lot in common. All four of them were academics. His dad was an administrator at UMass Dartmouth and his mom taught in the education department at Rhode Island College, one building over from where both my parents taught special ed. But look higher on the family tree and the differences grew stark.

Aaron is a Panofsky, which meant nothing to me at first. The significance of his surname would be teased out over the course of the early years in our friendship, usually quite literally: Aaron would do something dumb, and our funniest friend, Sean, would dig at Aaron for failing the family line. The kids in our friend group in our farm town were, as a Replacements song we used to listen to while driving around its back roads put it, "the sons of no one." That wasn't the case for Aaron.

Despite spending most of my youth over the border in Rehoboth and the last couple of decades happily in Los Angeles, I am a Rhode Islander at heart. I know that Rhode Island's smallness is its whole thing—it is forty-five minutes by fifty minutes on a traffic-free day; other places measure themselves by how many Rhode Islands can fit within them. But its smallness stretches beyond its mere dimensions, owing less to how much room it takes up on a map than to its placement on it. Wedged into the bottom-right corner of New England like a shim fixing a wobbly table, it isn't a place you ever need to go, unless it's your destination. If you want to travel from New York to Boston for work, or from New Haven to go to Kennebunkport for vacation, it's faster to bypass Rhode Island entirely. This makes it different from its tiny peers. New Jersey and Maryland and Delaware and Connecticut are wonderful in their own ways, but nonnatives typically experience them on the highway on the way to somewhere else. And most of the good people of each of those states find themselves aligning, by necessity, with a neighboring state: If you live in South Jersey, you get your media from Philadelphia; if you live in North Jersey, from New York. You get it. But not if you live in Rhode Island. This is, again, a quirk of its geography: For most of the twentieth century, the only clear radio and television signals Rhode Islanders could receive came from towers outside Providence. The signals could reach every corner of the state but couldn't make it up to Boston or Hartford in any meaningful way. The state's media spoke to and about only itself. Growing up in Rhode Island, I found it hard to understand that there were other places you could be (beyond Boston, if you were truly adventurous), and other lives you could lead beyond the ones you saw being lived around you. My mother's younger sister lived in New York for a few years after college before returning to Providence; she might as well have been an astronaut. One time she saw Sylvester Stallone and Dolly Parton filming a movie on the streets of Manhattan. For my part, one time I saw the sports guy from Channel 10 in the waiting room of my pediatrician's office. Both of these incidents filled me with odd wonder for years.

Aaron's stories astounded me when I first heard them in high school, despite the fact that he always told them with an endearing combination of a shrug and a little wide-eyed headshake that meant "Yeah, pretty wild, right?" This is how I remember them:

Aaron Panofsky came from a long line of intellectuals. His great-great-grandfather was a German Jewish legal scholar who in the late nineteenth century was brought over by imperial Japan to author its first constitution. Aaron's great-grandfather was Erwin Panofsky, known as the father of modern art history. He coined the word *iconography*. He wrote a book about the fifteenth-century artist Albrecht Dürer that pulled the German painter and printmaker out of obscurity and is why Dürer's pieces are in every major art museum

to this day. When Hitler ascended to power, Erwin Panofsky immigrated to the United States at the invitation of the president of New
York University. He left a relative behind in Germany. She worked
for the police in Berlin and, as a Jew and a lesbian, was spared from
the camps only as a special favor to the emperor of Japan for services
rendered by Aaron's great-great-grandfather to the nation. Meanwhile, Erwin was safe in New Jersey, having taken a position at
Princeton, and was palling around with his best friend, Albert Einstein. One time, the esteemed art historian asked the wealthy man
behind the Barnes Foundation's famed collection of impressionist
art if he could come and see his paintings. Mr. Barnes wasn't a fan of
Erwin Panofsky. He saw Panofsky as a stodgy gatekeeper, an old-
school, Old World elitist propping up an art world that Barnes and
the artists he championed were trying to dismantle; he wouldn't let
him see his collection. So Einstein called instead for his own tour.
Barnes would be happy to open his doors to the esteemed scientist.
Einstein showed up with his buddy Erwin dressed as his chauffeur,
and the pair took in the collection together and the two had a laugh
at Barnes's expense.

Erwin's wife, Dora, was also a renowned art historian. They had
two sons, Hans and Aaron's grandfather Wolfgang, who was always
known as Pief. Upon arriving in America, the boys enrolled at
Princeton, from which they graduated first and second in their class,
both with GPAs above 4.0, after which they were forever known in
the family as the Smart Brother and the Dumb Brother. Hans went
on to be one of the twentieth century's most important meteorolo-
gists, explaining how turbulence affected airplanes and how pollution traveled in the lowest parts of the atmosphere. Wolfgang
worked on the Manhattan Project and flew over the Trinity test in an
airplane to oversee the release of a device he'd created that would
measure radiation after the blast. As I remember it, he was a queasy
flier and he accidentally took too much antinausea medication and
was asleep when his invention deployed and the world changed forever beneath him. Aaron and his brother, Dave, slept in a hand-me-

down crib that had been previously occupied by the children of their grandfather's friend, J. Robert Oppenheimer.

I opened the *Playboy* on Aaron's coffee table and turned to the photocopied article inside. It had been sent to him by a friend, an art history grad student, who'd come across it during research for her dissertation. It was an obituary for Aaron's great-grandmother. Prior to her death after a long illness, there had been an extended period when she'd been unable to get out of bed. The article said that during her convalescence, she was read to each day by a rotation of three men: her esteemed husband, their dear friend Albert, and the novelist Thomas Mann. I finished the article and noticed for the first time that it had been placed there as a bookmark at the beginning of a long interview with Aaron's grandfather, the physicist, about his role as a leading proponent of nuclear disarmament. This was exciting, though not all that surprising.

One story about his family in particular has stayed with me since Aaron told it to me on one of those afternoons when I'd drive him home after school and we'd play catch for a while in his front yard, with my back always to the woods with all the poison ivy (I was immune and could go in there to get the ball if it sailed over my head). After the war, like so many of the young physicists who'd moved to Los Alamos to work under Oppenheimer, Pief Panofsky worked to ban the bomb. Aaron told me this story about how his grandfather—a man whose diminutive frame, face weathered by years in the New Mexico and California sun, and eyes magnified by the same kinds of lenses his grandson would need made Pief a dead ringer for Yoda—was such a powerful voice against atomic weapons that the Japanese government brought him to Hiroshima to honor him with a medal. During this visit, at some point between the state dinners and symposia and speeches, he was taken on a private tour of the Peace Memorial Museum. As I remember it, the honored scientist was trailed closely by Japanese colleagues and dignitaries as he moved through the displays in somber silence. Eventually, he came to a large glass case containing artifacts that had once been scattered around the devastated city. Fragments of American military hardware, each piece charred and twisted, melted, now meticulously mounted and labeled. As he looked through the case, probably trying to gauge just how long he should pause at each item, certainly feeling the weight of the eyes of his entourage, he saw a small mechanical object. Its tag read "Unidentified measuring device." I have always remembered this moment in the story, when the grandfather of my friend—my Einstein, my Thomas Mann—stood there and realized he could identify the object because he had made it. I can see him in that moment, deciding what to do, everyone watching his every move, this esteemed visitor who had been at Los Alamos and had gone on to become a hero in their eyes, his mind racing through his options while trying not to betray any reaction. A man of science who prized accuracy and truth. Who had played a part in building the atomic bomb, in changing history, in bringing an end to the war, in killing more than 140,000 people indiscriminately, old women, little boys, in the city where he stood right then. Whose work, in a material way, was one link in a chain of events that meant the entire world and every one of its creatures, right then, were threatened with literal destruction. A man who had spent so many of the previous years trying to prevent that very thing, and who had been brought to the other side of the world to be thanked for that work. He decided not to tell anyone.

The fact that Aaron, the dearest of friends and the most normal of dudes, had these connections to people who had played roles in changing the world, in ways big and small but real, helped me understand, in ways big and small but real, that the people I read about in the papers and history books were also real. His grandfather, there in the museum, in that moment, at least the one that existed in my mind, was human in ways I could understand.

I flipped through the article as the shower door opened and the air in the apartment shifted: steam and shampoo and the sound of my friend opening the refrigerator and asking me if I wanted a beer. There was a pull-quote splashed across the page. I don't remember what the quote itself was—"Richard Nixon could pull us back from the brink of apocalypse but utterly refuses to": something like that. The second part, though, I will never forget: "says Wolfgang Panofsky, perhaps the world's smartest man."

I laughed out loud, maybe made a small moan in disbelief. Aaron came in and let out a puff of breath through his nose, probably with an endearing look that was part shrug, part "Yeah, pretty wild, right?"

I asked him directly: "Is your grandfather the world's smartest man?"

He kind of pursed his lips and rubbed at the back of his still-damp hair while he considered the question. After a long beat he nodded gravely and said, "He's pretty fucking smart."

He then went on to explain how there are certain questions you can ask his grandpa about science, say, or about how an appliance works, or just something that requires a complicated answer, and you would marvel at how his brain works, pulling in disparate ideas and weaving them together to answer your question in a way that is both clear and authoritative but somehow infused with this spark of something you could only call genius. Aaron excelled in school. I had marveled to the point of intimidation at what seemed from afar like the ease with which he breezed through AP chemistry and calculus and into his pick of the best colleges in the country. But he also told me there were concepts in experimental physics and math that he could barely grasp, but that seemed no more challenging to his grandfather than the rule book to Hungry Hungry Hippos. So, yeah, Aaron said, his grandfather might be as smart as anyone on Earth.

I don't remember how I responded, just that I struggled to get my head around it.

He went on to say that his grandfather might well be the smartest man in the world, but was also "kind of a dumbass." An inveterate forgetter of socks and birthdays. Couldn't make heads or tails of Shakespeare, say. Was often misreading rooms and putting his foot in his mouth. "You know," he said, "it's like you and me. You know how there are ways that you're as smart as literally anyone?" I did not. "And same with me, same with Sean, Cary, my brother . . . ," he said, invoking close friends, "but we spend so much of our time being total knuckleheads?" That much I knew. He then gave some example of some apparently signature Nate DiMeo–style of higher reasoning or creative thinking that dazzled him regularly in ways of which I had been utterly unaware and now can't begin to recall, and how, for his part, he could manipulate certain kinds of complex information in his head and perform other feats of mental acrobatics in ways he'd never seen other people do, but the two of us were also the people who, when my 1982 Volkswagen Rabbit convertible broke down on an incline, got the passenger-side door wedged into the hillside, pushed the car in the wrong direction, and tore the door off its hinges.

His theory went that each of us has certain ways in which we are elite geniuses and others in which we are knuckle-dragging bozos. This wasn't a new concept to me. I had heard about different kinds of intelligence at that point in my life and had certainly rolled out Dungeons and Dragons characters and tallied scores for wisdom and dexterity and charisma and the rest. But what hit me like an epiphany was that Aaron walked around believing it. He understood that it was possible to be the smartest person in the world, but also that there were untold others who could claim that title in different ways. And, case in point, he knew this extreme intelligence wasn't embodied by some unknowable being but by a short old guy puttering about his bedroom in Northern California, wondering where his socks went. This was Aaron's birthright as much as his name or his own intellect or his bad eyesight: an understanding that the people who did things in the world were just people. And that meant that anyone could do things in the world. Even me.

We drank a beer and headed out. We walked over the Williamsburg Bridge. Took the train up to the Met. We looked at Dürers and knew why they were there. We saw world-famous masterpieces that were just all right; thought about how they got there too; wondered who was that painting's Panofsky, which curator had pulled together which exhibition at what time and why, which critic had hailed it in which publication, which audiences had read it, then dropped the critic's opinion at a dinner party as though it were their own, which museumgoers at which moment in time had stood in front of those flowers or that landscape or that bluish-orange-greenish square and thought, "Yes, that is it right there," and turned to their friend and tried to figure out why that image made them feel so deeply. We saw an Anselm Kiefer that seemed like everything that anyone would ever want to achieve in a painting. We walked through the American Wing and stumbled into a room filled with glass cases with row after row of stacked paintings and vases, headboards, and carved mantels, and so many images of Ben Franklin on dishware and in lockets and friezes, and I understood for the first time that he was just a man, too, just some dude who was maybe the world's smartest man but was also such a weirdo, horny and gouty, who couldn't see for shit without the bifocals he'd invented, and here in this room he had been turned into an icon, a concept that Erwin Panofksy had already put a name to but we were coming to it on our own.

I didn't know on that day that down the road I would be asked by the Met to write stories about its collection and would write about that room, but it might have been the day that set me moving in that direction. That had me beginning to realize that I might be one of those people who did things in the world. They were just people after all.

Six Waterlines

1.

The Providence River begins at the confluence of two similarly modest waterways, the Moshassuck and the Woonasquatucket, that trace their own origins to two ponds—one called Primrose and another that, I was surprised to learn, has never been given a name. It then runs for eight miles before emptying into Providence Harbor, whose tidal shifts shorten and lengthen the river significantly, depending on the moon and the seasons. Roger Williams named the river. In the winter of 1636, the Puritan exile from the Massachusetts Bay Colony came by boat, saw green hills along its banks, and thought it was the perfect place to found his community, based on the principles of religious liberty.

At right is the seal of the city that grew from that settlement:

Williams, in the peaked hat and coat familiar from elementary school Thanksgiving pageants, stands in the prow of a canoe, arriving in this place he'll call Providence, being greeted from the shore by two Narragansett men. One stands at relative ease, holding a spear he doesn't seem immediately inclined to use. The other is a sachem who holds his arms out in greeting. The "What Cheer?" floating above the scene is the city motto, a paraphrase of what an early historian of Rhode Island claims the chieftain called out from shore—"What cheer, *netop?*"—a blend of the then common equivalent of a casual "What's up?" and the Narragansett word for "friend" or "neighbor." The design of the seal has been rejiggered a few times but has been basically the same since it was first created in 1878. Its purpose seems clear: The image ties the modern city to an appealing and useful story drawn from the history of its own founding and to the iconography (thank you again for that word, Erwin Panofsky) of the founding of the United States. Once again, a Pilgrim-looking fellow arrives in another new world to live in accordance with his principles, with the assistance of friendly natives. In that story, the Narragansett didn't just welcome Williams but gifted him prime real estate.

It may not surprise you that this story isn't entirely true, and that, as with the émigrés up in Plymouth, the tangible assistance he did receive from the people that were there when he arrived wasn't entirely altruistic. The Narragansett who agreed to let him settle the land at the mouth of the river did so out of strategic necessity. They wanted a physical buffer between their lands and those of the Wampanoag, who lived across the Seekonk River, Providence's eastern border. The Narragansett and the Wampanoag had a recent history of violent conflict. They figured Williams could serve as a useful envoy between their tribe and the English colonies. They wanted the stuff he had to trade and hoped this alliance would open up other economic opportunities. The land wasn't a gift but rather represented the Narragansett's side of an exchange that established a strategic partnership.

He did not, as the seal suggests, come upon the Narragansett and soon-to-be Providence after a long *Mayflower*-like journey: In fact, he had spent a while on the other side of the not particularly wide Seekonk River living among the Wampanoag. But he was informed that where he'd been staying was still technically part of the Massachusetts Bay Colony, and since he had been banished as a heretic, he had to clear out. So Williams hopped into his canoe and rowed over. He probably could've heard the Narragansett shouting, "What cheer, *netop*?" (if indeed it was the Narragansett who said it and not, as a different early historian suggested, Roger Williams himself) from the shore of the future Rhode Island, before he'd even left Massachusetts.

And it will likely not surprise you either to read that this peace didn't hold. As with the Pilgrims and the Wampanoag, a few decades of mutually beneficial coexistence between Williams and the Narragansett were followed by horrors. After years of colonists breaking treaties, seizing Wampanoag land, and raiding their resources, the Wampanoag went to war against Plymouth and the colonists in Massachusetts. When that happened, Roger Williams, Rhode Island, and the Narragansett managed to remain neutral for a while. But the war escalated, pitted the Wampanoag and Narragansett against each other; pitted white settlers against both tribes; and even Roger Williams, paragon of religious tolerance and cultural acceptance, tried on atrocity: He approved the sale of Narragansett prisoners as slaves. He led the Rhode Island militia against his former allies and friends. In turn, the Narragansett burned his home to the ground.

But there was an era of peace and mutual prosperity that made Providence worthy of its name, for a while. The waters of the Moshassuck and the Woonasquatucket met in a salt cove teeming with eels and crabs and lobsters and quahogs and runs of salmon so dense in certain seasons, some say, that you could walk upon them from shore to shore. And the Providence River fed fields that fed a settlement that would become a city, pushed wheels that would fuel its industries, spilled out into a harbor that would host ships that would send out its wares, and let the blessings of the religious liberty that Williams had brought to its banks flow onward.

2.

They used to call them gales, the hurricanes that swept through and wreaked havoc along the Providence River. Without modern meteorological instruments, without Doppler radar or a soaked TV reporter doing a wind-whipped broadcast as the storm approached, the people who lived there wouldn't have known what was coming. A gale would blow in unannounced and the river would rise. Happened over and over. In 1764, 1815, 1878. The first major named hurricane to cause the river to flood was in 1954, when Carol brought floodwaters thirteen feet high. That's pretty much all I know about that one. But I do know about the gale in 1938. It was the one that overflowed the banks of the Pawtuxet River a few miles away, right by the Club Baghdad, and flooded the zoo in Roger Williams Park, and that was "The Day Dad Had to Get the Escaped Monkeys Off the Roof of the Nightclub."

3.

This story is being written in a monk's cell of an office off a guest bathroom by the entrance to my house in Los Angeles. I built a shelf for my laptop to keep the screen at a height that won't hurt my middle-aged neck. I type on a wireless keyboard. If I look down to make sure my hands are in the right place or to remember over which number I can find an ampersand, I see this picture leaning on my desk:

I'm not sure I've ever seen a better photograph taken inside an average home in the early nineteenth century. It is of my mother's father's family, clearly dressed for a holiday or wedding, I don't know which or whose. We assume it is in a family home in the fishing village of Rodi Garganico, on the Gargano Peninsula—the spur of the boot on a map of Italy. Interior photography was no easy feat back then. Knowing how humbly my forebears lived, and having personally walked the streets of Rodi and had relatives point out the balcony on which my great-grandmother would sit and sew while my great-grandfather looked up longingly from below, hoping to catch her eye, I find it remarkable that the photographer produced an image of such clarity and energy in what was certainly a small room.

I tend to write slowly, in fits and starts. I have had a lot of time to stare at this picture. It rewards repeated investigation. You, too, will find a lot to unpack in the dynamic between these people, if you want to take the time to look. But now I just want you to see my great-grandparents: They are seated to the left, Dominico Mancini and Antonia Palliano, who did indeed look down from her needle-work to notice him one day. They passed through Ellis Island not long after this picture was taken and were told, like many Italian immigrants during that time, that there wasn't room for them in New York and instead they should try Providence. They moved into the Pierce Street house. Antonia took care of the home and the five children they'd brought with them (one of those children would die in the flu of 1918; two more, including my grandfather, would be born in the United States). Dominico pieced together a living in the same way he had in Italy. He loved to play the violin and dabbled at composing, but it didn't pay the bills. He opened up a barbershop on the banks of the Providence River, cutting the hair of other immi-grant men who loaded and outfitted and crewed the ships that used to dock there.

4.

My parents grew up on Federal Hill, one of the seven hills upon which, it is said, Providence was built ("just like Rome," as people who like to puff up this small city are fond of saying, though people who like to look at topographical maps would consider that claim a stretch). Federal Hill was the place most of those rerouted Italian immigrants wound up. My mom lived in the nicer part of this working-class neighborhood in the house on Pierce Street; my dad lived in the rougher part off Atwells Avenue in a cold-water flat by a bowling alley where his father and two of my uncles set pins. He spent his childhood running around a very small number of blocks. There was a fair amount of trouble in the neighborhood, which oc-casionally pulled in those two pin-setting brothers (they were half brothers from his mother's previous marriage, and quite a bit older than him). My dad kept himself out of that trouble by reading Clas-sics Illustrated comic books and playing baseball and football by the public bathhouse in a park that wasn't big enough for either baseball or football, and playing basketball at Zuccolo Rec Center or for the team at Our Lady of Mount Carmel Church, one block from their apartment. His childhood was spent almost entirely on what they called, simply, the Hill. His family's biggest adventures were trips to his mom's eldest brother's house in the Connecticut suburbs, which might as well have been Tierra del Fuego. My dad once saw a car parked on Atwells with North Dakota plates. Still talks about it to this day.

His best friend, Jimmy, lived on the other side of the Mount Carmel rectory in the bottom floor of a triple-decker. One day when they were teenagers, they were hanging out in the little store Jimmy's mother ran out of a one-car garage, when they heard on the radio that there was a whale in the Providence River. A whale in the river? No one could believe it.

Now, there were Rhode Islanders who knew for whales, who spent their whole lives on the water, sailing Newport Harbor, trawling Block Island Sound for fluke and scup. But their boats weren't in Providence. The docks on the river along which my mom's grandfather had his barbershop had been torn down long before. My dad's people were not boat people. To see a whale! In the Providence River! A once-in-a-lifetime opportunity! Just down the hill, fifteen blocks across downtown, twenty minutes on foot, tops. My dad and Jimmy started walking over to see this marvel. Past my father's uncle Tony's own barbershop. Past the public library, where my dad had spent so many hours keeping out of trouble, reading and rereading *Ivanhoe*. Past the Majestic Theatre and the Albee, where he'd sometimes get an extra nickel to take his baby brother to the movies to get them out of their parents' hair. The city was electric. People streaming by, rushing to the river. Besuited bankers cutting out of work early, a pep in their step. Pontiacs pulling over, the news of the whale drifting from their radios through their open windows. A pushcart vendor pushing fast. A woman running out of the beauty parlor, curlers still in her hair, maybe. A city alive with that rarest of energies, when everyone knows that this, right here, right now, is a day no one will ever forget. My dad and Jimmy got about halfway and turned around. Felt too far. Which is their story of that day, as wonderful in its way as a whale in the river.

5.

I was a safari guide for Providence, Rhode Island. It was 1991. Kids in my rural town just over the Massachusetts border were getting their licenses and testing out their freedom and discovering the genuine magic of driving to the Cumberland Farms convenience store by Rehoboth's single stoplight. They were heading to Seekonk to see a movie, going to the Swansea Mall, getting soft-serve on Route 44. Tale was heard of some driving out to this clearing in the woods and drinking beers stolen from the snack bar at the public golf course and blasting Metallica in the glow of the headlights of a hand-me-down Chevelle. I drove to Providence.

I knew its streets by heart, knew all the spots, and felt cool being the guy who would introduce the Rehoboth kids to the record stores and that place on Thayer Street that sold Doc Martens and those fishnet gloves with the fingers cut out that the hot goth college girls wore. Why go to the Showcase Cinemas in Seekonk to see *Don't Tell Mom the Babysitter's Dead* when we could go to the Avon to see *Barton Fink*? I was a man of the world. Eager to share its many wonders with anyone who wanted to hop into my Volkswagen Rabbit—at least those wonders that existed within a forty-minute drive or from which I could return by ten on a weeknight, midnight on the weekend.

I loved this role as tour guide. And I found I loved that particular thrill of returning to places my parents and babysitters used to take me as a little kid, now that I was older and had *lived,* man. To sit under the canopy of a two-hundred-year-old tree by the private girls' school and climb and lie in its branches, hidden from the people on Blackstone Boulevard, is delightful at any age. The pocket-size playground built at the end of my old block in the nineteenth century—thick with old oaks and elms behind ornate wrought iron, where my grandmother used to push me on the swings as we sang— was a great place to be with my friends in the dark after seeing some band at a real club with real adults. It was fun to make out in a gilded-age graveyard, even if it didn't matter to my girlfriends that it happened to be the place where my parents taught me to ride a bike.

But it mattered profoundly to me. I would walk around Providence, intoxicated by the palimpsest of time, the layers of memory built up Troy-like over the city (as I now knew from twelfth-grade civilization class). I would be in my rattletrap Rabbit laden with friends, at a stoplight on Angell Street, on the steepest of the city's seven Rome-ish hills, attempting to do a nearly impossible hill start, feeling the eyes of every perfect art school girl on her way to class at RISD, trying to work the stick shift and the clutch like my dad had taught me and not roll backward, not crash into the car behind me, not burn out the clutch again, and I would realize that this was the exact spot where my grandfather had been in that story he'd told about the time he was driving a cab to make extra money during the Depression and his ride shouted from the back seat because the floor of the car had suddenly rusted through and his feet were touching the ground like Fred Flintstone's. I was feeling my own past and my family's past, the city's past, all around me.

I was alone in that feeling. I felt alone a lot. Feeling like the only one who noticed certain things, the only one who seemed to be aware that we are all products of the historic moments we are given. That in a different era maybe I wouldn't be thinking about going to college; maybe I would be drafted into a war, or would be getting on a boat, hoping to find a place by a river to put a barbershop; maybe I wouldn't be getting an easy cure for my Graves' disease. I wouldn't be meeting these friends. Now. This was our moment. These were the kinds of cars we drove. These were our songs. These were the lives we got to live. Timing *was* everything, it turned out, and it was a gift to notice beautiful moments as they happened, but I felt alone in holding that particular melancholy of knowing they were, in that same moment, becoming the past.

My friends weren't going to care about my learning to ride my bike in Swan Point Cemetery, but they did like the story about how my dad used to dig graves there as he was paying his way through Rhode Island College, and how there was a peculiar way people mourned their dead back then, at least in Providence. They'd place cardboard clocks with plastic hands on the graves that were set to the time their loved one had left them. After the burial and the funeral procession drove off, my dad would steal those clocks and bring them to my mom so she could use them in her student-teaching classes to help the kids in special ed learn how to tell time. They liked that story. I'd tell similar stories as we walked the city. They liked hearing about my dad and the whale. About how his older brother had lied and said he played drums in a band called B-Bop and the Four D's and it was funny to pretend to be in a band that didn't exist and be one of the four D's, as a DiMeo, and it was funny that no one knew who B-Bop was supposed to be, and it was funny because he didn't even know how to play the drums, but it was beautiful, too, because his real father, "the Irish Bastard," his mother called him, had vanished from his life and left him only with a set of drums that he never learned to play. They liked the one about that same half brother and how he loved the daughter of a guy that owned a pizza place on the Hill and would come by every day just to be around her, and then another pizza place opened up across the street and my uncle Russell threw a brick through its window to impress her, and still she would never love him, and his stepfather—who didn't vanish, who adopted him—paid for that window with money he did not have, to get his son out of trouble. They cared if I told the stories well. I learned that if I could keep them tight, infuse them with meaning, with enough context to make that meaning land, and could turn my family members or my younger self into characters with needs and wants and obstacles, they would care. If I told the story well, they would feel a little of the way that I did. I would feel connected. I would be less lonely. I do that to this day. I'm pretty sure it's what I'm trying to do right now.

6.

When I was about nineteen, they moved the river. I had forgotten they were going to do it. One morning when I was eight or nine, my mom showed me an article in the Sunday *Providence Journal*. It laid out an ambitious public works project to eventually reroute the Providence River. A couple of decades after my great-grandfather ran his shop on the riverfront, the shipping business had moved elsewhere, to larger ports and deeper waterways up and down the coast. Without the boats there, the city government thought Providence didn't need the river as much anymore. They expanded the roadways along the river. After building a hurricane barrier at the mouth of the harbor in 1961 to finally control the tides and keep the water from rising, they paved over even more of it, leaving very little of the river exposed.

This new project, I read on the floor, the paper spread out on the living room rug, would tear out most of the asphalt, clean out the old tires and half-submerged shopping carts that I could see in gaps in the roadway, and then redirect the flow of the river to mirror the way it had looked prior to the buildup of downtown and the creation of a railroad depot that had required filling in the Great Salt Cove, where the salmon once ran so thick you could walk across the water on their backs. The architectural renderings were beautiful. A gleaming walkway by a crystal-clear river that would stretch from the hurricane barrier and feed into a granite basin, whose elegant circular shape would echo that of the old cove. At the edge of the reborn cove would rise a grand amphitheater that would host theatrical productions, the Philharmonic, and international touring acts who'd perform while people paddled about in canoes. It was beautiful. I was thrilled. My mother cautioned me that a lot of things get proposed and don't get built.

I forgot all about it. But then one night I was walking around the city with my friend Jen from high school. We were leaving the next day on a cross-country drive so I could have a car during my sophomore year at UC Santa Barbara, and she could visit a friend in Sonoma. We felt excited and happy to be old enough and brave enough: We were two kids from our hometown, each with lovely and loving but, in the eyes our youthful selves, too parochial parents, going on a grand adventure. We talked about our futures and a little about the past. I showed her the garage that used to be my dad's friend Jimmy's mom's store, and how there was a spot on the wall, protected by an overhanging roof, where my dad had written his name in chalk when he was our age, and it still said "Johnny D," plain as day. I wrote my name beneath it. We walked down to the river past where my great-grandfather's barbershop used to be. We noticed the lines on the RISD building that mark where the water rose in 1938 and again in 1954, and I thought about how it doesn't rise anymore, ever since they put in the hurricane barrier, which was good, but how it meant there would never be another day when a whale swam through, which wasn't. But then I noticed that while I'd been away at school, they had actually started to move the river. We stumbled upon the construction site like we'd stepped through an opening in the back of an enchanted wardrobe. Here it was, that place I'd read about. They were really doing it. And, sure, it wasn't quite as grand as I'd imagined: The amphitheater was just a dozen rows deep; Prince wasn't going to play there, but someone would. It would be nice to sit and listen. It was nice that the city's resources had gone toward trying to undo some mistakes of the past and toward bending the city's future a bit toward beauty.

In order to move the river, they had to move a monument. A hundred-foot pillar topped with a robed figure meant to represent peace had been constructed in 1929 to honor Rhode Islanders who fought and died in World War I. For the first part of my life, it had stood at the center of a chaotic traffic circle in the middle of the road that covered a long section of the river. Jen and I came upon it shortly after it had been relocated to its new home across from the granite-lined river walk. Now it stood in the center of a rectangle of dirt and debris that would soon be seeded with grass to grow into a memorial park, where they would honor other dead from other wars and provide a place for bank employees and jurors on lunch break from the courthouse to eat chicken Caesar salads from plastic containers. There were small trees, then freshly planted, that are now majestic. The pillar was still held temporarily in position by four girders that suspended the monument in the air over a hole that would soon be filled with concrete. Here we were, two friends, reunited in the middle of our grand adventures at college, she in Florida, me in California, on the eve of another adventure, a cross-country drive, about to start the next part of our lives.

Just a couple of years after this night, I would wind up back in Providence. My undergraduate journey made more stops than most; the oddly ecstatic beginning of my Graves' disease diagnosis turned into a story about disease management and radioactive iodine and adjusting to the slowed-down metabolism of the thyroid-less. School and life got weird. After time at two Universities of California, I finished up at Rhode Island College, where my parents had met in Italian 101 and went on to teach special ed, which meant I could attend college for $267 a semester in fees; it wound up being the perfect place to find my footing again. As was Providence itself, where I found myself in the familiar role of de facto tour guide, this time for kids at Brown or RISD or for other transplants who came to the city to make art and music or just find their own footing as they made their way into adulthood. And along with showing them the locals-only lunch places, or that one junk shop outside of town that had a lot of old tube amplifiers and guitar pedals, I told stories.

I was falling in love with history then. My fascination with the past began to reach beyond my own narrow world, found purchase in books and documentaries and museums. I made a practice of going to every museum, every historic home and marker within driving distance, both because I loved them and because I felt my life slipping by every day, even at twenty-three. I found that engaging actively with history—with stories of the past, of lives with beginnings and middles and ends, with periods of strife that felt unending but weren't, or peace or joy that couldn't hold—kept present the most valuable thing I knew: the fact that we are all going to die. And living in awareness of that made me live better. More bravely. Made me more attentive. More considerate. It was the simplest, most eternal of lessons (I knew that, even then), but I had noticed it was one you needed to relearn over and over. To this day, I write these stories in part because doing so well requires that I remember it.

But I forget myself.

Anyway:

There we were, Jen and me, by the open pit beside the moved monument. We saw an opportunity. Jen asked a man, a lawyer-looking guy, probably just getting out of work after a long day at the courthouse across the street, for a pen. I tore a receipt in my pocket in half, and the two of us sat on the steps of the monument, by the open pit, and we each wrote down a wish for ourselves. We were entirely earnest. We would memorialize this moment. We composed lines that encompassed our feelings at that time in our lives and what we wanted for ourselves in this future into which we were boldly going. We folded up our papers. We closed our eyes. We tossed them down into the darkness below the floating column, knowing that they would soon be entombed forever, and we turned that monument into a tribute to our own young selves and to that moment, so that anytime, as the years went on, our lives, wherever they led us, brought us back to Providence, we would see that monument and we would think of those messages on those scraps of paper.

I have absolutely no idea what I wrote.

One last story . . .

These Words, Forever

Guglielmo Marconi is the father of radio. He didn't really invent it. He got much more credit than he deserves, but whatever. Guglielmo Marconi was the father of radio. He was a hero on a scale that the nation of Italy hadn't seen since the Renaissance. I have a postcard I found in my grandfather's attic after he died. It has a picture of Marconi on the front and a message in Italian on the back encouraging immigrants like my grandfather's family to express their pride in their countryman by investing in the Marconi Company.

He was celebrated all over the world. He dined with presidents and kings and captains of industry. Beautiful women. He shared a Nobel Prize. Got just about every honor the Italian government had to give. Benito Mussolini was the best man at his second wedding, which I'm sure felt like a good idea at the time.

But we're told that when he was in his sixties, somewhere around the time of his fourth or fifth heart attack, the inventor began to think about mortality. Or rather, he began to think about immortality.

Marconi became convinced that sound never dies. That sound waves, once emitted—from a radio, from the vibrating string of a Stradivarius, from whispering lovers or a baby discovering how to make a *bah* or a *guh* sound for the first time—lived on forever, flowing permanently but growing weaker and weaker with each moment. He just hadn't yet managed to build a radio powerful enough to tune in the signal.

This wasn't entirely foolish. One of the things that had made Marconi famous was the sinking of the *Titanic*. Seven hundred and five people were rescued from the icy water after radiomen on nearby ships heard its wireless distress signal. Newspapers around the world credited Marconi as those passengers' savior. One of those radiomen, working the night shift on a Russian steamer, heard the signal through his headphones more than an hour and a half after it was sent. It was a physical anomaly. Atmospheric conditions and whatnot.

But here was Marconi near the end of his life, growing weaker and weaker with each heart attack. Dreaming of a device that would let him hear these lost sounds, that would let him tap in to these eternal frequencies. He would tell people that if he got it right, he would be able to hear Jesus of Nazareth giving the Sermon on the Mount. He would be able to hear everything that had ever been said. Everything he himself ever said. At the end of his life, he could sit in his piazza in Rome and hear everything that was ever said to him or about him. He could relive every toast and testimonial.

We all could. Hear everything. Hear Marco Polo talk to Genghis Khan. Hear Shakespeare give an actor a line reading. Hear my grandmother introduce herself to my grandfather at a nightclub in Rhode Island. Hear someone tell you they love you, the first time they told you they loved you. Hear everything, forever.

Il famoso Inventore Italiano, Guglielmo Marconi, nacque a Bologna, Italia, il 25 di Aprile, 1874, e ricevette la sua educazione nelle Università di Livorno e Bologna. Il Signor Marconi comunque giovanissimo, ha l'onore della scoperta di una nuova scienza la quale viene riconosciuta da tutti gli uomoni per la più rimarchevole invenzione nella storia.

Il Signor Marconi ha dato grande onore all'Italia, e gli Italiani dovunque, dovrebbero prendere grande interessamento nel suo lavoro.

Le Compagnie Marconi che si sono organizzate sotto la sua direzione, quasi in tutte le parti del mondo, sono in azione commerciale.

Il meraviglioso successo che hanno incontrato queste compagnie prova senza dubbio che le Compagnie Marconi, in pochissimi anni saranno più grandi di quelle dei Telefoni, Telegrafi, o telegrafiche compagnie di oggi.

Cento dollari investiti nelle azioni del Bell Telephone, in 25 anni aumentarono a 2 mila dollari. 100 dollari di azioni nella Edison Electric Light in un anno salirono a 4 mila dollari. La Western Union Telegraph ha pagato un dividendo in 8 anni ammontante a 71½ per cent. in contante, e 707.99 1-3 per cent. in capitale. Noi crediamo che le azioni della Compagnia Marconi verranno ad un maggiore aumento, e mostreranno una maggior potenza : di guadagno.

Voi dovreste immediatamente chiedere informazioni a queste Compagnie e divenire un azionista di una di esse. Se siete interessato, scriveteci per maggiori schiarimenti, che noi vi mandiamo senza alcuna spesa.

MUNROE & MUNROE

AGENTI PER LA VENDITA DELLE AZIONI MARCONI

25 BROAD STREET, NEW YORK   50 CONGRESS STREET, BOSTON

CANADA LIFE BUILDING, MONTREAL

Acknowledgments

They wanted me to write *Seabiscuit*.

It was the same thing, nearly every time. I would get an email from an editor at a publishing house who had heard my podcast and wanted to meet about maybe doing a book. I would be thrilled. A book! I have always wanted to write a book and see it in a bookstore window, on a blanket on a beach beside a sleeping stranger, on the shelf of a junk shop next to a faded Windows 95 manual, anywhere. But on some real, kind of embarrassing, probably pathological level, I didn't necessarily believe that could be a real thing for a very long time. So, as my podcast audience grew, I would be tickled to get an email from and a breakfast with a real editor or agent who was in the business of making books. The people would be lovely—they'd like the show, they'd like the writing, they'd like the platform, and then they'd want me to write *Seabiscuit*. Or *The Devil in the White City,* or *Hidden Figures,* or *Cod,* or some other history book for general readers in which a deep dive into a single subject somehow explains America. I couldn't blame them. Those books were big hits. But they were also *big. The Memory Palace,* hit potential aside, is small. And it's what I do. It's how my brain works. I don't know if I have it in me to write *Seabiscuit* (a terrific book, by the way; another wonderful title in the Random House catalog; you should buy several copies), but, either way, I knew I didn't want to. I wanted to write a book like this one. But there hadn't been a book like this one, not really. True short stories isn't a thing. How do you market that?

Plus, the show was never that big. A beloved cult object at best. It was going to be a tough sell, the editors and agents would tell me. Was I sure there wasn't a story I wanted to go long on? Was I sure there wasn't a horse I wanted to write about? An old-timey serial killer? A horse that was an old-timey serial killer? The idea of a book of stories like the ones I write just never quite added up.

I don't know if this book is going to sell. All those people may have been right all along. But I am extraordinarily happy that it is a book at all and deeply grateful to the people who helped make it. That starts with two dudes for whom the idea of a *Memory Palace* book felt like a no-brainer: my dear friend Mike Schur, who, while we sat watching the Sacramento Kings defeat the Memphis Grizzlies at a basketball arena named after a regional bank, sent an introductory email to the other dude, Richard Abate, the best kind of agent (offhandedly projecting a well-earned air of client-calming confidence, sharp and funny and warm and altogether un-agent-like). Which led to a Zoom in 2021 with Andy Ward, Tom Perry, and Robin Desser at Random House, who, while all completely up-front and aware of the many pitfalls of publishing a book without a natural comp and a straightforward path to the bestseller list, wanted to read the book I wanted to write and saw it as a challenge worth taking on. And that meeting led to any number of meetings behind the scenes at Random House with all the folks who do the work of making a book; I want to particularly thank Rebecca Berlant, Evan Camfield, Kevin Garcia, Monica Rae Brown, Erin Richards, Michael Hoak, Ralph Fowler, Lucas Heinrich, Alison Rich, Ben Greenberg, and Andy Ward.

Now, there was a fourth person on that Zoom, and hers was a familiar face. Molly Turpin was one of those people who had sent me an email over the years. That was in 2016. She was an associate editor. She took me to breakfast. She was relatively new to the publishing business then, but she knew enough to know that the best way for me to get a book published was for me to write *Seabiscuit*. But she was the only book person I'd talked to who followed that up with "But that's not what you do. I wonder what version of what you do might work?" Five years later, she was in a window in a video conference, smiling quietly as it became clear that her bosses also thought the version I was pitching could be something. Since then, she has become a wonderful editor and friend. The most insightful and open-hearted reader. The sharpest eye. The steadiest hand (in the "on the rudder, steering through rocky waters" way, in the "surgeon making precise cuts" way, and in the way of the best partner for someone trying to juggle a ton of stories/chainsaws). Patient and nimble and kind.

I also want to thank the wonderfully talented, good-natured, and shockingly efficient Jill DeHaan, who created the illustrations inside the book and designed its cover.

I'm not sure where I would be had my friend Avery Trufelman, when I spoke in a semipanic about how I kept losing photo researchers to full-time employment, not directed me to the thrillingly competent and knowledgeable Jane Yeomans, who swept in and made every complicated thing easy. (I also want to thank Than Saffel for some fantastic photo guidance on my way to finding Jane.)

This book, like *The Memory Palace* podcast, owes a great deal to the smarts and care and drive of the whole team at Radiotopia and PRX, but especially Audrey Mardavich and Yooree Losordo for their support and friendship, and Melissa Garcia-Houle in ad-ops, who met my occasional frantic emails wondering if it was possible to move things around with the podcast so I could carve out time for the book with warmth and patience.

When I was a kid, I was an obsessive viewer of the Oscars. Even when I was too young to have seen most of the movies or have any opinions about the relative merits of *The Trip to Bountiful* or *Kiss of the Spider Woman* as they competed for Best Adapted Screenplay in 1986. I loved all of it. Particularly the speeches, and at some point, maybe in middle school, I had an epiphany: People might make jokes about the way the actors thanked their agents and stylists and whomever, but these people were important to the actors. These were the people in their lives. And even though their names didn't mean anything to us at home, each was a real relationship. Worthy of a moment out of one of the most important in their lives. And so I give you this list, surely incomplete, of people whose names aren't important to you, but whose advice or encouragement or mere love helped immeasurably during the creation of this book: Guadalupe Ruano, Nancy Farghalli, Eliza McGraw, The Ambrose Pals, Hrishikesh Hirway, Helen and Martin, Nick and Marie, JJ and John and Arianne, the Savage sisters and Phil, Ethan Sandler, Jeff and Dave, Pilates Jill, Dhavi and Raphael, Steve Belber, Amy Nicholson, Madeleine Mazé, Lucy Cotter, Roman Mars, Jody Avrigan, Chris Bannon, the Rebeccas and Gail and Colin, Dave and Jessica, Walnut and Goldie and dear, sweet Flower, Matt and Tamara and Eric and Katya, Wilson and Liesl, Gersteins and Jarretts and a Weaver and a Matzkin and a Gilbert, Phil Klay, Daniel Alarcón, Uncle Pete, Uncle Matt, Julianna Castigliego, the unstoppable Mancini Sisters, Aaron and Sean (who, even when not name-checked, are all over this book), and always and forever, my mom, my dad, and Leila and Quinby.

A Brief Note on Sources and Process

I decided to try to break into radio when I was twenty-five. I had spent the previous several years hanging out in underground music and art scenes, playing in bands and mostly thinking about art I was too afraid to actually try to make. But after the best of those bands broke up, I was in the throes of one of those fairly typical midway-to-midlife crises where you're just sure you need to figure everything out immediately. I had heard some particularly inventive and moving stories on the public radio shows *This American Life* and *All Things Considered* that made me realize that there might be a way for me to make beautiful things for a living after all. When I finally managed to get my foot in the door, I stumbled into deadline journalism. I took to it. I was a quick study. And I found that the act of starting the workday not knowing what that day would bring and then going off and working hard to make the very best story I could and just putting it out into the world when time was up was both exhilarating and the perfect antidote for my fear-based perfectionism. It got me out of my own way. I did that for nearly a decade, all the while wanting to get back to the original dream: I wanted to make beautiful things. *The Memory Palace* has been my attempt to do that.

I came to the project as a journalist, and since the first story I have applied my journalistic practice in my artistic practice. In short: Use reliable sources, don't plagiarize, figure out the truth and tell it as best you can. It is not quite the same as a historian's approach, I think; where she might take on the obligation of laying out conflicts that might arise between sources and historical accounts and walking the reader through the trail of evidence that leads to her conclusions as she has best been able to reach them, I choose to leave that process off mic. All that public weighing weighs down the story. Therefore, my goal in my show notes has always been to simply point the person who might come away from the story wanting to know more to the best sources that I found useful and to acknowledge the sources without which any given story could not have been written. So that is what is happening next here.

And one final note: I've been doing this for fifteen years. Between untransferred files that are now on old laptops with missing chargers, a botched website update, and the like, there are older stories for which I have, to my regret, lost the trail that originally led me to their facts.

Including the first story:

"Distance"—I do not have a record of how I first came upon this story over a decade ago, but the story was greatly helped by my poring through an old paperback of Morse's letters, printed by Da Capo Press in 1973 as *Samuel F. B. Morse: His Journals and Letters* and edited by Morse's son Edward Lind Morse, a painter in his own right.

"Gigantic"—I highly recommend searching through the archives of the old *American Heritage* magazine, which include some spirited back-and-forth and fact-checking in letters to the editor debating whether Old Bet was the first or second elephant to set foot in North America.

"The Nickel Candy Bar"—I put this story together like a Halloween bag of fun-size candy bars from a biographical article, "Doug Davis—Air Racer, Barnstormer, Airline Pilot," written by Clair C. Stebbins for *Aviation Quarterly* in 1989; from another covering Otto Schnering by Samantha Chemlik for immigrantentrepreneurship .org; and from *The Oxford Companion to American Food and Drink*, edited by Andrew F. Smith and released in 2007, as well as other sources.

"Hercules"—The website of the George Washington Presidential Library at Mount Vernon and the Papers of George Washington Project at the University of Virginia are great entry points for documents and scholarly work on Hercules Posey. I found Fritz Hirschfeld's book *George Washington and Slavery: A Documentary Portrayal* particularly useful, and enjoyed further reading in W.E.B. Du Bois's *The Philadelphia Negro: A Social Study.*

"A Brief Eulogy Written After Noticing That *The New York Times*'s Obituary for Carla Wallenda, the Last Surviving Child of the Founders of the Flying Wallendas Acrobatic Troupe, Said That the Cause of Death Was Unknown"—This one was pieced together, as many *Memory Palace* stories are, through numerous contemporary articles documenting the Wallendas' exploits that I found in newspaper archives. You can find a thorough, if charmingly hagiographic, history of the Flying Wallendas at Wallenda.com.

"A History of Martian Civilization, 1877–1906"—I found that the most thorough way to explore this episode in humanity's relationship to Mars was by reading David Strauss's *Percival Lowell: The Culture and Science of a Boston Brahmin* from 2001. The most fun way, however, is to go to newspaper archive websites and search for "Mars" and watch the whole thing unfold over time.

"Zulu Charley, Romeo, a Love Story"—I originally came upon this story in a brief mention in a wonderful old book called *Theatrical and Circus Life; or, Secrets of the Stage, Green-Room, and Sawdust Arena,* written by John Joseph Jennings. Two articles—"Zulus Abroad: Cultural Representations and Educational Experiences of Zulus in America, 1880–1945" by Robert Trent Vinson and Robert Edgar, published in the *Journal of Southern African Studies* in 2007, and "Beyond the Exhibit: Zulu Experiences in Britain and the United States, 1879–1884," a graduate thesis submitted to Carleton University in Ottawa in 2011 by Erin Elizabeth Barbara Bell—were critical in making Jennings's mention concrete and contextualized.

"At the White House Egg Roll of 1889"—The egg roll of it all was pulled together largely from contemporary newspaper accounts and from the many timelines of the history of the White House

Easter Egg Roll published on the many websites dedicated to presidential history. The Eastman of it all was informed by Elizabeth Brayer's *George Eastman: A Biography,* from 2011, and Douglas Collins's 1990 book *The Story of Kodak.*

"The Glowing Orbs"—In 2014, I was asked to join the writing staff of a television miniseries for ABC, an adaptation of Lily Koppel's book *The Astronaut Wives Club,* a sharp group biography. The show's creator, Stephanie Savage, tapped me in part because there was a strict mandate from Disney, the network's parent company, to stick to the facts as closely as possible, as there was a perception, right or wrong, that a wife or two was particularly litigious; Stephanie knew *The Memory Palace* and felt like it displayed a useful knack for finding relatively deep drama from seemingly shallow factual pools. It was a great experience. My co-workers and I were handed stacks of books about the space program. I now know a ton about the space program without caring much about the space program. Somewhere in there, in one of those books, likely in one of the fading old issues of *Life* that were piled up on the table in the writer's room, was the thing about the pee.

"The Prairie Chicken in Wisconsin: Highlights of a Study of Counts, Behavior, Turnover, Movement, and Habitat"—I first learned about Frances Hamerstrom in the kids' section of Counterpoint, our local used bookstore. My daughter was ten at the time and a big fan of middle-grade historical biographies. I found a terrific little book with brief stories about female naturalists by Jeannine Atkins called *Girls Who Looked Under Rocks* and bought it for two bucks. If you want to learn more about Frances (and you should), I could not recommend her autobiography, *My Double Life,* enough. It features wonderful illustrations by her daughter, Elva Paulson, with whom I had the great pleasure of corresponding during the production of my own book.

"A Timeline of the History of the Temple of Dendur"—In 2015 I was invited to be the artist in residence at The Metropolitan Museum of Art and produce stories related to and inspired by the collection. Each of the stories was drawn from its American Wing, except this one. The museum itself is by far the best repository for information about the temple and how it came to the Met. You can find pretty much everything you'd want on its website, including a brief book it commissioned in 1978 from the art historian Cyril Aldred, which I found indispensable. The most enjoyable take on Dendur comes from *Making the Mummies Dance,* the 1993 autobiography of the Met's former director Thomas Hoving. It is dishy and fun and, I've been informed by folks who knew Hoving, perhaps not entirely reliable. His account of his interactions with Jackie Onassis have been refuted. This story first appeared as an episode of the podcast thanks to the support of The Metropolitan Museum of Art's Chester Dale Fund, and was executive produced by Limor Tomer, general manager of live arts at the Met.

"Points Excised from the Timeline of the History of the Temple of Dendur"—The go-to sources on this aspect of Dendur's time at the Met are *Empire of Pain: The Secret History of the Sackler Dynasty* by Patrick Radden Keefe, Barry Meier's *Pain Killer: An Empire of Deceit and the Origin of America's Opioid Epidemic,* and Laura Poitras's documentary about and with Nan Goldin, *All the Beauty and the Bloodshed.*

"Dreaming Caroline"—The most comprehensive work on Brooks was done by Pamela H. Simpson in her article "Caroline Shawk Brooks: The Centennial Butter Sculptress," published in the Spring/Summer 2007 issue of *Woman's Art Journal.*

"Seven Stories"—Probably the best thing I read on Otis was the appropriately titled *Otis: Giving Rise to the Modern City,* from 2001, by Jason Goodwin.

"Elizabeth"—I found *Bittersweet: Diabetes, Insulin, and the Transformation of Illness* by Chris Fuedtner and *Breakthrough: Elizabeth Hughes, the Discovery of Insulin, and the Making of a Medical Miracle* by Thea Cooper and Arthur Ainsberg particularly useful and humane.

"Butterflies"—A couple of sources I want to flag here are the dissertation of William J. Kovarik, titled "The Ethyl Controversy: How the News Media Set the Agenda for a Public Health Controversy Over the Use of Leaded Gasoline, 1924–1926," and Thomas Midgely IV's biography of his grandfather, *From the Periodic Table to Production: The Life of Thomas Midgely, Jr., Inventor of Leaded Gasoline and Freon Refrigerants,* which is much more substantive and readable than one might imagine.

"Fifty Words Written About the Arctic Bowhead Whale After Learning That They Can Live up to Two Hundred Years"—Dunno. It's fifty words.

"Peregrinar"—I relied heavily on *The Crusades of Cesar Chavez* by Miriam Pawel as well as on Jacques E. Levy's oral history *Cesar Chavez: Autobiography of La Causa.* I also recommend going back through the original newspaper accounts of the march; *The Sacramento Bee* did a particularly good job of covering it at the time.

"New England Granite"—A fun place to start learning about the strange life of Plymouth Rock is a delightful article by Francis Russell called "The Pilgrims and the Rock" in the October 1962 issue of *American Heritage.*

"1,347 Birds"—This is based on the work of Shane DuBay and Carl Fuldner as laid out in their article "Bird Specimens Track 135 Years of Atmospheric Black Carbon and Environmental Policy," published in *Proceedings of the National Academy of Sciences,* vol. 114, no. 43 (October 24, 2017).

"Natural Habitat"—I came to this story as I often do: Something caught my eye in a museum. Here, it was Su Lin, stuffed at the Field Museum in Chicago. That led me to Vicki Croke's *The Lady and the Panda,* which does a good job with Ruth's story, and *Chasing the Panda,* Michael Kiefer's book about Quentin Young's experience of the same events. Ruth's own book, *The Baby Giant Panda,* is delightful, if you can get your hands on it. I also found Elizabeth Hanson's *Animal Attractions: Nature on Display in American Zoos* especially illuminating.

"Crazy Bet"—The best source on this one is probably Elizabeth R. Varon's *Southern Lady, Yankee Spy: The True Story of Elizabeth Van Lew, a Union Agent in the Heart of the Confederacy* from 2003.

"Enlargement"—With scant information about the men on the roof, I'd suggest you spend your time with the boy; Barnard's life gets a thorough treatment in William Sheehan's *The Immortal Fire Within: The Life Work of Edward Emerson Barnard,* published in 2007.

"The Surfman"—My favorite account of the life of Richard Etheridge is David Wright and David Zoby's book, *Fire on the Beach: Recovering the Lost Story of Richard Etheridge and the Pea Island Lifesavers.*

"Guinea Pigs"—Colin Burgess and Chris Dubbs's *Animals in Space: From Research Rockets to the Space Shuttle* does a good job placing these animals in their historical and scientific context.

"Betty Robinson"—My favorite book on Betty is Roseanne Montillo's *Fire on the Track: Betty Robinson and the Triumph of the Early Olympic Women.*

"A Washington Monument"—John Steele Gordon's *Washington's Monument: And the Fascinating History of the Obelisk* is quite thorough on the monument.

"George Meléndez Wright"—Jerry Emory does a beautiful job telling the story of Wright's life in *George Meléndez Wright: The Fight for Wildlife and Wilderness in the National Parks.*

"Né Weinberg"—The most comprehensive work on Weyman is found in the November 8, 1968, issue of *The New Yorker,* in a profile by St. Clair McKelway called "The Big Little Man from Brooklyn."

"Below from Above"—David McCullough's utterly transporting *The Great Bridge: The Epic Story of the Building of the Brooklyn Bridge* was both crucial to writing this story and an early influence on *The Memory Palace* in general.

"Stories About the *St. Louis*"—The contemporary accounts of the voyage of the *St. Louis* are worth reading in any major newspaper's archive. I'd also recommend *Refuge Denied: The St. Louis Passengers and the Holocaust,* by Sarah A. Ogilvie and Scott Miller.

"Full Circle"—There's an excellent book by Kevin J. Avery about Vanderlyn's work, called *John Vanderlyn's Panorama of the Palace and Gardens of Versailles.* This story also first appeared as an episode of the podcast thanks to the support of The Metropolitan Museum of Art's Chester Dale Fund, and was executive produced by Limor Tomer, general manager of live arts at the Met.

"Looking Up"—I pieced this story together using newspaper archives.

"As They Were in Life"—Peter Manseu does a terrific job with Mumler's story (I'd highly recommend his lengthy discussion of the court case) in *The Apparitionists: A Tale of Phantoms, Fraud, Photography, and the Man Who Captured Lincoln's Ghost*. For more on Mary Todd Lincoln, I personally enjoyed the time I spent with Jean H. Baker's *Mary Todd Lincoln: A Biography*.

"Six Scenes from the Life of William James Sidis, Wonderful Boy"—There's an expansive but, to my mind, oddly judgmental biography of Sidis by Amy Wallace called *The Prodigy: A Biography of William James Sidis, America's Greatest Child Prodigy*, from 1986. Speaking of judgmental, there's Jared L. Manley and James Thurber's "Where Are They Now?" article from the August 6, 1937, issue of *The New Yorker*. But mostly I'd highly recommend going to the ramshackle but lovingly curated site www.sidis.net.

"Alexander Graham Bell . . ."—The most comprehensive work I've found on Bell's work with tetrahedral kites was released in 1964 by the University of Toronto Press: *Bell and Baldwin: Their Development of Aerodromes and Hydrodromes at Baddeck, Nova Scotia* by J. H. Parkin. ("Baldwin" refers to the Canadian aviation pioneer, Frederick Walker Baldwin, who partnered with Bell on a number of projects in their later years.) Less germane to this story but highly recommended on Bell is Katie Booth's *The Invention of Miracles: Language, Power, and Alexander Graham Bell's Quest to End Deafness*.

"Four Hundred Words for 79th Street"—Nothing has done more to keep Minik's memory alive than Kenn Harper's work in his book *Give Me My Father's Body: The Life of Minik, the New York Eskimo*.

"Snakes!"—This one was done nearly entirely with newspaper research. The September 28, 1953, edition of *Life* has a charming photo spread.

"The Wheel"—There's a lot written about Robert Smalls, often with quite a bit of contradictory information. I found Edward A. Miller's *Gullah Statesman: Robert Smalls from Slavery to Congress, 1839– 1915* helpful in sorting it out.

"AKA Leo"—This one was pieced together with contemporary news accounts and texts on the history of aviation in Arizona, which love a dramatic plane crash.

"Dreamland"—There is no shortage of engaging books about the history of Dreamland and Coney Island (I enjoy Oliver Pilat and Jo Ranson's *Sodom by the Sea: An Affectionate History of Coney Island* and John F. Kasson's *Amusing the Million: Coney Island at the Turn of the Century* quite a bit). But if you want more depth about the world of Dreamland itself, you'll find it in Dawn Raffel's book about the man behind the baby amusement and his vital role in developing methods of care for premature babies. That's called *The Strange Case of Dr. Couney: How a Mysterious European Showman Saved Thousands of American Babies.*

"These Words, Forever"—I've loved the anecdote about Marconi and his magical history-hearing machine for many years since coming upon it in an aside in Greg Milner's *Perfecting Sound Forever: An Aural History of Recorded Music.*

Art Credits

Illustrations on pages 21, 52–57, 59–60, 75–81, 111–12, 115–18, 122, 124, and 184–87 are by Jill De Haan.

214–16 Library of Congress

236–37 Kobal/Shutterstock

250, 253, 254, 256 Author's personal collection

274 Creative Commons

278, 293–94 Author's personal collection

About the Author

NATE DIMEO is the creator, producer, and host of *The Memory Palace,* a podcast from Radiotopia and PRX. He was previously the artist in residence at the Metropolitan Museum of Art and has performed stories from *The Memory Palace* in theaters all over the United States as well as Canada, England, Ireland, and in a field at a rock festival in Tasmania. He has reported stories for National Public Radio's *Morning Edition* and *All Things Considered* and American Public Media's *Marketplace,* as well as numerous other public radio programs. He is the co-author of *Pawnee: The Greatest Town in America,* for which he was a finalist for the Thurber Prize in American Humor. He has written for NBC's *Parks and Recreation* and the ABC miniseries *The Astronaut Wives Club.* He lives in Los Angeles by way of Providence, Rhode Island.

thememorypalace.us

About the Type

This book was set in Dante, a typeface designed by Giovanni Mardersteig (1892–1977). Conceived as a private type for the Officina Bodoni in Verona, Italy, Dante was originally cut only for hand composition by Charles Malin, the famous Parisian punch cutter, between 1946 and 1952. Its first use was in an edition of Boccaccio's *Trattatello in laude di Dante* that appeared in 1954. The Monotype Corporation's version of Dante followed in 1957. Though modeled on the Aldine type used for Pietro Cardinal Bembo's treatise *De Aetna* in 1495, Dante is a thoroughly modern interpretation of that venerable face.